Herbal Magic

by Coby Michael

Herbal Magic For Dummies®

Published by: **John Wiley & Sons, Inc.,** 111 River Street, Hoboken, NJ 07030-5774, www.wiley.com

For general information on our other products and services, please contact our Customer Care Department within the U.S. at 877-762-2974, outside the U.S. at 317-572-3993, or fax 317-572-4002. For technical support, please visit https://hub.wiley.com/community/support/dummies.

Wiley publishes in a variety of print and electronic formats and by print-on-demand. Some material included with standard print versions of this book may not be included in e-books or in print-on-demand. If this book refers to media that is not included in the version you purchased, you may download this material at http://booksupport.wiley.com. For more information about Wiley products, visit www.wiley.com.

Library of Congress Control Number: 2026937982

ISBN 978-1-394-37018-4 (pbk); ISBN 978-1-394-37020-7 (ebk); ISBN 978-1-394-37019-1 (ebk)

SKY10151713_040726

Table of Contents

Introduction

My interest in the natural world began at a very young age. I spent a lot of time in the garden at my grandparent's house helping pick vegetables, plant flowers, and collect seeds. These times are some of my most peaceful and cherished childhood memories. Something about being out in the garden in the summer evenings, with the lightning bugs flashing around me, struck a deep chord within myself. I felt this affinity and connection to the plants that populated the garden before I had the words to describe what I was experiencing.

I remember my grandfather telling stories about his mother, who tended to her own garden growing all sorts of things to feed the family. One thing that always stuck out to me when he would tell me these stories was the deep and intimate connection she had with her garden, something that was impressed upon by my grandfather and passed on to me. It was more than just a source of food or a means to an end; it was a sacred place.

Another childhood memory that I still carry with me is sitting on the swing in the backyard with my grandfather and my sisters, and he would sing a song to us: "*In the Garden*" written by Charles A. Miles in 1913. I'll never forget that song, and its lyrics will forever be woven into the memory of that magical place, my grandpa's garden.

I share these stories to not only give a little backstory on my own early connection to the world of plants and herbs, but also to show that this sacredness is universal. Anyone from any background, time period, or belief system can tap into this connection to the natural world, whether by gardening, enjoying walks in Nature, or working with plants and herbs in other ways. It is part of our human nature and our role as stewards of this amazing planet that we live on. It doesn't matter whether you call it Magic, Mother Nature, God, Spirit, or Consciousness. The truth is self-evident, and anyone can experience it.

About This Book

When I began writing *Herbal Magic For Dummies,* I set out with the intention of providing a resource that anyone could pick up and feel comfortable working with herbs in a magical way.

The sacredness of the natural world is universal, and we (humans) are part of that sacredness and deserve to take part in that and be empowered by it regardless of religious, philosophical, or spiritual beliefs. It was important for me to present the idea and practice of herbal magic outside of the context of any spiritual tradition or belief system, to make it practical and approachable for everyone.

I start by defining some important terms and concepts such as "What is magic?" and "Connecting with plant intelligence" to provide the reader with the framework to begin this journey. In Chapter 1, I list some of the major traditions of herbalism from around the world, including Traditional Chinese Medicine, Ayurveda, and Western Herbalism to show that while these traditions use many different herbs in their practice and different terminology, at their core they share a lot in common. One of those common elements, while not always explicitly stated and in some cases lost in modernization, is the recognition of the subtle energetic (spiritual) nature of disease and the ways that disease is treated. Understanding this energetic or spiritual component is important because of the influence that medicinal herbalism has had on magical herbalism throughout human history. It's only until relatively recently that the two have become distinctly separate things in the realm of clinical herbalism. However, traditions of herbal knowledge that maintain these unseen connections at work are still practiced today.

Herbal knowledge is a legacy that has been transmitted throughout human history. Predating the written word, this knowledge was transmitted orally. It's a legacy that has astonishingly survived all of the ups and downs of human history, so I thought it important to begin this book with some of the most influential people that have contributed to our collective herbal knowledge. My focus is on Western Herbalism because of the vastness of the subject matter and also my personal perspective as a person living in the Western Hemisphere. However, I would be remiss not to mention that I haven't mentioned many individuals who belong on this list and many others whose contributions have been lost to history.

This book gives you all the tools necessary to begin practicing herbal magic on your own and also develop your own practices in creative and personal ways. Through working with herbs in this way, you can develop an intimate understanding of the spirit or consciousness within each plant and thereby strengthen your connection to the natural world. This very connection in the web of life makes magic possible, and nothing is more empowering than this simple but profound realization.

My hope is that after reading this book, you'll feel empowered to pursue all the wonderful things that life has to offer and be able to see the magic that exists in the world all around you!

Foolish Assumptions

We all make assumptions, and when writing this book I gave myself the task of assuming that you're new to the world of herbalism as well as the world of magic. I also assume that if you found your way to this book that you have some level of interest in working with herbs in a magical way or understanding more about this practice and what it has to offer. I don't assume that you have a background in herbalism or botany, and I provide as much information as possible to fill in the blanks.

The following are additional assumptions I've made. If you fit into any of these categories, this book is for you:

- You feel called to develop a deeper connection with the natural world through working with herbs.
- You have dreams, desires, and goals that you want to bring into your life.
- You understand that the natural world is full of beings that are as conscious and alive as humans are.
- You are aware that some things in the universe cannot be seen or explained, but that does not mean they don't exist.

Icons Used in This Book

All *For Dummies* books feature icons (little pictures that grab your attention) in the margins to serve you well. Think of them as road signs pointing to different kinds of information in the chapters.

REMEMBER

This icon alerts you to concepts, terms, and ideas about herbal magic that are of particular importance.

This icon points out helpful information that you can use if you continue to practice herbal magic.

WARNING

This icon points to misconceptions about herbs that have certain interactions or need extra care when working with them. Read this information carefully!

Beyond the Book

In addition to the abundance of information that we provide in this book, you get access to even more help and information online at `Dummies.com`. Check out this book's online Cheat Sheet. Just go to `www.dummies.com` and search for "Herbal Magic For Dummies Cheat Sheet."

Where to Go from Here

You can begin this book wherever you like. But you may want to start with the following suggestions:

- If you want to jump right in to casting specific spells or trying a variety of rituals, start with Part 2.
- If you're interested in cultivating a connection to the herbs that you want to work with by growing them first, read Chapters 11 and 12.

Regardless of your interest in herbs and magic, you can gain so much from cultivating a connection to Nature and all of its wonders. Herbal magic is such a vast area of study, with many different angles and avenues to pursue. I invite you to follow what calls out to you and see where it takes you. Enjoy the journey and all the magical herbs you will meet along the way!

1

Planting the Seed

IN THIS PART . . .

Discover the foundations of herbal magic.

Create herbal formulas.

Explore how herbs are connected to magic.

IN THIS CHAPTER

» Meeting magical herbal allies

» Tapping into the energy of herbs

» Understanding the diversity of herbal traditions

» Building the foundations of herbal knowledge

Chapter 1 Meeting Your Herbal Allies

Magical herbalism conjures images of bubbling cauldrons and shimmering potions from childhood fairy tales, but when you take a closer look, you discover that it's not something from the supernatural realm. Magical herbalism is based on an ancient and intuitive understanding of the world that you live in.

In this chapter, you find that magic, like science, operates on its own system of rules. This chapter explores traditions of herbal magic from around the world and the beliefs and concepts that form the foundation of those traditions. You get to know some of the most influential figures in Western Herbalism and discover how their theories and practices, which may seem rather fantastical from today's perspective, have formed the basis of modern medicine.

Aligning Intention through Magic

Magic, in its most essential form, is the practice of aligning intention with unseen forces to produce change in the physical, mental, emotional, or spiritual realms. Magic is one of humanity's oldest beliefs found in every culture and is not merely superstition or fantasy, but a complex system of interaction between the human will and the subtle energies that permeate all levels of existence. From occult, metaphysical, and spiritual perspectives, magic is a technology of the universe, an ancient and evolving art that seeks to harness the deeper laws of Nature, spirit, and consciousness.

In occult traditions — *occult* meaning hidden — magic is often understood as the manipulation of hidden forces. Occult practice involves ritual, symbolism, and the use of sacred texts, tools, and formulas to influence reality. Practitioners view the universe as a web of interconnected energies governed by universal laws, and these laws are applied to affect magical acts. Magic, then, becomes a disciplined method of working within these systems, using precise rituals, divine names, planetary timing, and esoteric symbols to apply spiritual forces to create material effects.

The metaphysical perspective emphasizes magic as a natural expression of the mind's power to shape reality. Metaphysical practitioners view consciousness as the primary creative force, drawing on *New Age thought* — a movement focused on individual spiritual awakening, psychology, and *mysticism* (inner transformation through communion with the Divine). *Belief* (acceptance of something's truth or existence), *intention* (will or desire directed toward a goal), *visualization* (holding a mental image of something), and *vibration* (the energetic frequency found in all) are the core mechanisms through which reality is shaped. According to this view, thoughts are energy, and when focused with clarity and emotion, they manifest outcomes in alignment with the practitioner's inner state. Magic, therefore, isn't supernatural, but an extension of the laws of cause and effect operating on more subtle planes.

In traditional spiritual contexts, magic is often viewed as a sacred act that arises from communion with the divine, the higher self, or the spirit world. Magic was part of humankind's earliest religions and still exists today taking on new forms. Magic becomes prayer in motion, ritualized reverence, and co-creation with spiritual allies, deities, ancestors, and *elemental forces* (the creative and destructive forces of Nature). This approach emphasizes harmony, spiritual ethics, and the soul's journey toward growth and union with the greater whole. Magic isn't just a tool for getting what you want, but a way of living in alignment with spiritual truth and cosmic balance.

Across all these perspectives, magic is ultimately a participatory art and spiritual science, one that calls the practitioner into a deeper awareness of self, Nature, and the unseen patterns that shape life. Whether through candle spells, herbal formulas, or meditation, magic allows you to engage with reality in a way that is co-creative.

Discovering that Not All Plants Are Herbs

While the terms *plants* and *herbs* are often used interchangeably, they refer to different levels of classification. All herbs are plants, but not all plants are considered herbs. A *plant* is a broad term that includes all living organisms in the plant kingdom, ranging from towering trees and ornamental flowers to grasses, shrubs, and aquatic vegetation. An *herb*, on the other hand, is typically defined as a plant with soft, nonwoody stems that is valued for its flavor, fragrance, medicinal properties, or spiritual significance. Herbs are often used in their fresh or dried form and may include leaves, flowers, seeds, or roots, depending on the specific plant and its purpose.

In medicinal and culinary contexts, herbs are highly prized for their practical applications. Culinary herbs, such as basil, rosemary, and thyme, enhance flavor and aroma in food, while medicinal herbs, like echinacea, chamomile, and peppermint, are used in teas, tinctures, and salves for their healing properties.

Unlike many other plants, herbs are often used in small quantities but have potent effects. Their essential oils and other chemical compounds that are responsible for an herb's medicinal properties make them powerful tools in both traditional and modern herbal medicine. While many trees and shrubs also offer medicinal value, they're not always referred to as herbs unless the soft parts of the plant are used for healing.

Spiritually, herbs have long held a central place in rituals, ceremonies, and energetic practices across cultures. Whether burned as incense, placed in charms, or used in baths and anointing oils, herbs like sage, mugwort, and frankincense are used to purify, protect, and attract specific energies.

While the distinction between plant and herb is useful in certain contexts, such as botanical classification or gardening, all herbs are, fundamentally, plants. The terms are often used interchangeably in everyday language, especially when referring to botanical materials used for healing, cooking, or spiritual work. However, recognizing the unique role that herbs play within the larger plant kingdom can deepen one's appreciation for their versatility and potency.

Treating Herbs as Magical Allies

In magical practice, herbs are far more than passive ingredients or symbolic additions to spellwork: They're conscious, living allies (a concept known as *animism*). Just as practitioners may work with deities, ancestors, or elemental forces, herbs are part of the vast network of spirits and energies that can be called upon for assistance. Each plant carries its own intelligence, personality, and spiritual essence. These plant spirits are ancient, wise, and often eager to form relationships with those who approach them with respect and sincerity. When you include herbs, roots, woods, or resins in your rituals, you're entering into a form of partnership, inviting the presence and power of the plant's spirit into your magical workings.

Animism is the belief that all things possess a spirit or consciousness. This worldview sees the natural world as animated by an unseen spiritual essence, recognizing trees, rivers, rocks, animals, and even weather patterns as sentient or spiritually alive. Rather than placing humans above Nature, animism emphasizes interconnectedness, relationship, and reciprocity between all beings. Rooted in many Indigenous and ancient traditions across the globe, animism forms the spiritual foundation for viewing the world not as a collection of inert objects but as a living web of relationships in which each part holds meaning and agency.

In the context of plant-based spiritual practices, animism invites the practitioner to engage with herbs, roots, and trees not merely as tools or ingredients, but as conscious allies. Each plant is approached with reverence, as a being with its own unique energy, wisdom, and preferences. This perspective transforms magical herbalism into spiritual partnership where you're not using the herbs but working with them.

By honoring the spirit of the plant, practitioners can deepen their intuitive connection, receive guidance, and build more effective and ethically grounded rituals. Animism encourages you to listen to the plants you work with, fostering a practice that is not only spiritually enriching but also rooted in humility and gratitude.

Each herb has its own unique qualities and area of expertise. Some are protective guardians, such as rosemary or basil, while others are known for opening the heart to love, like damiana or rose. Mugwort may enhance dreams and psychic insight, while patchouli anchors spells in physical reality. Understanding these energetic signatures allows the practitioner to work in harmony with the natural strengths of each plant. However, simply using herbs as tools is not enough — you must also honor them as *sentient beings,* able to perceive or feel things. You can do so through offerings, spoken gratitude, conscious harvesting, or taking a moment to connect with the plant's energy before use. In doing so, you deepen your connection to the green world and cultivate a more reciprocal and respectful form of magic.

Working with herbs in this way transforms spellwork into sacred partnership. It reminds you that Nature is not inert or impersonal, but filled with spirit and agency. When you treat herbs as allies rather than objects, you unlock the full depth of their magic and enter into a lineage of herbal wisdom that spans generations, cultures, and lifetimes.

Discovering the Magic of Herbs

Humans have likely been aware of the magical, spiritual, and transformative properties of herbs, plants, and fungi since before humans had written language. Working with herbs hearkens back to a time when people were still very much a part of Nature and lived in harmony without the perceived separation that modern society has forced upon them. Incorporating herbs into magical practice is a powerful way to reconnect with primal natures and the ability to cocreate with the universe.

The act of choosing, handling, and working with specific herbs brings focus to your intentions and creates a tangible channel through which you can direct energy. Herbs serve as natural transmitters of energy that help translate your thoughts, feelings, and magical goals into something that can move beyond the self and take root in the world around you. This physical and spiritual connection grounds your magic in the living world and helps bridge the gap between the seen and unseen.

Thousands of herbs, each with its own associations, traditions, and folklore, are available and vary widely depending on the cultural or spiritual context. While many herbs carry broadly agreed-upon magical themes, other associations are much more specific, rooted in local customs, personal experiences, or the teachings of a particular tradition. Magical herbalism is not a one-size-fits-all practice and is rich with varied perspectives and approaches, shaped by lineage, geography, and personal relationship. What works in one tradition may differ significantly in another, and it's this diversity that gives magical herbalism both depth and flexibility.

REMEMBER

While it is important to honor and recognize traditional knowledge and have an understanding of the basic framework of the system you're working within, herbal magic is as alive as the herbs that you work with, and personal insight and intuition is just as valid and valuable.

Herbs aren't just tools you use to express our intentions, they are active participants in the magical process. When you engage with them as conscious, living beings, you open the door to a deeper level of communication. Just as you use herbs to speak to the world, herbs speak back to you. Through meditation, intuition, dreams, and direct experience, you can receive unique insights into how a particular plant wishes to work with you. This reciprocal relationship allows your practice to evolve beyond what books or traditions alone can teach.

Just as different schools of thought are in medicinal herbalism, magical herbalism also allows for a wide range of interpretations and applications. A single herb may be used in vastly different ways depending on the practitioner, their intention, and the spiritual framework they operate within. This openness invites experimentation, intuition, and individual creativity.

Looking at Herbal Traditions

In this section, I look at a variety of herbal traditions from around the world. While many more are out there, by covering just a few, you can begin to see remarkable patterns emerge that point to a shared, intuitive understanding of the energetic and spiritual qualities of plants.

Despite vast cultural differences, many systems recognize herbs not only for their physical effects, but also for their ability to shift energy, balance emotions, and connect people to the sacred. Noticing these commonalities helps you deepen your relationship with herbs, allowing you to move beyond memorization and toward intuition. By studying how various traditions perceive herbal *energetics* (how the characteristics of an herb effect the body), plant spirits, ritual uses, and symbolic correspondences, you can begin to see the deeper nature of the plants themselves. This pattern recognition invites you to cultivate your own insight and sensitivity, honoring the wisdom of your ancestors while developing a personal language of plant medicine rooted in reverence and respect.

African Traditional Herbalism

African Traditional Herbalism is one of the oldest and most diverse healing systems in the world, rooted in the continent's vast cultural, spiritual, and ecological landscapes. It encompasses a wide range of regional practices developed over thousands of years by various ethnic groups, each with their own rich traditions of plant medicine, spiritual healing, and ancestral knowledge. Healers serve as intermediaries between the physical and spiritual worlds, using herbs not only to treat physical ailments but also to restore spiritual balance and community harmony. These practices are deeply holistic, viewing illness as an imbalance that affects both body and spirit.

The diversity of African Traditional Herbalism reflects the continent's immense biodiversity and cultural complexity. Remedies and rituals may vary significantly from one region or ethnic group to another, yet many share common elements: the use of sacred plants, spiritual diagnosis through divination, and a deep reverence for Nature and ancestral guidance.

This rich heritage has had a lasting influence on global herbal and spiritual traditions, most notably in the Americas, where the transatlantic slave trade carried African herbal knowledge into systems such as Hoodoo, Santería, and Obeah. Today, African Traditional Herbalism continues to thrive both on the African continent and across the *diaspora* (places where people have been dispersed from their original homeland), preserving a living legacy of healing, resistance, and spiritual resilience.

Ayurvedic medicine

Ayurveda originated in India more than 3,000 years ago. The word *Ayurveda* comes from the Sanskrit words *ayur* (life) and *veda* (knowledge or science), meaning "the science of life." Rooted in the Vedic spiritual tradition, Ayurveda developed alongside yoga and other philosophical systems that emphasize balance, consciousness, and harmony with Nature. Ancient Ayurvedic texts detail thousands of herbal remedies, surgical techniques, and lifestyle practices that are still in use today. Traditionally, Ayurvedic knowledge was passed down orally through generations of healers and scholars before being codified in written form.

REMEMBER

At the heart of Ayurveda is the belief that health is achieved by maintaining balance between the body, mind, spirit, and environment. This system identifies three primary energies, or *doshas*:

- *Vata* (Air and ether)
- *Pitta* (Fire and Water)
- *Kapha* (Earth and Water)

These doshas govern physiological and psychological functions. Each person has a unique constitution, made up of these doshas in different proportions. Imbalances in the doshas are believed to lead to illness, and treatments aim to restore equilibrium through personalized combinations of diet, herbal medicine, yoga, meditation, detoxification practices, and lifestyle adjustments. Ayurveda continues to be a widely respected and practiced system of medicine both in India and around the world, influencing modern integrative and holistic health approaches.

Indigenous plant medicine practices

Indigenous plant medicine comprises many different traditions across the Americas, developed over thousands of years by Native American communities who cultivated profound relationships with the natural world. In North America, Native American herbalism includes a wide range of healing practices passed down through oral traditions, ceremonies, and apprenticeships. Healers, often referred to as medicine men or women, worked with local plants to treat illness, maintain spiritual balance, and foster connection with the land. Herbs like sage, cedar, sweetgrass, and tobacco hold not only medicinal value but also ceremonial and spiritual importance. These ancestral traditions have had a lasting influence on modern herbalism, holistic healing, and spiritual practices, yet they remain deeply specific to the cultures that created them and should be approached with respect and cultural sensitivity.

In Central and South America, sacred plant medicine traditions continue to thrive among Indigenous peoples who work with powerful plant allies, such as ayahuasca, tobacco, wachuma, and coca. These plants are not used casually but within specific ceremonial frameworks guided by experienced shamans or healers, who serve as mediators between the spiritual and physical realms. These traditions emphasize ritual purification, ancestral connection, and purging of unhealthy energies and offer healing on emotional, energetic, and physical levels.

DECOLONIZING HERBALISM

Decolonizing herbalism means shifting away from a purely extractive or commodified view of plants and instead approaching them with respect for their cultural contexts, ancestral lineages, and spiritual significance.

This process also includes giving credit to the communities who have preserved this knowledge, supporting BIPOC herbalists, questioning Eurocentric standards in herbal education, and being mindful of cultural appropriation.

As these Indigenous plant medicine practices gain global attention, it is crucial to recognize their cultural origins and avoid appropriation. Engaging with Indigenous plant medicine should always be done with humility, permission, and awareness of the historical and spiritual significance these plants hold. Honoring the knowledge-keepers and protecting the integrity of these traditions is essential to preserving their sacred value and ensuring they are not exploited.

Traditional Chinese Medicine

Traditional Chinese Medicine (TCM) is a comprehensive healing system that has been practiced in China for over 2,500 years. Its roots lie in ancient Taoist philosophy and observations of the natural world, emphasizing the interconnectedness of the body, mind, and environment. TCM includes a variety of modalities, such as acupuncture, *qi gong* (a practice working with the body's vital energy), *qi/chi* through gentle movements and focused breathing to promote health and well-being, massage, dietary therapy, and most notably, herbal medicine.

Herbal medicine is central to TCM and is guided by a sophisticated system of herbal energetics. Rather than focusing solely on the chemical properties of a plant, TCM classifies herbs based on their energetic qualities, such as temperature (hot, warm, neutral, cool, or cold), taste (sweet, bitter, pungent, sour, and salty), directionality (ascending, descending, inward, and outward), and the organ systems they affect. For example, you might use a warming herb to treat a cold condition, such as fatigue or poor circulation, or a cooling herb to clear heat, reduce inflammation, or calm excess *yang* (active/masculine) energy. This energetic framework allows practitioners to tailor herbal formulas to an individual's unique pattern of imbalance, aiming not just to treat symptoms but to restore harmony throughout the body.

The influence of Traditional Chinese Medicine has extended far beyond Asia, shaping holistic health practices around the world. Many commonly used herbs, such as ginseng, licorice root, and astragalus, have been integrated into Western herbalism, while TCM's energetic approach has inspired more nuanced understandings of plant medicine in various traditions. As interest in integrative and preventative medicine grows, TCM continues to offer valuable insight into the subtle dynamics of health, emphasizing balance, harmony, and a deep respect for the natural world.

Folk practices

Folk herbal traditions in North America are rich, varied, and deeply rooted in the blending of Indigenous knowledge with European and African influences. In the Appalachian region, herbal practices evolved from a combination of British Isles folklore, Native American plant wisdom, and African folk healing. Appalachian herbalists often relied on plants that were abundant in the mountainous terrain, such as burdock, yarrow, black cohosh, and yellow dock. These remedies were passed down through oral tradition and family lineages, used not only for physical ailments but also for protection, cleansing, and spiritual well-being. The use of signs, charms, prayers, and moon phases to guide planting and harvesting is common, reflecting a worldview in which Nature, spirit, and health are intimately connected.

The Pennsylvania Dutch tradition, which stems from German-speaking immigrants who settled in the region during the 17th and 18th centuries, includes a unique blend of Christian mysticism, astrology, and folk medicine. Known for practices such as *braucherei* or powwow, Pennsylvania Dutch healers used herbs alongside blessings, symbolic gestures, and Bible verses to treat ailments and ward off harm. Common herbs in this tradition include mugwort, tansy, comfrey, and plantain, often grown in home gardens or wildcrafted. Herbal remedies were prepared in simple, accessible ways and were seen as gifts from God that worked in concert with faith and divine will.

In the Ozark Mountains, folk herbalism closely resembles that of the Appalachians due to similar geographic and cultural roots. However, Ozark traditions also emphasize the role of *granny women* — folk healers who served as midwives, herbalists, and spiritual counselors. Herbal knowledge was closely guarded and often shared only within families or with trusted apprentices. Plants like boneset, elderberry, and poke root were staples in the Ozark herbal cabinet, used for both physical healing and magical protection. As in other folk systems, spiritual beliefs were woven into daily life, with herbal practices guided by dreams, signs, and seasonal cycles. Together, these North American folk traditions reflect a profound respect for the land and a deeply embedded belief in the power of plants to heal both body and spirit.

Wortcunning

Wortcunning is an Old English term that translates to plant wisdom or herb knowledge, derived from the words *wort* (meaning plant or herb) and *cunning* (meaning knowledge or skill). In Anglo-Saxon England, *wortcunning* referred to the practice of using plants for both healing and magical purposes, blending herbal medicine with spiritual and mystical traditions. This knowledge was passed down through oral tradition and written texts, and it played a central role in the healing practices of early medieval England. Practitioners of wortcunning were often called *leeches,* a term that originally referred to healers rather than the blood-sucking creature, and they held respected roles in their communities as both herbalists and spiritual workers.

Much of what we know about Anglo-Saxon herbalism comes from *leechbooks,* medical manuscripts compiled by monastic scribes between the ninth and tenth centuries. The *Leechbook of Bald*, one of the most famous, includes remedies using herbs, animal parts, and prayers to treat a wide variety of ailments. These texts reflect the blend of Christian, Germanic, and folkloric influences that shaped Anglo-Saxon healing. One of the most fascinating survivals of this tradition is the Nine Herbs Charm, an Old English poem found in the *Lacnunga*, a tenth-century collection of medical and magical texts. The charm invokes nine sacred herbs, such as mugwort, nettle, and fennel, combined with incantations and references to the god Woden, illustrating the fusion of pagan and Christian elements. It was used both to heal and to protect, showing that wortcunning was never just about the physical properties of herbs, but also their spiritual power and connection to the divine.

Rootwork

Rootwork is a form of African-American folk magic and herbalism rooted in the blending of African spiritual traditions with Native American plant knowledge and European folk practices. Emerging in the Southern United States during the era of slavery, rootwork developed as both a spiritual and practical system of survival, healing, and resistance. Enslaved Africans brought with them a rich understanding of plant medicine and spiritual practices, which they adapted to the new environment by incorporating local herbs, roots, and minerals — often learning from Indigenous peoples and borrowing from European folklore when necessary. Over time, this unique blend evolved into what is now commonly referred to as *Hoodoo,* though the terms rootwork, conjure, and Hoodoo are often used interchangeably depending on the region and practitioner.

In the context of magical herbalism, rootwork places a strong emphasis on the use of roots, herbs, and *curios* (natural or symbolic objects) to affect change in one's life whether for protection, love, money, justice, or spiritual cleansing. Plants such as High John the Conqueror root, devil's shoestring, and angelica are considered powerful allies, each with specific uses and spiritual associations.

Rootworkers create charm bags (see Chapter 2), oils, baths, powders, and candle rituals using these materials, often accompanied by spoken prayers or psalms. While not a religion, rootwork often draws upon Christian elements, especially the Bible, as a source of spiritual authority, reflecting the syncretic nature of the tradition. Today, rootwork remains a vital and living tradition, passed down through families and communities, continuing to serve as both a magical and cultural expression of resilience, wisdom, and connection to ancestral power.

Green witchcraft

Green witchcraft is a Nature-centered path of magical herbalism that emphasizes working in harmony with the Earth, plants, and natural cycles. It weaves together practical herbal knowledge with intuitive, spirit-based approaches to magic, often drawing on elements of kitchen witchcraft, conscious gardening, and plant spirit communication.

At its core, green witchcraft is about forming a deep, reciprocal relationship with the land and the plants that grow upon it. Green witches often grow or wildcraft their own herbs, harvesting them from the wild with their spiritual intentions in mind; prepare teas, tinctures, and infusions; and use these botanicals in both healing and spellwork. They may keep a garden as a sacred space, tending it not only for nourishment and medicine but as a living altar where offerings, blessings, and rituals are performed in rhythm with the Moon, seasons, and natural world.

In green witchcraft, herbal correspondences are studied and applied with both tradition and intuition. But beyond symbolic uses, green witches also engage in plant spirit work, treating herbs as conscious beings with whom one can build a spiritual relationship. Practices such as meditating with a plant, listening for its guidance, or journeying through trance work are common, rooted in the belief that plants have wisdom to share when approached with respect. This belief blends seamlessly with spiritual ecology, the idea that all life is interconnected and that healing the Earth is a sacred act. By incorporating magical herbalism into daily life through cooking, crafting, gardening, and ritual, green witchcraft becomes a living, evolving practice grounded in both the physical and the spiritual.

Whether working from a windowsill garden or deep in the forest, green witches are stewards of plant magic, using their craft to foster healing, harmony, and balance between themselves and the Earth. Their magic is personal, Earth-honoring, and deeply rooted in the cycles of growth, decay, and renewal reflecting the green world itself as both teacher and ally.

Western herbalism

Western herbalism is rooted in the medical traditions of ancient Europe and the Mediterranean. Its origins can be traced to early Greek, Roman, and Egyptian medicine, where healers like Hippocrates, Galen, and Dioscorides laid the foundation for herbal theory and practice. These traditions were preserved and expanded throughout the Middle Ages by monastic herbalists and Islamic scholars, eventually influencing European folk medicine, Renaissance medical astrology, and later, colonial-era healing practices in the Americas. One of the earliest and most influential texts in Western herbalism, *De Materia Medica* by Dioscorides, cataloged hundreds of plants and their medicinal uses, many of which are still recognized today. Over centuries, Western herbalism grew into a rich blend of formal medical systems and localized folk knowledge, ultimately shaping the foundations of both modern herbalism and allopathic medicine.

A central component of early Western herbal theory was the humoral system, developed by Hippocrates and expanded by Galen. This system proposed that health depended on the balance of four bodily humors: blood, phlegm, black bile, and yellow bile. Each humor was associated with specific qualities — hot, cold, wet, and dry — and illnesses were believed to result from excesses or deficiencies of these elements. Herbs were classified by these same qualities, and treatments were designed to restore equilibrium. While humoral theory has largely been replaced by modern biomedical models, its emphasis on constitutional balance and energetics continues to influence traditional herbalism today.

In addition to humoral theory, planetary correspondences and astrological herbalism (see Chapter 3) played a significant role in Western herbal traditions, particularly during the Middle Ages and Renaissance. Pioneers like Paracelsus and Nicholas Culpeper developed systems in which plants were ruled by planets and zodiac signs, with each celestial body influencing the medicinal and magical properties of certain herbs. For example, Mars governed fiery, stimulating plants, such as nettle and garlic, while Venus ruled over gentle, harmonizing herbs, like rose and violet. Practitioners would consult astrological charts to determine the best times for harvesting, preparing, and administering remedies, believing that cosmic alignment affected both plant potency and patient receptivity.

The Foundations of Medicinal Herbalism in the West

In this section, I explore some of the most influential figures in the evolution of Western herbalism and examine how their contributions have shaped both traditional and magical approaches to working with plants. From the foundational theories of Hippocrates and the humoral system to the esoteric insights of Paracelsus and the astrological correspondences emphasized by Nicholas Culpepper, each of these individuals has played a critical role in establishing the frameworks still used by herbalists today. Their understanding of herbal energetics, planetary influences, and the spiritual qualities of plants has deeply informed the development of magical herbalism. From ancient Greece to early 20th-century practitioners like Maud Grieve, these trailblazers have laid the groundwork for modern herbal practice, blending science, folklore, and metaphysical insight into a living tradition that continues to evolve.

Hippocrates

Hippocrates (c. 460 BCE–c. 370 BCE) is often referred to as the Father of Medicine and was a pioneering figure in the development of Western medical thought. He is credited with shifting the understanding of disease and healing from superstition and divine punishment to natural causes and empirical observation. Although much of what is known about him comes from later sources and the *Hippocratic Corpus*, a collection of texts attributed to him and his followers. His legacy had a profound impact on both medical and herbal traditions in the Western world. Hippocrates emphasized the importance of diet, lifestyle, and the use of natural remedies, in the maintenance of health and treatment of illness.

One of Hippocrates' major contributions to herbal medicine was his development of the humoral theory, which proposed that the human body is governed by four fluids or humors: blood, phlegm, black bile, and yellow bile. Health, according to this theory, was a state of balance among these humors, while disease was the result of imbalance. Herbs were used to correct these imbalances based on their perceived energetic properties: hot, cold, moist, or dry; establishing a framework that would influence herbal and medical practice for centuries. This approach laid the groundwork for later systems of herbal energetics and was a cornerstone of Greco-Roman medicine, continuing to influence European herbalism well into the Renaissance and beyond.

Pedanius Dioscorides

Pedanius Dioscorides (c. 40 CE–90 CE) was a Greek physician, pharmacologist, and botanist whose work became one of the most influential foundations of Western herbalism and medicine. His most significant work, *De Materia Medica*, compiled around 50–70 CE, described over 600 plants along with their medicinal properties, preparations, and applications. This text became the authoritative herbal reference for more than 1,500 years, influencing medical practice throughout the Byzantine Empire, the Islamic Golden Age, and into Renaissance Europe.

Avicenna

Avicenna, known in Arabic as Ibn Sina was a Persian polymath who lived from 980 to 1037 CE. He is considered one of the most influential figures in the history of medicine, philosophy, and science. Avicenna's most celebrated work *The Canon of Medicine* became a foundational medical text in both the Islamic world and medieval Europe.

In terms of herbalism, Avicenna placed great emphasis on the energetic properties of herbs and their effects on the body's internal balance. He developed a complex system of herbal energetics based on the theory of the four humors: blood, phlegm, yellow bile, and black bile. Each herb was understood in terms of its heating, cooling, moistening, or drying effects.

Hildegard von Bingen

Hildegard von Bingen (1098–1179) was a Benedictine abbess, mystic, composer, and healer whose writings made significant contributions to Western herbalism and natural medicine. Living in medieval Germany, she combined monastic healing traditions, Christian theology, and empirical observation of Nature into a holistic approach to health. Her major works on natural history and medicine, including *Physica* and *Causae et Curae*, catalogued the medicinal uses of plants, animals, and minerals. Hildegard's writings preserved valuable herbal knowledge through the Middle Ages and continue to influence modern herbalists and magical practitioners, blending practical medicine with spiritual ecology.

Paracelsus

Paracelsus, born Philippus Aureolus Theophrastus Bombastus von Hohenheim (1493–1541), was a Swiss physician, alchemist, and philosopher who played a transformative role in the development of Western medicine and herbalism. Breaking away from the rigid doctrines of Galenic and scholastic medicine, Paracelsus advocated for a more empirical and spiritually informed approach to healing. He believed that observation, experience, and the study of Nature were essential to the practice of medicine.

Deeply immersed in alchemy, astrology, and esoteric philosophy, Paracelsus believed that the healing power of herbs came not only from their physical constituents but also from their spiritual essence. He taught that everything in Nature carried a divine signature, a concept later known as the "Doctrine of Signatures," which revealed its intended use in healing.

REMEMBER

The Doctrine of Signatures also plays a role in magical herbalism, covered in Chapter 2, which provides a sense both the medicinal and magical properties of an herb.

John Gerard

John Gerard (1545–1612) was an English herbalist and botanist best known for his influential work *The Herball, or Generall Historie of Plantes*, first published in 1597. This extensive volume was one of the most comprehensive English-language herbals of its time, cataloging over 1,000 plants with detailed descriptions of their appearance, habitat, and medicinal uses. His herbal included many woodcut illustrations and became a widely used reference for both laypeople and medical practitioners in the early modern period.

Gerard's contributions to Western herbalism lie not only in the breadth of botanical knowledge he helped preserve but also in his emphasis on practical application.

Nicholas Culpeper

Nicholas Culpeper (1616–1654) was an English herbalist, physician, and astrologer whose contributions to Western herbalism remain highly influential. His most renowned work, *The English Physician* (later expanded as *The Complete Herbal*), combined traditional herbal knowledge with astrological theory, making herbal medicine accessible to the general public in a time when medical knowledge was largely controlled by academic institutions and the elite. Culpeper translated complex Latin texts into English and challenged the exclusivity of medical knowledge, advocating for the empowerment of common people to take charge of their own health using the plants around them.

Culpeper's most distinctive contribution was his integration of astrological correspondences into herbal medicine. He believed that each plant was governed by a specific planet, and that the energetic and medicinal qualities of herbs could be better understood through their celestial rulers.

REMEMBER

Historically, astrology has played a role in medicinal herbal treatment throughout history and is part of the systems of traditional herbal medicine around the world. While planetary correspondences were originally focused on an herb's medicinal qualities, as we will see they also help to categorize an herb's magical qualities.

Carl Linnaeus

Carl Linnaeus (1707–1778), often referred to as the "father of modern taxonomy," was a Swedish botanist, physician, and zoologist whose work laid the foundation for the classification of plants and animals. Born on May 23, 1707, in Sweden, Linnaeus had a lifelong passion for the natural world and dedicated his career to bringing order to its immense diversity.

One of Linnaeus's most significant contributions was the development of binomial nomenclature — the formal system of naming species using two Latin names. In this system, each plant (or animal) is identified by its genus and species, such as *Rosa canina* for the dog rose. The genus refers to the broader group to which the plant belongs, while the species identifies the specific organism within that group. This system not only simplified the chaotic naming practices of the time but also created a universal language that allowed scientists and herbalists across the world to communicate clearly about plants and their uses.

In cases where multiple species exist within the same genus, the abbreviation spp. (meaning "species pluralis") is used to refer collectively to all species in that genus. For example, writing *Mentha* spp. would include all species of mint without specifying a particular one, such as *Mentha spicata* (spearmint) or *Mentha piperita* (peppermint). This is especially useful in herbalism when a general property of a plant family is being referenced rather than a single species. Linnaeus's classification system, still in use today with modern refinements, provided a critical framework for herbalists to identify, categorize, and study plants for both their medicinal and magical properties, ensuring consistency and accuracy across generations of practitioners.

Maud Grieve

Maud Grieve (1858–1941) was a prominent English herbalist, author, and educator whose work laid a critical foundation for modern Western herbalism. She is best known for her monumental text *A Modern Herbal*, first published in the 1930s. This extensive compendium offers detailed information on hundreds of medicinal plants, including their botanical characteristics, traditional and contemporary uses, preparation methods, and therapeutic actions. Grieve compiled her herbal during a time when traditional plant medicine was at risk of being overshadowed by the rise of pharmaceutical drugs, and her work served to preserve and revitalize interest in herbal remedies in the 20th century.

TIP

You can view *A Modern Herbal* online at `https://www.botanical.com`.

Connecting with Plant Intelligence

Plants have complex ways of communicating with one another and their environment. One of the most fascinating examples is found in the behavior of trees, which exchange information through an underground system known as the *mycelial network*. This network is formed by the subterranean part of fungi, thread-like structures known as *mycelium* that connect the roots of trees and other plants. Through these fungal networks, trees can share nutrients, send warning signals about pests or disease, and even assist younger or weaker trees by supplying them with needed resources. This cooperative behavior reveals a level of mutual support and awareness that challenges the notion of plants as isolated, unconscious organisms.

The existence of such communication systems supports the idea that plants possess a form of consciousness, not necessarily in the human sense, but as a subtle awareness that enables them to respond intelligently to their surroundings. Trees, for example, can differentiate between their own relatives and unrelated individuals, altering their growth patterns or nutrient sharing accordingly. Plants can also react to touch, sound vibrations, and even the presence of specific insects or animals, suggesting a kind of sensory intelligence. In spiritual and animistic traditions, this responsiveness is often interpreted as evidence of a plant's spirit or consciousness. By recognizing and honoring the ways plants communicate in Nature, practitioners can cultivate deeper, more respectful relationships with the botanical world, tapping into an ancient dialogue that exists all around them.

Plants also communicate with humans through their color, shape, scent, and growing habits — features that have long been used to draw symbolic connections between the plant world and human experience. These natural traits allow you to make intuitive and cultural associations that reveal a plant's potential uses or energetic qualities. Such associations are known as *correspondences* and form the foundation for many systems of magical herbalism. Correspondences can be categorized in various ways, including astrological influences, planetary rulerships, and elemental affinities, each offering insight into how a particular plant might support specific intentions or rituals. Chapter 3 explores these symbolic connections in greater detail.

Looking at Magical Plant Anatomy

The magical anatomy of plants refers to the idea that a plant's physical characteristics, such as its leaves, roots, flowers, color, scent, and growth pattern, can offer valuable insight into its spiritual and energetic properties. For example, plants with thorns or protective oils may be associated with warding and defense, while those with heart-shaped leaves or fragrant blossoms are often linked to love and attraction.

This concept is deeply rooted in the *Doctrine of Signatures*, a historical belief that the form of a plant reflects its intended use, both medicinal and magical. By observing a plant's structure and behavior, practitioners can intuit how it might be applied in ritual or spellwork, using its physical form as a language through which its spiritual essence is revealed. This symbolic interpretation allows you to engage with herbs not just as tools, but as living allies with distinct magical personalities and functions.

Parts of a plant

The anatomy of a plant holds symbolic meaning about its occult, energetic, and magical virtues. Each part of the plant reflects a stage or force that plays a role in both physical and spiritual growth. At the base, the roots represent the foundation, stability, nourishment, and vitality. They ground the plant just as your personal foundations ground you, making growth possible from a place of security and sustenance. Roots are often viewed as the seat of the plant's spirit, the vessel of its power and potency.

Moving upward, the stem symbolizes growth and forward movement. It supports and elevates, allowing the plant to reach for the light while distributing energy throughout the organism. The leaves, often vibrant and full of life, are symbols of energy, power, and dynamic force. They are where the plant breathes, gathers light, and transforms it.

The leaves of a plant are most often used in the form of loose herbs for both medicine and magic. The leaves echo the action of magical practice and represent the process of channeling and focusing personal power.

The buds of a plant are potent emblems of new beginnings, creativity, and untapped potential. They hold the promise of what is to come, representing new ideas and ventures waiting to bloom. Once opened, the flower reveals the spirit of the plant in its most refined form, its essence and beauty. It speaks to the higher or spiritual nature of a matter, serving as a metaphor for the soul or purpose.

Finally, the seed holds the power of renewal and preservation. It carries the memory of the plant, the potential for future life, and the ability to begin again.

Each part plays an integral role in the greater cycle, offering deep insight into Nature's wisdom and its reflection in human life.

The language of flowers

The language of flowers, also known as *floriography*, is a symbolic tradition in which flowers are used to convey specific emotions, messages, or sentiments without the use of words. This practice reached its height of popularity during the Victorian era, when complex floral arrangements were carefully crafted to communicate affection, grief, desire, secrecy, or forgiveness, among many other feelings. Each flower held a specific meaning: Roses signified love, lilies purity, violets modesty, and marigolds grief. The selection, color, and even number of flowers in a bouquet were chosen with intention, allowing individuals to express deeply personal emotions in a socially acceptable and often poetic form.

Beyond this historical context, flower symbolism remains an important aspect of spiritual and magical practices. Flowers are powerful carriers of emotional and energetic resonance, making them ideal for use in rituals, offerings, charms, and divination. Their colors, shapes, and natural associations help evoke particular states of mind or call in specific energies. Whether placed on an altar, infused in oils, or given as heartfelt tokens, flowers continue to serve as a universal medium for expressing the full range of human experience — grief and joy, longing and hope, celebration and remembrance.

Flower petal numerology

A flowering plant is believed to be at the peak of its magical potency. The flowers themselves contain the most refined version of the plant's spiritual energy and allow people to convey emotions, sentiments, and messages through the careful selection and arrangement of flowers and plants. In a time when direct expression of feelings, especially romantic ones, was often considered improper or too forward, flowers offered a discreet and elegant way to communicate. Each bloom carried a specific meaning and even the color, number, and manner of presentation could alter or enhance the message. Bouquets were often exchanged as coded messages between lovers, friends, and family, with an entire social language built upon the symbolism of Nature.

Flowers could convey a spectrum of human emotion, from joy and admiration to grief, regret, or even rejection. For example, a yellow rose might symbolize friendship or jealousy depending on context, while a sprig of rosemary represented remembrance. This symbolic language also intertwined with magical and folkloric traditions, where plants were believed to carry energetic properties corresponding to their meanings. Today, the language of flowers continues to influence floral arrangements, rituals, and herbal magic, allowing plants to act as messengers of emotion and intention, bridging the gap between the physical and the symbolic.

The number of petals on a flower carries symbolic and magical significance, reflecting the spiritual qualities and energetic signature of the plant. In plant magic, *petal numerology* is an approach that combines sacred geometry and numerical symbolism to better understand the nature of a plant spirit. Each petal number expresses a unique frequency that can inform how the plant is used in healing, ritual, or spiritual practice.

Flowers with two petals speak to the theme of duality. They teach you to recognize opposing forces and strive for balance between them. These flowers are often aligned with harmony between polarities, such as light and shadow, self and other.

Three-petaled flowers, on the other hand, encourage the unification of body, mind, and spirit, fostering inner harmony and holistic well-being.

Four-petaled flowers are deeply symbolic of balance and sacred geometry. They correspond to the four directions, four elements, and four seasons, making them powerful allies for grounding, protection, and working within cycles. These flowers also echo the medicine wheel and magic circle, emphasizing integration of body, mind, emotions, and soul.

Flowers with five petals hold special significance in magical traditions. Representing the pentagram, they're associated with the life force, gateways, and transformation. These flowers tend to exist on a spectrum — on one end, deeply healing, while others are dangerously toxic. Their energy is often visionary, working with the forces of initiation and protection.

Six-petaled flowers reflect the union of the Universe and the individual, blending celestial and planetary forces into human consciousness. The hexagram geometry they embody can be viewed as a gateway used to invoke or banish planetary energies, assisting in integrating cosmic wisdom and facilitating transformation, especially during times of transition or shock.

Finally, seven-petaled flowers are connected to the mystical realms: fairies, spirits of Nature, and ancestral powers. Their sacred energy opens portals to the unseen, making them potent allies in magical and intuitive work.

Working with Herbal Energetics

Herbal energetics and herbal action are typically used in medicinal herbalism to refer to an herb's medicinal properties, the way it affects the body, and the specific body systems that it influences. For example, an herb like ginger, which has a fiery energy, helps to stimulate the digestive system and can also be used topically to stimulate blood flow to the surface of the skin. You can see how its fiery energetics give ginger the herbal action of getting things moving through its stimulating properties.

TIP

As you become more familiar with the energetic correspondences of herbs, you'll develop a better sense of which herbs to incorporate into your rituals through your own intuition, matching the characteristics of an herb with the energy of your intention.

Through an understanding of herbal action, you can also gain magical insight into a plant's energetics through its association to particular parts of the body. For example, an herb with an affinity for the heart would be useful in rituals for love, courage, and heart healing, while an herb with a bitter action that affects the digestive system would be helpful for spells to remove unwanted energies or break unhealthy patterns.

Table 1-1 list commonly used terms that refer to an herb's action:

TABLE 1-1 Common Herbal Actions

Herbal Action	What it does	Examples
Adaptogen	Helps the body adapt to stress and restore balance	Ashwagandha, ginseng, holy basil
Analgesic	Relieves or reduces pain	Meadowsweet, willow bark, clove
Anti-inflammatory	Reduces inflammation and swelling	Chamomile, turmeric, ginger
Antimicrobial	Fights or inhibits growth of microbes, such as bacteria, fungi, or viruses	Cinnamon, garlic, thyme
Antioxidant	Protects cells from oxidative stress caused by free radicals	Sage, green tea, rosemary
Antispasmodic	Relieves or prevents muscle spasms or cramps	Black cohosh, chamomile, valerian
Astringent	Contracts tissues, reduces secretions, and tightens skin or mucous membranes	Raspberry leaf, witch hazel, oak bark
Carminative	Eases digestive discomfort by reducing gas and bloating	Cardamom, fennel, peppermint
Diaphoretic	Promotes sweating, aiding detoxification and fever management	Ginger, elderflower, yarrow

(continued)

TABLE 1-1 *(continued)*

Herbal Action	What it does	Examples
Diuretic	Promotes urine production and supports the urinary system	Juniper berries, dandelion leaf, nettle
Emmenagogue	Stimulates or regulates menstrual flow	Angelica, yarrow, mugwort
Expectorant	Helps clear mucus from the respiratory tract	Eucalyptus, mullein, licorice root
Nervine	Supports the nervous system, often calming or sedative	Passionflower, lemon balm, skullcap
Rubefacient	Stimulates blood flow to the surface of the skin, creating warmth and redness	Rosemary, cayenne, mustard
Sedative	Calms the body and mind, often promoting sleep	Lavender, valerian, hops
Stimulant	Increases activity of the body or its systems	Yerba mate, coffee, guarana
Tonic	Strengthens or invigorates a specific organ or overall vitality, preventing illness, helping with stress or fatigue	Dandelion, nettle, astragalus

REMEMBER

Consult with your physician or a qualified herbalist before you begin taking any new herbs internally to avoid any contraindications. The herbal actions provided here aren't intended as medical advice but meant to demonstrate the connection between medicinal action and magical energetics.

IN THIS CHAPTER

» Concocting formulas for magic

» Infusing and extracting herbal properties

» Blending herbs for magic and wellness

» Developing an herbal magic repertoire

Chapter 2
Working with Herbal Magic Formulas

Herbs are wonderfully versatile allies for magical practice, offering a multitude of ways to channel their energies and enhance ritual work. Their versatility allows you to incorporate them into nearly any aspect of spellcraft, and plants almost always play some role in spiritual practices around the world. An herb's medicinal properties, fragrance, and taste confer the ability to connect with you on a physical level, which help you tap into its spiritual properties as well. Whether you're brewing an herbal tea, blending a loose incense, or creating a charm to carry with you, the natural properties of herbs provide both physical and energetic qualities that support your magical goals.

In this chapter, I explore a variety of herbal formulas and the techniques for preparing them, drawing on foundational methods of herbal formulation. My focus in this chapter is on how you can intentionally craft these preparations to serve your magical goals rather than solely for your physical well-being.

I also look beyond the basics to explore ways of working with herbs that are unique to magical practice, such as crafting herbal charms, burning ritual incense, or creating flower essences to capture a plant's energetic properties. By understanding these foundational techniques, you gain the skills to incorporate herbs more effectively into your rituals, spellwork, and daily spiritual practices.

Blending Herbal Tea

Tea is one of the most popularly consumed beverages in the world. Originating in Asia, tea comes from the tea plant *Camellia sinensis*, and depending on how it's harvested and prepared, it makes green, black and white varieties. Tea has been consumed for thousands of years, and the process of preparing and consuming tea has become highly ritualized in some parts of the world.

Tea is prepared using a hot water infusion technique that involves pouring hot water over dried tea leaves and allowing it to sit and infuse, pulling its flavor into the hot water. Because of its popularity, tea has come to be a general term for any herb that has been prepared in this way. Herbal teas, or *tisanes*, refer to hot water infusions that are prepared from herbs other than the tea plant. Examples of herbal teas include lavender, lemon balm, or chamomile tea. You can prepare herbal teas using single or multiple herbs.

Drinking herbal tea is a simple and effective way to benefit from an herb's medicinal properties and promote general well-being. By ritualizing the process of preparing and consuming herbal tea and infusing it with your intentions, you can effectively connect with the energy and spirit of the herbs you're working with both physically and spiritually. Blending, brewing, and consuming herbal tea with intention is a powerful way to incorporate herbal magic into your daily life.

WARNING

Before consuming any herbal formula, remember that not all herbs are safe to consume internally.

Blending herbal teas can be a very creative and personal process, especially when those blends are created for magical purposes. By bringing together multiple herbal ingredients, you can create tailored formulas to match your magical intentions. Just remember that while a carefully thought out magical tea blend may have all the components you're looking for in your spellwork, not all magical blends are going to have the nicest flavor.

TIP

When blending herbal teas for magical purposes, I recommend working with three to five ingredients at most, which helps to keep the overall energy of the blend more focused. Select each individual herb based on your intention or desired goal, making sure that it's safe to make into herbal tea.

TIP

Go to the tea aisle in the grocery store and read the labels so that you can become familiar with herbs that are commonly sold as teas. Herbs like hibiscus, passionflower, chamomile, and lemon balm will likely be present, indicating these herbs are likely safe to add to your formulas.

After you decide on your magical intention (see Chapter 10) and choose your herbs, you can prepare your magical herbal tea. You will need an electric or stovetop kettle to heat your water in, a teacup or mug, and a tea-ball infuser, tea bag, or tea pot with strainer.

The amount of each herb depends on the size of your container, and how much tea you're making. For example, to make a tea blend for happiness and well-being, I use 1 tablespoon of lemongrass, 1 tablespoon of chamomile, and 1 tablespoon of jasmine flowers.

TIP

If you're using a smaller tea-ball infuser, you may not be able to fit 3 tablespoons in it; in that case, just use equal parts. The same applies if you're making a larger pot of tea; you can use more than 1 tablespoon of each herb. The most important thing is that each herb is present.

Follow these steps to make an herbal tea:

1. **Heating your water in the electric or stovetop kettle.**
2. **While the water is heating take each of your herbs individually in the palm of your hand while focusing on your intention and ask the herb to support your magical goal.**

   After you have connected with each herb, place it in the strainer.
3. **When the water has finished boiling, pour it into the container with the herbs and allow it to sit and infuse for 15 minutes.**

While the herbs are infusing, you can sit with your herbal tea and meditate on your magical intention, adding your own energy to the energy of the herbs.

4. **After the herbs have finished infusing and the tea is cool enough to drink, mindfully sip the tea feeling the energy and influence of the herbs mingle with your physical body.**

TIP

When you have finished, be sure to thank the plant spirits for their support.

Brewing herbal tea can be performed as a ritual on its own or as part of a larger magical working to attune your body and spirit to a specific vibration. Drinking herbal teas is also a great way to connect with a plant spirit and develop a deeper relationship with it.

Infusing Herbs into Oil

Infused oils are used for culinary, medicinal, and cosmetic purposes. These formulas extract an herb's flavor and aromatic and medicinal qualities into a carrier oil. In herbal magic, infused oils form the basis for formulas often referred to as *ritual oils* or *anointing oils*. In addition to an herb's physical qualities, these formulations also contain an herb's energetic and spiritual properties as well. Simply put, oil infusions are created by adding plant material to a carrier oil and allowing it to infuse over time.

You can apply these formulas to the body or use them to anoint ritual tools, such as candles, jewelry, or crystals, to confer their unique energies. To *anoint* something is to apply a formula — in this case, an infused oil — with the intention of imbuing the object or person with the formula's energy.

Infused oils are very versatile and often combine a number of herbal ingredients that create specific combinations based on each herb's magical correspondences. You can use infused oils to create an infinite number of formulas for use in spellwork.

Carrier oils

Carrier oils are the medium in which the properties of the herbs are extracted. Some carrier oils absorb into the skin more effectively, others are odorless, and certain carrier oils are able to be heated to a higher temperature than others. As you become more advanced in your practice, you can also get more specific with the magical correspondences of the carrier oils that you're using.

A few common carrier oils that you can use effectively for all the formulas in this book are grapeseed oil, jojoba oil, olive oil, and sweet almond oil.

TIP

If you'd like to get more specific with the carrier oils you're working with, you can definitely do that, or you may choose one and stick with that same oil throughout your magical practice. I personally use grapeseed oil in the majority of my oil infusions because it's inexpensive, accessible, and odorless. It also has a high burn temperature, which can be helpful if you need to heat the oil to a high temperature.

Cold-infusion method

The cold-infusion method, sometimes referred to as the folk method, is the more traditionally used method for creating infused oils. The cold-infusion method takes more time than the hot-infusion method that I discuss in the next section, usually taking four to six weeks to complete. When creating infused oils for magical use, this longer completion time allows for the opportunity to add more energy and intention into the creation of the oil and also incorporate magical timing. Many magical practitioners will work with the 28-day lunar cycle for timing their infused oils. For example, you may choose to start your infused oil during the New Moon and allow its energy to accumulate throughout the entirety of the lunar cycle.

To create a cold-infusion oil, you need a clean glass jar with a lid, such as a mason jar or recycled pasta sauce jar. Then select all your herbal ingredients and your carrier oil. For this purpose, I use dried herbs, although in some instances, you can use fresh. Make sure all the herbal ingredients are completely dried. You don't have to be specific with the amounts of ingredients. The amounts depend on the size of your jar and how much oil you want to make. Keep in mind the more plant material that you use, the more concentrated the oil will be.

After you gather your dried herbs and carrier oil, you're ready to make the infused oil:

1. **Crush or tear your herbs into smaller pieces to fit them into the jar, focusing your intention and asking each herb to imbue the ritual oil with its energy.**
2. **Add your herbs to the jar until it's one-third to halfway full.**

   TIP

   You may want to use the handle of a wooden spoon to help push the herbs down into the jar.
3. **Cover the herbs entirely with carrier oil, pouring enough oil into the jar to cover the herbs by at least ½ inch.**
4. **Put the lid on the jar and allow to sit and infuse for four to six weeks, shaking the jar occasionally and checking that the plant material remains completely covered in oil.**

   Optionally, you can sit the jar in a sunny spot to help with the infusion process. Depending on the type of oil you're preparing, you may choose to keep the jar out of the sunlight and expose it to the light of the Moon instead.
5. **(Optional) After four to six weeks, strain out the plant material using cheesecloth.**

TIP

Four to six weeks is the average amount of infusion time, although some herbs infuse faster than others. Some people may also choose to allow their oils to infuse perpetually, which is how I do mine. How can you tell the infusion process is complete? Sometimes the oil will change color depending on the type of plant material, or the fragrance of the plant material will be transferred to the oil.

TIP

Because these are magical formulas, I typically don't strain out the plant material and allow it to continue infusing indefinitely. As long as the plant material is properly dried and there is no prior contamination or moisture in the jar, you should not have any issues with mold or rancidity.

TIP

You can also add other ingredients to the jar, such as essential oils for a stronger scent or other magical materials, such as crystals or bones, to incorporate their unique energies into your formula.

Hot-infusion method

The hot-infusion method is similar to the cold-infusion method (see preceding section) with the benefit of it being much faster because of the incorporation of heat in the infusing process. With this method, you can create infused oils in just a few days instead of weeks.

This method does have a few downsides, however. The infusion may not be as strong. It also won't have as much of a scent as cold infusion techniques because the heat causes the essential oils to evaporate more quickly. Also, the cold infusion technique offers more opportunity for magical timing and bringing in extra energy because it takes longer to create and put effort into shaking it on a regular basis.

To begin the creation of your infused oil, select all your herbal ingredients and your carrier oil. Make sure all the herbal ingredients are completely dried. The hot-infusion technique does allow for fresh plant material to be used because the heat evaporates any water present in the plant material, which prevents contamination and keeps the oil from spoiling. Just as in cold infusion, you don't have to be specific with the amounts of ingredients being used. It just depends on the size of your jar and the amount of oil that you want as an end result. Keep in mind the more plant material that you use, the more concentrated the oil will be.

To create a hot-oil infusion, you will need a clean glass jar with a lid, a slow cooker, a carrier oil, and dried herbs. Then follow these steps:

1. **Crush or tear your herbs into smaller pieces to fit them into the jar, focusing your intention and asking each herb to imbue the ritual oil with its energy.**
2. **Add your herbs to the jar until it's one-third to halfway full.**

   You may want to use the handle of a wooden spoon to help push the herbs down into the jar.

3. **Cover the herbs entirely with carrier oil, pouring enough oil into the jar to cover the herbs by at least ½ inch.**

4. **Put the lid on the jar, but do not seal the jar completely.**

WARNING

Not sealing the jar completely allows heat and moisture to escape so that pressure doesn't build up inside the jar.

5. **Place the jar inside the slow cooker and add water to the slow cooker until it reaches the same level as the oil inside of the jar; do not put the lid on the slow cooker.**

REMEMBER

The water is only going inside the slow cooker, not the jar with the oil.

6. **Set the slow cooker to a low and heat the jar for three to four days, keeping an eye on the water level and adding more water as needed.**

REMEMBER

Turn the slow cooker off at bedtime and turn it back on in the morning each day. Doing so makes it easier to monitor the water level in the slow cooker.

7. **After the oil has finished infusing, allow it to cool and add any other ingredients, such as essential oils, crystals, bones, or other charms.**

Making Your Own Herbal Tinctures

Herbal tinctures are formulas that are frequently used in medicinal herbalism. Tinctures are made using alcohol to extract the medicinal compounds from either fresh or dried herbs. They're typically made using a high-proof alcohol. Vodka, which is 80 proof (40 percent alcohol) is most frequently used, but you can also use other liquors, such as gin, brandy, and whiskey. Everclear, which is 190 proof or 95 percent alcohol, is also sometimes used but because of its high alcohol content, it's not recommended to be taken by itself and is typically diluted. To start out, I recommend working with vodka or one of the previously mentioned liquors, as 80 proof alcohol is sufficient to extract the chemical compounds of most plant material.

For medicinal purposes, tinctures are generally taken internally with multiple different tinctures being combined to support an overall purpose. Because of their alcohol content, tinctures absorb rapidly into the bloodstream, making them effective medicines. They also have an indefinite shelf life because the alcohol acts as a preservative.

WARNING

Be sure to do your research before taking any new herbs internally. It's always a good idea to consult with a qualified herbalist or physician before taking tinctures for medicinal purposes.

Because tinctures are potent extracts containing an herb's active constituents, they're also energetically potent and can be incorporated into magical practice in different ways. Like all these formulas, tinctures are essentially vehicles for an herb's energetic properties, and the ways that you can use them depend on your magical goals. For example, you can add a few drops of a tincture to herbal tea to increase its potency and incorporate additional herbal ingredients to the blend. You can also add a few drops of a tincture to a ritual bath to infuse the properties of the herb into your bath water if you don't have any of the actual herbs on hand. You can also use tinctures similarly to anointing oils by applying them to ritual objects, or you can use tincture to wash your ritual tools by adding the formula to some water to imbue the tools with the energy of a particular herb.

Weight-to-volume ratios

Because tinctures are concentrated in their chemistry and typically used in the context of medicinal herbalism, specific measurements are used to determine the concentration of a formula for more exact dosing. These measurements are called a *weight-to-volume ratio,* and it refers to the amount of plant material used in relation to the amount of alcohol used.

REMEMBER

If you're avoiding the use of alcohol for any reason, you can also make tinctures using either apple cider vinegar or vegetable glycerin. However, these options don't always extract as readily as alcohol and don't have as long of a shelf life.

When creating magical formulas, you can typically default to the folk method, which doesn't use specific measurements. (For more on the folk method, see Chapter 1.) This technique is safe and effective for most general use herbs. Some herbs are called *low-dose herbs* and have a much more potent chemistry and whose dosing must be more exact to avoid adverse effects and potential poisoning. The topic of low-dose herbs is much more advanced and outside the scope of this work, which focuses on general use herbs that are safer to work with. If you're interested in learning more about low-dose herbs in magical practice, I recommend my book *The Poison Path Herbal* (Park Street Press).

TIP

The weight-to-volume ratio is determined by the amount of tincture you want to create for your end result. They're typically written in the form of a ratio — for example, 1:5. The first number represents the amount of plant material in grams, and the second number represents the amount of alcohol in milliliters. So, for a 1:5 ratio, 1 gram (g) of plant material is present for every 5 milliliter (ml) of alcohol. You can do this conversion for any amount of alcohol. For example, if you're making a 100 ml tincture, you would use 20 grams of plant material.

- **Fresh plant material 1:2:** If you happen to be working with fresh plant material for whatever reason, the weight-to-volume ratio is 1:2. This ratio reduces the amount of alcohol to plant material to compensate for the fresh plant material's water content. When working with fresh plant material, you'd also use a higher alcohol percentage (95 percent alcohol, such as Everclear) to account for the plant's water content. Fresh plant material extracts differently than dry plant material and can have different medicinal properties, which is why an herbalist may choose to use fresh plant material versus dry. It is typically just for medicinal uses that this distinction matters.
- **Dried plant material 1:5:** Unless you're using herbs that you've grown in your garden or plants that have been wild-harvested, you'll most likely be working with dry plant material in your herbal formulas. The standard weight-to-volume ratio for making tinctures with dry plant material is 1:5 using alcohol that is at least 80 proof, typically vodka or one of the other liquors mentioned at the beginning of this section.
- **Folk method:** The folk method is more intuitive and effective for use with most herbs in general. The folk method for tincture-making is essentially the same as the folk method for making an infused oil. The dry plant material is added to a glass jar until it's around halfway full. The alcohol is added until the plant material is completely submerged, with the alcohol level being at least a ½ inch above the plant material.
- **Maceration:** Maceration refers to the process and time period during which the alcohol extracts the properties from the plant material. Most tinctures will be ready within four to six weeks. Some tinctures, especially those made with tough

roots and resins like frankincense, can take months to fully extract the chemical constituents of the plant material, but for this purpose, four to six weeks is a sufficient maceration time.

Lemon Balm Tincture

For this Lemon Balm Tincture, I am using lemon balm (*Melissa officinalis*) as an example. Lemon balm has a variety of medicinal uses and is generally safe to work with. It's also a versatile plant ally for magical practice, valued by alchemists and magical practitioners alike.

You can use this tincture to connect with the wisdom of lemon balm by taking a few drops in a cup of water before meditation. You can also add to other alcohol or water-based formulas to increase their magical potency and synergize the other ingredients.

Gather a clean glass jar with a lid, cheesecloth, coffee filter or parchment paper, 20 grams dried lemon balm, 100 ml vodka, and dropper bottles. Then follow these steps:

1. **Crush the dried lemon balm until it's a fine consistency.**

   Crushing makes it easier for the alcohol to cover it.

2. **Add 100 ml of vodka, using the handle of a wooden spoon to push down the plant material until it's completely covered.**

   If needed, you can add a little extra vodka because some will be lost in the straining process.

3. **Place the coffee filter or parchment paper over the rim of the jar before putting on the lid.**

   This step helps reduce the contact of the alcohol with the metal in the lid, which can affect the quality of the tincture.

4. **Store the jar in a cool dark place for four to six weeks, shaking it every so often and adding more vodka, if needed.**

5. **When the maceration is complete, strain the tincture using the cheesecloth, squeezing the cheesecloth to remove any remaining alcohol that the plant material has absorbed, and then discard the plant material.**

When you finish the tincture, distribute it into dropper bottles and label the bottle with the name of the herb, the weight-to-volume ratio used, and the date of bottling.

Store your finished tinctures in a cool, dry place away from direct sunlight to prevent evaporation. Even when the dropper bottles are sealed, small amounts of alcohol will evaporate over time.

Making and Burning Incense

Throughout history, all cultures have used incense and herbal fumigations to create sacred space and promote healing of the body and spirit and as offerings to the spirit world and the divine. Incense typically consists of fragrant woods like sandalwood and *tree resins* (the aromatic sap excreted by trees), such as frankincense and pine resin. *Herbal fumigations* refer to the burning of aromatic plant material, such as sage, mugwort, or juniper.

You can use incense and herbal fumigations similarly, and the terms are often used interchangeably. Incense and herbal fumigations can consist of a single ingredient or blends of multiple ingredients, such as resin, wood, and plant material. Incense also comes in other forms ready to use, such as stick incense, incense cones, and powdered incense.

Incense ingredients

The main purpose of incense is to create a specific atmosphere. Typically, incense blends are used for their pleasing aroma to create a sacred space, provide an offering, or convey an uplifting or healing quality. Not all herbs are going to have a pleasing aroma when burned, and an herb that smells nice when fresh may smell very differently when dried and burned. This is why incense blends typically make use of aromatic resins, woods, and fragrant herbs.

Tree resins, such as frankincense, myrrh, copal, and pine, have been valued for thousands of years as powerful incense materials in both ritual and everyday practice. These aromatic exudates are collected from the bark of trees and, when burned on charcoal or added to incense blends, release fragrant smoke that is often used for purification, protection, spiritual elevation, and offerings to deities or spirits. Because resins are rich in volatile oils and natural compounds, their smoke carries potent energetic and aromatic properties, making them ideal for consecrating sacred space, enhancing meditation, or supporting spellwork.

Aromatic woods, such as sandalwood, cedar, palo santo, and agarwood, are prized in incense-making for their rich fragrances and their ability to hold and release scent slowly when burned. These woods are often used as a base material in loose incense blends, powdered for sticks and cones, or burned directly as chips on charcoal. Each type of wood carries its own energetic qualities, making them versatile tools for a wide range of ritual and magical purposes. Their aromatic smoke is used for creating sacred space, promoting relaxation, and connecting with the spirit world.

Not every herb is going to have a fragrant scent when burned. However, you can incorporate fragrant herbs with resins and woods as part of an incense blend, adding their own magical correspondences. Herbs have been burned throughout human history for their ability to cleanse a space, raise energy, and prevent and cure illness. Mugwort, rose, juniper, myrtle and spikenard are just a few examples of herbs used in incense blends or burned alone in herbal fumigations.

Incense Blend

You can create your own incense by blending ingredients and burn it to purify your space and promote relaxation and focus during meditation. The following formula is a simple example, using only three ingredients, but as you become more experienced, you can create more complex incense blends using multiple ingredients.

TIP

I recommend using one ingredient from each of the categories — resin, wood, and herb — to create a well-rounded and aromatically pleasing incense blend. Woods that are frequently used in incense-making are usually already available in powder or chip form.

This formula uses the resin known as copal. Although there are many varieties of copal, I like to use white or gold copal.

To create this Incense Blend, gather 1 ounce copal resin, 1 tablespoon sandalwood chips or powder, and 1 tablespoon mugwort. I recommend using mugwort that is cut and sifted because it's already at the right consistency. If you're using mugwort that you have grown or harvested, you may have to use a pair of scissors to cut it into smaller pieces.

You also need a mortar and pestle and a glass jar with a lid for storage. A *mortar and pestle* is a tool, usually made of stone, wood, or marble, that is used to grind up solid ingredients like incense resin. The *mortar* is the bowl, and the *pestle* is the handheld tool used to do the grinding. I recommend using one made of stone or marble.

After you gather your ingredients, follow these steps:

1. **Add the copal resin to the mortar and pestle and grind it until it reaches a fine consistency.**

   This step is a good time to focus on your intention and begin putting your energy into the incense blend.
2. **Add the sandalwood to the mortar and mix with the resin.**
3. **Add the mugwort to the mortar and mix with the other ingredients, blending all the ingredients together until they're evenly distributed.**
4. **Transfer the incense blend to your glass jar for storage.**

Burning incense

Burning incense seems like it's straightforward, but you need to remember a few important things when burning loose incense blends. When the incense is burned, the smoke is believed to carry prayers and petitions to the spirit world. It also releases powerful aromatic compounds that assist in altering consciousness to aid in meditation and spellwork.

Incense blends are burned by placing a small amount of the incense blend on charcoal. The charcoal used to burn incense is a special kind of charcoal that is very different from the charcoal briquettes used for grilling food. Charcoal briquettes should never be used for burning incense. Incense charcoal is safe to burn indoors and is circular in shape. It's the same charcoal that is used when smoking out of a *hookah* (a water pipe, originated in the Indian subcontinent that is used for smoking), and you can find it online at metaphysical stores and smoke shops.

To burn incense, you need an incense burner, which can be a specially made burner meant for loose incense or a fireproof dish made from clay or metal. You also need incense charcoal, metal tongs, sand, incense, and a lighter or matches.

After you gather these items, follow these steps:

1. **Prepare your incense burner.**

   To prepare your incense burner, add sand to the burner or dish so that it fills the bottom. The sand helps absorb the heat from the charcoal so that the incense burner doesn't burn the surface it's sitting on.

2. **Light the charcoal.**

   Hold the charcoal with the metal tongs before lighting. The charcoal is self-igniting and will begin to spark. Hold the flame to the charcoal until the sparks begin to ignite the rest of the charcoal and then place the charcoal on the sand in the center of the incense burner.

   Don't hold the charcoal with your fingers when igniting. The charcoal heats up very quickly and will burn your fingers.

   The charcoal begins to glow red.

3. **When the charcoal is ready, place a small pinch of your incense blend on the charcoal, adding more as needed.**

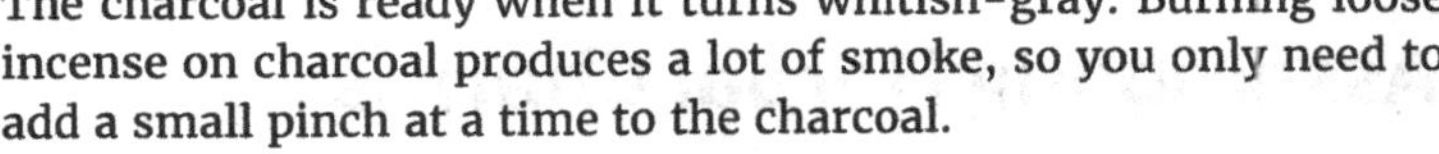

The charcoal is ready when it turns whitish-gray. Burning loose incense on charcoal produces a lot of smoke, so you only need to add a small pinch at a time to the charcoal.

Crafting Stick and Cone Incense

You can burn Stick and cone incense in an incense burner without charcoal. Light the tip of the incense stick or cone and blow it out when you see the tip glowing red.

The Crafting Stick and Cone Incense formula uses powdered aromatic wood, such as sandalwood or cedar. It also uses *Makko powder,* a combustible binder powder that holds everything together and makes it burn.

To create this formula, you need 4 tablespoons powdered aromatic wood, 1 tablespoon Makko powder, 1 teaspoon powdered herbs and or resins for additional scent, distilled water, and (optional) a small amount of alcohol for faster extraction/drying. Also gather parchment paper, mixing bowls, and bamboo incense sticks (for stick method). Then follow these steps:

1. **Mix the dry ingredients.**
2. **Add a small amount of distilled water and stir until it's a thick paste-like consistency.**

   Continue adding water or powder until you have achieved the desired consistency.
3. **Prepare a workspace with parchment and lay out the bamboo sticks.**
4. **To make incense sticks, take a small amount of paste and roll it around a bamboo stick with your fingers forming an even layer about 2 to 4 mm thick; to make incense cones, take grape-sized amounts of paste and form them into tiny cones.**

   Work from one end to the other so that the stick or cone is evenly coated.
5. **Place coated sticks or cones on parchment or on a drying rack, turning them every so often.**

TIP

Drying time will vary based on humidity and the thickness of the paste applied to the stick.

Assembling Herbal Charms

Charms are magical objects that you can carry, hang in a home, or place in specific locations to cause a variety of magical outcomes ranging from prosperity to protection.

Charms can take on a variety of forms, including charm bags, herb bundles, and spell jars. They're different from other magical objects, such as amulets and talismans, which are singular objects of a more permanent nature typically worn as jewelry or carried. Charms are often comprised of multiple components, including herbs, roots, bones, and other small objects of a symbolic significance. Amulets are usually crafted to be worn as jewelry and are used for protection and keeping away unwanted influences, while talismans are ritually constructed objects that can be created for a variety of different uses. The latter are often created using astrological timing and specific symbols engraved on metal, clay or wood and can be carried on the person or fashioned into talismanic jewelry once imbued with the desired energy.

Charm bags

When it comes to herbal magic, the most commonly crafted charm is the charm bag. Charm bags are used in many magical traditions and go by many different names. They're often called herbal sachets, gris-gris bags, mojo bags, hexentaschen, or medicine bags.

You can create a charm bag for divine protection using dried angelica root, hyssop, frankincense resin, and rue. Gather the following supplies:

- Small drawstring bag
- Three white chime candles with holders
- A plate
- Protection incenses (see Chapter 5 for formulas)
- Incense burner
- Protection oil (see Chapter 5 for formula)

After you gather your herbs and supplies, you're ready to create your charm bag for divine protection:

1. **Prepare the space.**

   On a stable surface, arrange the three white chime candles in a triangle. Place the heat-safe plate in the center. Light your charcoal and, after it's gray at the edges, add a pinch of incense, adding more incense as needed.

2. **State your intention.**

   Stand or sit comfortably. State your purpose plainly: "I consecrate this work for divine protection and blessings."

3. **Awaken the ingredients.**

   Take each ingredient in your hand individually and ask the plant spirit to lend its power to your ritual. Blow on the plant material in your hand three times, offering it your breath to awaken it. Place the plant material on the plate inside the triangle of candles.

4. **Cleanse the bag.**

   Hold the empty drawstring bag over the incense smoke, allowing the smoke to saturate it inside and out.

5. **Build the charm.**

   Add each herb to the bag one by one. As each goes in, name the herb and offer a brief petition reciting the desired qualities of each herb. For example:

   - *Angelica:* To connect to the divine and confer blessings
   - *Hyssop:* To purify and remove all unwanted energies
   - *Frankincense:* To raise the vibration and bring spiritual protection
   - *Rue:* To banish harmful energies and influences

TIP

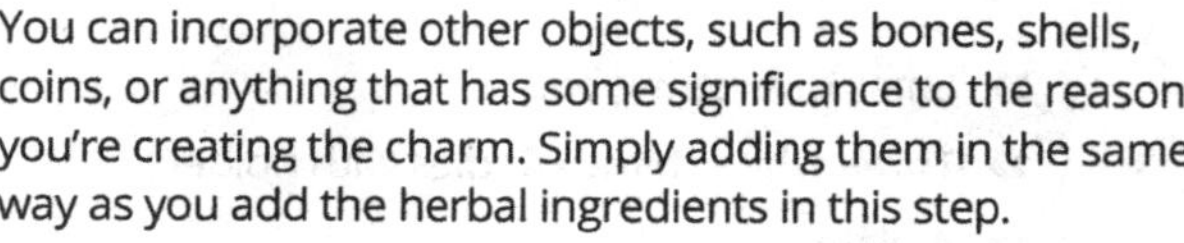

You can incorporate other objects, such as bones, shells, coins, or anything that has some significance to the reason you're creating the charm. Simply adding them in the same way as you add the herbal ingredients in this step.

6. **Consecrate the finished bag.**

   Hold the filled bag over the incense smoke and then place it on the plate at the center of the candle triangle. Meditate, pray, or chant your intention for protection until the candles burn down safely.

7. **Seal the bag.**

   Tie the bag closed. (You can knot three times, repeating your intention.) Optionally, anoint the outside with a few drops of protection oil. Hang it by the front door or in the bedroom or carry it with you.

8. **Recharge.**

   Every full moon, refresh the charm: cleanse it in incense smoke, place it inside a new triangle of three white candles, and pray your petitions as they burn. You can also feed the bag between recharging by applying a few drops of protection oil to the outside.

Spell Bottle for Keeping Away Unwanted Visitors

Spell bottles have become a popular component of modern magical practice. Like charm bags and other containers, spell bottles bring together magical ingredients dedicated to a specific purpose. The container is then kept in a specific place to confer its influence.

Historically, these container spells were known as *witch bottles.* Witch bottles were used as protective charms, particularly in early modern Europe and colonial America, to ward off malevolent magic, curses, or the evil eye. They were often filled with sharp items, such as pins, nails, thorns, and personal elements, such as hair and urine, and were then buried beneath the hearth, threshold, or hidden in the walls of a home to trap and neutralize harmful influences.

Originating in the 16th and 17th centuries, these bottles acted as both a spiritual decoy and a magical barrier, reflecting or returning ill will to its source while safeguarding the household. Witch bottles have been discovered hidden in or near old homes into the 20th century. Today, spell bottles, like charm bags (see preceding section), are constructed for a variety of magical purposes.

The charm in the next formula is an adaptation of the historical witch's bottle and makes use of herbal ingredients to repel unwanted visitors from the home. You can create this charm to keep away a specific person or to act as a general protective measure.

TIP

Construct the charm on a Tuesday or Saturday while the Moon is waning.

To create the Spell Bottle for Keeping Away Unwanted Visitors, you need the following: glass bottle with tight cork or lid, black chime candle, white or apple cider vinegar, wormwood, slippery elm bark, thorns, mustard seed, and valerian root. Then follow these steps:

1. **Set your focus.**

   Stand or sit quietly for a few breaths. Envision your home being surrounded by a field of energy that repels any unwanted persons or those with negative intentions. Keep this image in mind throughout the ritual.

2. **Prepare the ingredients.**

   Lay your herbs and materials out before you in the order you'll use them, focusing on your intention.

3. **Add your herbs to the bottle, speaking a petition as you add each one.**

   One at a time, pick up an ingredient, hold it briefly in your hands, and focus your intention on repelling unwanted visitors. Speak a short petition as you add each item to the bottle. For example:

   Wormwood, bitter and sharp, I turn you against all those who would disturb my peace.

   Slippery elm bark, hidden from view, tie the tongues of those who would speak against me.

   Thorns, to rip and tear at those who would ignore my boundaries.

   Mustard seed, bring confusion and distraction to those who would approach with ill intent.

   Valerian root, bring discomfort and repel those who are not welcome here.

4. **Fill the bottle with vinegar.**
5. **Seal and charge.**

   Put the cork or lid on snugly. Hold the sealed bottle in both hands and shake it while mentally filling it with the energy of repulsion: Imagine a barrier forming around your home and unwanted visitors turning back. Shake until you feel the charge has been set.

6. **Burn the candle on top of the bottle, allowing the candle to burn down.**

   Melt a little wax and drip a small pool onto the center of the lid; press the bottom of the black chime candle into that wax to anchor it upright. Allow the wax to set enough to hold the candle steady. Ideally, allow the candle to consume itself fully while you keep focus on the intent.

7. **Bury or hide the bottle.**

   Bury the bottle on your property in the front yard or tuck it under the front porch or doorstep. If burying is impossible, hide the jar indoors near the front door, behind a mat, in a recessed space by the threshold, or in a small niche that isn't easily disturbed. Always keep the bottle where it will not be broken or accessed by children or pets.

Incorporating Essential Oils and Aromatherapy

Essential oils are concentrated plant extracts that capture the aromatic compounds responsible for a plant's characteristic fragrance and many of its therapeutic properties. These volatile compounds, including terpenes, aldehydes, and phenols, not only provide the distinctive scent but also interact with the human body on both physiological and psychological levels. Terpenes, for example, are known to influence mood by promoting relaxation, alertness, or emotional uplift depending on their chemical structure.

Essential oils are most commonly obtained through *steam distillation,* a process that separates the plant's aromatic essence from its fibrous material using heat and water vapor. From an alchemical perspective, the resulting essential oil represents the Sulphur, or the soul, of the plant, while the distillation process itself is seen as a means of separating and purifying the three alchemical principles: Sulphur, Mercury, and Salt, which each represent a different aspect of the plant's spiritual essence. This connection to alchemy reflects the ancient understanding of distillation as both a physical extraction and a spiritual refinement and the potential that essential oils have in magical practice.

TIP

The sense of smell is one of your most powerful tools when it comes to altering consciousness, whether it's promoting relaxation, bringing back a childhood memory, or putting someone in a desired state of mind for a ritual. Essential oils are an effective means of working with a plant's natural aromas.

Aromatherapy harnesses the volatile compounds of essential oils to influence both mental and physical well-being through the sense of smell and, in some cases, topical application. When inhaled, aromatic molecules travel through the olfactory system, directly stimulating the brain, which governs emotions, memory, and the stress response. Certain scents, such as lavender or chamomile, can promote relaxation and reduce anxiety, while others, like citrus or rosemary, may enhance alertness, focus, and mood elevation. On a physiological level, some essential oils have been shown to affect heart rate, blood pressure, and hormone levels, creating a measurable impact on the body's stress and relaxation cycles. The unique chemistry of each oil plays a key role in determining these effects.

Essential oil blends

You can use essential oils individually or blend them into infinite combinations based on personal preference and magical intention. These oil blends, mixed with a carrier oil, are versatile tools that you can wear on the body as a personal fragrance, use to anoint candles and other ritual objects, or add to ritual baths. Mix all essential oils with a carrier oil before applying to skin.

Carrier oils are neutral or lightly scented plant-based oils used to dilute essential oils when creating blends, ensuring safe application to the skin and allowing for easier absorption. Because essential oils are highly concentrated and can cause irritation or sensitivity if applied undiluted, carrier oils provide a stable base that helps disperse the aromatic compounds without compromising their therapeutic or magical properties.

Common carrier oils include:

- Sweet almond oil, valued for its light texture and skin-nourishing vitamin E content
- Jojoba oil, which closely resembles the skin's natural sebum and has excellent moisturizing properties
- Coconut oil, prized for its antimicrobial qualities and smooth glide in massage
- Grapeseed oil, a lightweight option with a mildly astringent effect
- Olive oil, which offers deep nourishment and is used in many traditional formulas

To formulate essential oil blends:

1. **Determine your purpose.**

   Begin by identifying the intention or desired effect of the blend. Is it for relaxation, focus, protection, love, or magical workings? Your purpose guides your selection of essential oils and carrier oils.

2. **Select essential oils.**

   Choose two to five essential oils that complement each other in both scent and purpose. When blending, it helps to consider the aromatic hierarchy:

- *Top notes* are the first scents you notice, light and fresh, but they fade quickly (citrus, eucalyptus).
- *Middle notes* form the heart of the blend, giving it character and balance, often floral or herbal (lavender, rosemary).
- *Base notes* are rich and grounding, lingering the longest and providing depth (patchouli, sandalwood).

3. **Choose a carrier oil.**
4. **Measure your ratio.**

   A standard dilution is about 20 drops per 30 ml of carrier oil for topical application. For magical or aromatic purposes only (not direct skin application), you may use slightly higher concentrations.
5. **Blend the oils.**

   In a clean, dark glass bottle dropper bottle, add the essential oils first, starting with the base notes, then the middle notes, and finally the top notes. Swirl gently to mix.
6. **Add your carrier oil.**

   Pour in your carrier oil to fill the bottle. Cap tightly and shake gently to combine.
7. **Allow to mature.**

   Let the blend rest for at least 24 hours (or up to a week) in a cool, dark place, which allows the scents to meld and the energies to harmonize.
8. **Label and store.**

   Clearly label the blend with its name, ingredients, and date. Store in a dark glass bottle away from direct sunlight to preserve its potency.

TIP

Adding *scent fixatives* (ingredients that help hold the fragrance blend together) to your base note can help extend the longevity of the blends aroma. Using rich and long-lasting essential oils, such as patchouli or vetiver, or essential oils from resins like frankincense, benzoin, and myrrh can help increase the lasting ability of the overall fragrance. You can also add a pinch of orris root or gum Arabic powder to the formula to preserve its scent without changing the fragrance of the formula.

Autumnal Simmer Pot for Prosperity

Essential oils are naturally present in fresh and dried plant material. In addition to working with ready-made essential oils, you can also extract the beneficial aromatic compounds from plants in other ways, too. Simmer pots are a great way to make use of the naturally occurring essential oils of aromatic herbs and fill your home with some amazing scents.

The following formula shows you how to create an Autumnal Simmer Pot for Prosperity and requires the following ingredients: fresh orange peel from 1 to 2 oranges, lemon peel from 1 lemon, 2 to 3 cinnamon sticks, 1 tablespoon allspice berries, 2 to 3 bay leaves, and water. Then follow these steps:

1. **Prepare the ingredients.**

   Peel the orange and lemon, setting aside the peels. Break cinnamon sticks in half if desired to release more aroma.

2. **Fill your pot.**

   Place the orange peel, lemon peel, cinnamon sticks, allspice berries, and bay leaves into a medium-sized pot.

3. **Add water and simmer gently.**

   Fill the pot with 4 to 6 cups of water, ensuring the ingredients are fully submerged. Place the pot on the stovetop over low heat. Bring the water just to a gentle simmer, avoid a rolling boil.

4. **Maintain and refresh.**

   Allow the pot to simmer uncovered, releasing its warm, spiced fragrance into the air. Add more water as needed to prevent the mixture from drying out.

TIP

You can also use the same instructions to create a spring simmer pot for cleansing the home. Simply substitute the following ingredients: lemon peel (from 1 lemon), lime peel (from 1 lime), a few sprigs of fresh rosemary, 1 tablespoon fresh or dried lavender flowers, and 1 tablespoon fresh or dried lemongrass. This formula is great for the end of winter when doing spring cleaning as it has a clean and uplifting scent consisting of ingredients that bring light and a gentle uplifting energy.

Dressing and Fixing Candles

Candle dressing or *fixing* is a practice that comes from Hoodoo (see Chapter 1) and has become popular among magical practitioners. Candle dressing involves the ritual preparation of candles using herbs, oils, and waters to infuse the candles with your intention. You can use any kind of candle in this ritual, but you traditionally use glass-encased seven-day candles, also known as *novena candles*. You can also use smaller chime candles, taper candles, tea lights, or other store-bought candles that come in glass jars.

REMEMBER

You may have to adapt the steps for candle dressing depending on the type of candle that you're using.

You can create a candle dressing for healing by using lavender flowers, rose petals, lemon balm, and Holy basil and following the basic steps for candle. You can also come up with your own candle dressing preparations to set your intention and fix your candle to your desired magical outcome. You can choose the color of your candle based on your magical goal. You can also use white candles universally for any situation.

To create a candle dressing, you need a white or green candle, a dish of water, Florida water or rose water, incense and burner, mortar and pestle, and a baking sheet or tray lined with parchment paper or aluminum foil. Also gather a ritual oil for healing (see Chapter 8) and dried herbs aligned with your intention for the candle dressing (for example, love, protection, health, and so on). Then follow these steps:

1. **Bring all your tools and ingredients together on your workspace.**
2. **Focus on your intention.**

   Set your intention while holding your candle in your hands. Hold your intention in mind during the entirety of this process.
3. **Light your incense.**

   You can make the incense specifically for healing or as simple as burning pine resin or frankincense.

4. **Prepare your dish of water.**

   Add some Florida water or rose water to the dish of water that you've prepared.

TIP

   Florida water is a perfume commonly used in cleansing rituals. You can buy already made Florida water or make your own (see Chapter 6). You can easily make rose water by infusing fresh rose petals in water overnight.

5. **Bathe your candle.**

   Cup your hand and sprinkle some water on the outside of your candle while focusing on cleansing it of any previous energies creating a blank slate for your intention. Rub the water all over the candle. If the candle is encased in glass, do the same thing to the glass the candle is held in.

6. **Fumigate the candle.**

   Pass the candle through the incense smoke while focusing on your intention, allowing the smoke to come into contact with every surface of the candle.

7. **Anoint the candle.**

   Take some ritual oil and apply it to the outside of the candle. If your candle is encased in glass, apply the oil to the glass container. The intention and direction of the spell you're preparing the candle for determines the direction that you'll anoint the candle. For example, if you're attracting healing energy for yourself, anoint the candle from the tip (where the wick is) to the base in a downward direction to pull the energy in. If your goal is to send healing energy out toward a specific person, anoint the candle from base to wick (bottom to top) to project its energy outwards.

8. **Prepare the herbs.**

TIP

   When candle-dressing, it will help if the herbs are finely powdered to a uniform consistency, which makes sticking easier and prevents larger pieces of dried herb from catching on fire when the candle is lit. Mix all your herbs together and grind them in a mortar and pestle until they're at the desired consistency.

9. **Sprinkle the herbs.**

   Working over your tray, sprinkle the herbs on your candle. If your candle is encased in glass, simply sprinkle a pinch or two of your herb blend onto the top of the candle. Avoid using too much, or it will prevent your candle from burning properly. You can also omit this step and just sprinkle the herbs around your candle before burning.

10. **Roll the candle.**

    If you're using chime or taper candles or another type not encased in glass, sprinkle the herbs onto your tray and roll the candle in the herbs so that they stick to the outside.

    TIP

    Adding more anointing oil to the outside of the candle helps the herbs stick.

11. **Burn the candle.**

    After infusing the candle with your intentions, you're ready to burn it on a fire-safe plate or in a candle holder.

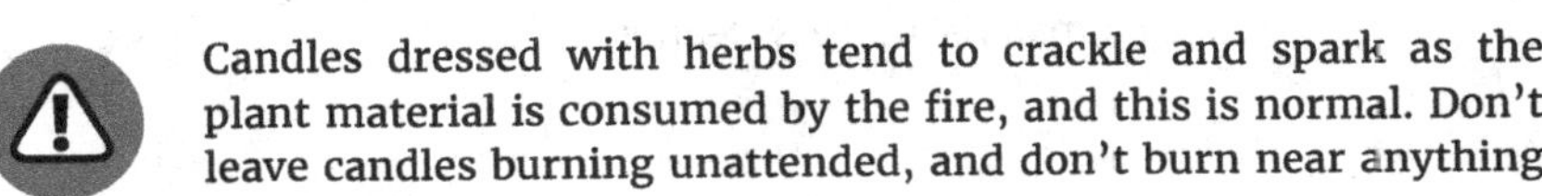

WARNING

Candles dressed with herbs tend to crackle and spark as the plant material is consumed by the fire, and this is normal. Don't leave candles burning unattended, and don't burn near anything flammable.

Taking Herbal Baths

Ritual bathing is something that has been practiced for millennia for its profound healing and transformative properties for both body and spirit. Early on humans have recognized the effectiveness of combining herbal ingredients with their baths for general healing and wellness as well as for specific magical intentions. You can effectively incorporate herbs into ritual baths in a variety of ways:

- **Herbal sachets:** You can fill cloth and organza drawstring bags with herbs and add them to bathwater to allow the herbs to infuse in the hot water without having to worry about cleaning the bathtub afterwards. Essentially, you're making a giant tea bag that you add to hot bath water, allowing it to infuse for five to ten minutes. Alternately, if you want to avoid loose plant material floating around in your bathtub, you can brew a pot of tea using your selected herbs and add them to your bath water.
- **Fresh flowers:** Few things are as luxurious as submerging yourself into a warm bath full of fresh flower petals. Roses

are often the go-to choice for ritual baths. Roses come in countless colors and varieties that you can pair with your desired intention. You can also make rose water by filling a large bowl with water and adding fresh rose petals to it. Allow it to sit overnight, preferably under the light of the full moon, and add the water to your next bath.

- **Bath salts:** Several bath salt formulas throughout this book pair with a variety of different intentions, from attracting love to banishing unwanted energies. Bath salts are an easy way to incorporate herbal magic into your baths. By adding dried herbs, anointing oils, or essential oils to Epsom salt, you can create ritual bath salts for any magical goal. You can add bath salts to bathwater directly or put them in drawstring bags and allow to infuse the water while hanging onto any plant material for easy cleanup.

Creating Flower Essences

Flower essences are subtle yet profound energetic remedies that work on the level of the emotions, mind, and spirit rather than the physical body. Unlike herbal tinctures or teas, flower essences don't rely on the plant's chemical constituents; instead, they capture the plant's unique energetic imprint or vibrational signature. Because of their energetic nature, flower essences are considered safe to use even when made from plants that would be too potent or toxic to ingest in their whole form. Flower essences are primarily used for emotional healing, spiritual growth, and energetic support, helping to shift thought patterns, release trauma, and open pathways for transformation.

The theory behind flower essences is that each plant carries a distinct energetic signature that can interact with the human energy field. When this essence is taken, it helps to harmonize discordant emotional or mental states with the plant's higher vibration. Their influence is often gentle but profound, creating gradual shifts that can lead to lasting change over time.

Flower essences are prepared through a ritualized process that honors the plant spirit. This process often involves selecting a living, vibrant plant ally, offering prayers or blessings, and asking permission for its essence to be shared. Three primary methods of preparation are:

- **Direct method:** Fresh flowers are placed on the surface of pure spring water in a clear glass vessel.
- **Indirect method:** The vessel of water is placed near the plant rather than in direct contact, used especially for toxic or rare plants.
- **Pour-over method:** Water is poured over the living plant and collected, allowing the plant to remain intact.

The vessel is then placed in sunlight or moonlight for a full cycle to capture the plant's energetic essence, often accompanied by petitions or intention-setting. Because the process transfers primarily the plant's vibrational qualities, only trace, if any, physical plant constituents remain in the water.

This infusion becomes the mother essence once stabilized with an equal part of brandy or another preservative. From this mother essence, a few drops are diluted into a *stock bottle*, and the process is repeated to make a dosage bottle, which is the finished product that is consumed. The idea is that the more times the formula is diluted, the stronger its energy becomes. A single mother essence can last a lifetime, as only minute quantities are needed to create many dosage bottles.

Flower essences are generally taken orally, either dropped directly onto the tongue or diluted in water several times a day over a set period of time. Many practitioners recommend a cyclical approach, allowing periods of rest and integration between courses. A common dosage is five to seven drops three times daily, although this dosage can vary based on the individual, the essence, and the purpose of the work. You can also incorporate ritual correspondences, such as planetary hours, numerology, or lunar phases, to deepen the energetic alignment of the process.

To create a flower essence, you need:

- Fresh flowers from the plant you want to work with (or a healthy living plant for indirect method)
- Pure spring water (not distilled or tap, if possible)
- Clear glass, crystal, or copper bowl or vessel
- Brandy
- Small funnel

- Large bottle or jar for the mother essence
- 30–60 ml dropper bottles
- Labels and pen
- (Optional) Cloth or mesh to protect the water from debris
- (Optional) Altar items for offerings or intention

1. **Select your plant ally.**

   Choose a vibrant and healthy plant in full bloom. Take a moment to connect, offer a prayer, thanks, or small offering. Ask permission to partner with the plant spirit to create this flower essence.

2. **Prepare your workspace.**

   Work in a quiet, natural setting when possible. Clean your tools and fill your clear glass bowl with fresh spring water, leaving room near the top.

3. **Choose your method.**

   - *Direct method:* Snip fresh blooms and float them on the water's surface.
   - *Indirect method:* Place the bowl of water near the plant without cutting it (best for toxic or endangered species).
   - *Pour-over method:* Gently pour the water over the plant, catching it in the bowl placed beneath.

4. **Infuse with sunlight or moonlight.**

   Place the bowl in a safe spot where it will remain undisturbed for a full cycle of at least three to four hours, traditionally from late morning to early afternoon for solar essences using the energy of sunlight or under a full moon for lunar essences using the energy of moonlight. During this time, hold your intention in mind, burn incense, or create an altar using crystals, fresh cut flowers and other sacred objects.

5. **Strain and preserve.**

   After the infusion period, carefully remove the flowers (or simply collect the water if using indirect or pour-over methods). Strain through a fine mesh or cloth, if needed. Fill the larger bottle halfway with brandy and top off with the infused water. This bottle is your mother essence.

6. **Prepare your stock bottle.**

   To make a stock bottle, place three to nine drops of the mother essence into a dropper bottle filled halfway with brandy and topped with spring water.

7. **Prepare your dosage bottle.**

   Repeat Step 6 but use a 30 to 60 ml dropper bottle. This bottle is the dosage bottle.

8. **Label and store.**

   Clearly label the name of the plant, date, and what it is (the mother essence, stock bottle or dosage bottle). Store in a cool, dark place.

For dosage and ritual use, take three to nine drops directly under the tongue or in water, usually three times daily, or use in baths, sprays, or other formulas.

Aligning your dosing with moon phases, planetary hours, or specific numbers can help reinforce your magical intention (see Chapter 10).

Making Herbal Powders

You can make *herbal powders*, sometimes called *sachet powders*, by finely powdering herbal ingredients and adding them to a base of talcum powder, cornstarch, or flour.

Herbal powders are nice because they're discreet, and you can use them in so many different ways. You can sprinkle these powders in specific places to deploy their magical influence or in charm bags to feed them and recharge their energy. You can use herbal powders to dress candles, create the boundaries of a ritual circle, or draw symbols on the altar. You can sprinkle an herbal powder for protection across the threshold at your front door or hidden under your welcome mat. You can sprinkle an herbal powder for romance around the bedroom or between your sheets. You can create an herbal powder for success and prosperity and dust your hands with it before going on a job interview or forming a new business partnership.

You can use the following herbal powder to increase your powers of persuasion by dusting yourself with it after taking a bath or shower. (Apply the powder to dry skin.) Alternately, use this powder to attract customers or general financial success by sprinkling it at your place of business or using it to dust your cash and credit cards.

You need 1 cup cornstarch, talcum powder, or flour and 1 teaspoon each of calamus root powder, finely powdered bay leaves, cinnamon powder, and powdered sugar. (If the herbs aren't already finely powdered, you need a coffee grinder.) Also, make sure you have a dish for mixing and a container with a lid for storage.

TIP

You can also add small amounts of mica powder, which comes in every imaginable color, to add the appropriate color correspondence to your herbal powders. For the following formula, use green or purple mica powder.

To create this Herbal Powder for Increasing Influence, follow these steps:

1. **Grind up the ingredients.**

   Make sure that everything is ground as finely as possible so that it mixes easily with the powder you're using as a base.

2. **Mix your ingredients.**

   Blend all your herbal ingredients together in the mixing bowl while focusing on your intention. Ensure everything is mixed easily.

3. **Add the finished product to your storage container to keep for future use.**

TIP

Apply this powder before going into work or before coming into contact with individuals that you want to influence. Apply the powder to the palms of your hands before meeting new people or use it to dust your entire body before going into social situations.

IN THIS CHAPTER

» Tracing energetic signatures

» Bringing in the four elements

» Drawing down planetary energy

» Reaching for the stars

Chapter 3 Understanding Herbal Correspondences

Herbal correspondences tell you what an herb is potentially used for and can seem confusing at first. For example, you can use multiple different herbs for protection. You may also notice the same herb being listed for different uses depending on your source. While herbal correspondences do follow recognizable patterns, they're also subjective. In addition, many herbs may not have an existing body of magical correspondences to draw from.

These categories can help you see the nuance of the many characteristics and personalities that you can find in an herb. After you have a sense for those characteristics, you can see how you can bring them together to create formulas for herbal magic.

In this chapter, you find out about some of the most common ways that herbal correspondences can be understood, drawing from the themes and energies associated with the four elements, as well as astrological and planetary associations. You also discover formulas that you can create to connect with these energies and the plants that represent them. (Chapter 2 offers more detailed information on creating and working with a variety of recipes for incense, infused oil, and essential oil formulas.)

The Doctrine of Signatures

The *Doctrine of Signatures* is a metaphysical and symbolic framework that suggests a plant's appearance — its shape, color, texture, or growth habit — offers clues to its medicinal and magical uses. This concept, rooted in ancient philosophy and theology, gained prominence during the European Renaissance and was later adopted by many herbalists and physicians, including Paracelsus and Nicholas Culpepper. The underlying belief is that the Divine placed signs within nature to guide humans in their use of plants for healing and spiritual purposes. For example, a plant with heart-shaped leaves might be used to treat heart conditions or enhance emotional healing, while a yellow flower might be associated with the liver, digestion, or the element of fire.

The formalization of the *Doctrine of Signatures* is often attributed to Paracelsus (1493–1541), a Swiss physician and alchemist who believed that natural objects carried divine signatures indicating their purpose. Paracelsus is known for incorporating alchemy, astrology, and mysticism into his theories of healing. This holistic view emphasized a correspondence between *macrocosm* and *microcosm* — that which exists in the larger cosmos is reflected in a smaller scale in the human body and mirrored again in nature. The *Doctrine of Signatures* became a useful interpretive tool in both medicine and magic, helping practitioners build intuitive and symbolic relationships with herbs.

In magical herbalism, the *Doctrine of Signatures* offers a practical method for intuiting a plant's spiritual and energetic properties. For example, plants with protective thorns, such as hawthorn or nettle, are often used in protection magic. Red-colored plants, like cayenne or hibiscus, may be used in spells involving passion, vitality, or courage due to their natural heat or their resemblance to blood. The round, sun-like shape of calendula flowers makes them ideal for solar magic, promoting joy, clarity, and protection. Through observation and symbolic association, magical practitioners learn to read the language of nature and build relationships with herbs based on both empirical experience and esoteric understanding.

All these characteristics and symbols are referred to as *correspondences*. Correspondences represent the energetic, spiritual and magical associations between things, such as herbs, planets, colors, elements, and other objects, and concepts with the forces that they connect to. It is through the correspondences that you can draw specific energies into your rituals and formulas.

While not a strict scientific principle, the *Doctrine of Signatures* continues to be a valuable guide in herbal magic, encouraging deep engagement with the natural world. It teaches practitioners to listen, observe, and reflect on what plants reveal about themselves. By studying a plant's form and behavior, magical herbalists can align their intentions with the plant's essence, creating more meaningful and effective rituals.

Practicing with Elemental Correspondences

The four elements represent the basic building blocks of the universe in a physical, symbolic, and spiritual sense. They consist of Fire, Air, Water, and Earth and are found in many forms throughout the cosmos. Each element is connected to numerous concepts and energies and can be considered a universal form of expression.

While various cultures have other elemental systems, with slight variations, I focus on the four classical element system commonly credited to the ancient Greek philosopher Empedocles (c. 495–435 BCE). He proposed that these four elements were the fundamental building blocks of all matter in the universe. These elemental theories deeply influenced Western thought, medieval alchemy, medicine, astrology, and magical traditions. Herbs are typically given an elemental association based on their appearance, energetics, and even their medicinal action, which also informs their magical uses.

Fire

Fire is the element of transformation, passion, and willpower. It brings energy, protection, courage, and vitality to magical workings. Fire herbs are typically hot, stimulating, spicy, or thorny and are ideal for spells of purification, manifestation, strength, or sudden change. Magical practices that make use of fire include candle work, pyromancy (fire divination), and rituals involving smoke, heat, and burning things.

TIP

Common herbs aligned with Fire include ginger, nettle, tobacco, pepper, cinnamon, dragon's blood, and angelica. These plants are used to boost energy, encourage boldness, and confer spiritual protection. Fire is particularly useful when the circumstances involving the ritual feels stagnant or blocked, as these herbs get the energy moving.

In magical herbalism, Fire represents the spark of divine will, the internal flame that drives action and fuels creative drive. By working with Fire plants, practitioners tap into a current of motivation, inspiration, and power that fuels transformation. The element of Fire represents the spiritual source, and Fire is typically present in almost every ritual in one form or another.

You can create a simple incense recipe to incorporate the magic of elemental Fire into your rituals. Combine the following ingredients in equal parts:

rosemary, frankincense resin, dragon's blood resin, and cloves. Grind all the ingredients to a uniform consistency using a mortar and pestle and add one pinch at a time to your charcoal to burn.

TIP

Use this incense to connect with the energy of elemental Fire. Incorporate it into your rituals for extra energy, willpower, and vitality and for protection. You can also use it to burn away obstacles.

Air

Air represents the realm of thought, communication, intellect, and spiritual insight. It is the element of movement, expansion, language, and wisdom. In magical herbalism, Air corresponds to herbs that disperse seeds via wind, have feathery or delicate structures, or release strong, clean fragrances. These plants stimulate the mind and support clarity, eloquence, and mental agility. Air magic is expressed through smoke, incense, feathers, windchimes, hanging charms, and tools suspended in trees or left to drift in the wind, all of which mimic the lightness and movement of this element.

TIP

Herbs associated with Air, such as dandelion, dill, lavender, yarrow, peppermint, and sweetgrass, are used to enhance intuition, improve communication, and bring clarity during divinatory work. Air is also the element of divine inspiration, making its associated herbs useful in dreamwork, visualization, breathwork, and rituals for shifting mental patterns or gaining new perspectives. These plants help lift stagnation, clear mental fog, and connect the practitioner to higher realms of thought and spirit.

You can create a simple incense to incorporate the magic of elemental Air into your rituals. Combine the following ingredients in equal parts: lavender flowers, juniper berries, sage leaves, and lemongrass. Grind all the ingredients to a uniform consistency using a mortar and pestle and add one pinch at a time to your charcoal to burn. Use this incense to connect with the energy of elemental Air.

TIP

Incorporate this incense into your rituals for cleansing, enhancing communication, and moving stagnant energy. It's also a great incense to burn before meditation or to purify your space before and after rituals.

Water

Water is the element of emotion, intuition, dreams, and healing. It rules over the subconscious, psychic awareness, love, and purification. Herbs associated with water tend to be soothing, moist, and gentle in nature, helping to balance emotions, regulate the sleep cycle, and promote inner peace. Magical practices associated with Water include potion-making, baths and washes, libations, mirror magic, *water scrying* (a form of divination that involves gazing upon the reflective surface of water to access psychic impressions), and ancestor connection. The sea, rain, ice, and snow are all expressions of Water's properties of depth and fluidity.

TIP

Herbs such as lobelia, lotus, coltsfoot, spearmint, willow, and lady's mantle embody the essence of Water. These plants support practices involving emotional healing, dreamwork, and spiritual cleansing. Water is also associated with fertility and the divine feminine, making its herbs especially potent in rituals related to love, compassion, and psychic development. When incorporated into magic, Water herbs help soften boundaries, dissolve emotional blockages, and connect to the subconscious. Their gentle, flowing energy guides the practitioner through cycles of release and renewal, mirroring the ever-shifting tides.

You can create a simple infused oil to incorporate the magic of elemental Water into your rituals. Combine the following ingredients in equal parts and add to a carrier oil allowing it to infuse for one lunar cycle (28 days): chamomile flowers, jasmine essential oil (20 drops), star anise pods, and blue lotus petals. Add all ingredients to a 30 ml bottle with a lid and cover with carrier oil.

TIP

Use this anointing oil to call upon the soothing and healing energies of elemental Water. Add it to ritual baths, wear it on the body before meditation or dream work, or use it to anoint blue candles to call upon the power of water in rituals for healing or cleansing.

Earth

The Earth element in magical herbalism represents stability, structure, physical manifestation, growth, and the tangible aspects of existence. It governs manifestation, grounding, fertility, and abundance. Herbs that correspond with the Earth element support practices related to prosperity, luck, employment, and physical healing. These herbs are typically sedative or slow-acting, with dense, moist, or fertile characteristics, helping to root the practitioner in the present moment and cultivate a deep connection with the material world. Earth magic often involves burying objects in the ground or hiding objects in the home, creating images from clay, and is present in all herbal magic because the herbs that herbal practitioners work with all come from the Earth.

TIP

In magical workings, Earth energy is channeled through garden magic, knot magic, and the use of stones, magnets, and other natural materials. Herbs like oak, ivy, sage, patchouli, and poppy petals align with Earth due to their grounding and stabilizing properties. Mosses and lichens, slow-growing and moisture-rich, offer a sense of stillness and endurance. These plants are ideal for rituals that require patience, protection, or steady growth. Working with herbs associated with Earth helps practitioners build a solid foundation for magical intention, encouraging inner strength, resilience, and a respectful connection to the cycles of nature.

You can create a simple infused oil to incorporate the magic of elemental Earth into your rituals. Combine the following ingredients in equal parts and add to a carrier oil allowing it to infuse for one lunar cycle (28 days): oakmoss, patchouli essential oil

(20 drops), and pine resin. Add all ingredients to a 30 ml bottle with a lid and cover with carrier oil.

Use this anointing oil to call upon the grounding and abundant energies of elemental Earth. You can add it to ritual baths and wear it on the body before meditation or going outdoors to connect with nature or use it to anoint green candles to call upon the power of Earth in rituals for growth or prosperity.

Herbal Magic and Planetary Correspondences

The seven classical planets, celestial bodies known to the ancient world and visible to the naked eye, serve as foundational archetypes in both astrology and magical herbalism. Each planet embodies a distinct constellation of energies, rulerships, and symbolic flavors that blend physical, esoteric, and mythological attributes. These planetary forces offer a lens through which practitioners can better understand the nature of herbs, their magical affinities, and their roles in ritual practice. By aligning plant spirits with the energetic signatures of the Sun, Moon, Mercury, Venus, Mars, Jupiter, and Saturn, practitioners tap into a universal framework that allows one to access these energies and weave them into magical workings.

You can further enhance this pairing of herbs and planetary energies by performing spells on the appropriate day of the week that is associated with the respective planet. Each planet holds rulership over a specific day of the week.

Moon

The Moon governs the intuitive, emotional, and mystical realms. In magical herbalism, lunar plants support psychic awareness, dreamwork, divination, and emotional healing. These herbs are often sedative or cooling, working with the water element to soothe the nervous system, regulate hormones, and encourage sleep. Plants ruled by the Moon typically grow near water, have high moisture content, or exhibit nocturnal blooming patterns. Their effects are often subtle yet profound, supporting rituals of introspection, protection, and connection to the subconscious.

Rituals related to the Moon are best performed on a Monday or based on the phases of the Moon.

Examples of lunar herbs include jasmine, lavender, mugwort, sandalwood, lily, and moonflower. Plants aligned with the Moon are especially beneficial for female reproductive health, and their calming influence is key in emotional healing and spiritual cleansing. These herbs aid in opening the practitioner to inner vision, heightening psychic sensitivity, and navigating the spirit world.

You can create a simple ritual oil to incorporate the magic of the Moon into your spellwork. You can use this ritual oil immediately because you're making them with essential oils.

Create this ritual oil on a Monday, the day ruled by the Moon. Combine the following ingredients into 30 ml of carrier oil in a glass bottle with a lid: jasmine essential oil (20 drops), sandalwood essential oil (10 drops), rose essential oil (5 drops), and mugwort essential oil (10 drops).

After you blend all ingredients together, you can apply a few drops of the oil to your skin to test the fragrance, adjusting the blend of essential oils to suit your preference. You can use this oil to draw the energy of the Moon into your rituals by anointing white or silver candles, applying it to ritual objects such as crystals, or wearing it on the body to deepen one's connection to the psychic and spiritual realms.

Mercury

Mercury is the planet of communication, intellect, wit, and travel between realms. In magical herbalism, Mercurial plants support memory, speech, nervous system function, and the clarity of thought required for both mundane and spiritual exchanges. These herbs are often fast-growing, aromatic, or creeping in growth habit, and they frequently display characteristics resembling the human nervous system. Mercurial herbs act as catalysts, enhancing the effectiveness of other herbs and quickening magical results.

Examples include licorice, various mints, cardamom, eucalyptus, skullcap, juniper, and lemongrass. These plants stimulate the lungs and brain, and their effects are often swift and energizing, though not necessarily long-lasting. Mercury also rules over trickery, invisibility, and deception, making these herbs valuable in glamour, illusion, or concealment spells. Spells drawing on the energy of Mercury are most effective when performed on a Wednesday. With their light, mobile energy, Mercurial herbs are ideal for practitioners seeking quick mental clarity, heightened perception, or spiritual messages from guides or the otherworld.

You can create a simple ritual oil to incorporate the magic of Mercury into your spellwork. You can use this ritual oil immediately because you're making it with essential oils.

TIP

Create this ritual oil on a Wednesday, the day ruled by Mercury.

Combine the following ingredients into 30 ml of carrier oil in a glass bottle with a lid: lavender essential oil (10 drops), peppermint essential oil (10 drops), fennel essential oil (10 drops), and yarrow essential oil (5 drops).

After you blended all ingredients together, you can apply a few drops of the oil to your skin to test the fragrance, adjusting the blend of essential oils to suit your preference. You can use this oil to draw the energy of Mercury into your rituals by anointing yellow candles, applying it to ritual objects such as crystals, or wearing it on the body to enhance communication and success in business. You can also apply it to your body before studying to sharpen your mental faculties.

Venus

Venus rules love, beauty, fertility, abundance, and the power of attraction. Herbs associated with Venus are often fragrant, lush, and flowering, designed to please the senses and invoke harmony. These plants support romantic and sensual magic, enhance personal magnetism, and promote both physical and emotional healing. Venusian herbs also relate to pleasure, luxury, and artistic expression, making them powerful tools for glamour, charm, and drawing in beneficial energies.

TIP

Common Venus herbs include rose, vervain, burdock, apple, damiana, thyme, passionflower, violet, and lemon verbena. These plants are typically mild in action, with soothing and beautifying qualities. They benefit the kidneys, skin, and reproductive system, and often work against harsh influences from Mars. In magic, Venus herbs are used in love spells, offerings, fertility rites, and abundance rituals, helping the practitioner align with the natural rhythms of attraction and creation. Spells related to Venus are most powerful when performed on a Friday.

You can create a simple ritual oil to incorporate the magic of Venus into your spellwork. You can use this ritual oil immediately because you're making it with essential oils.

TIP

Create this ritual oil on a Friday, the day ruled by Venus.

Combine the following ingredients into 30 ml of carrier oil in a glass bottle with a lid: rose essential oil (10 drops), lemon verbena essential oil (20 drops), ylang-ylang essential oil (5 drops), and bergamot essential oil (5 drops).

After you blended all ingredients together, you can apply a few drops of the oil to your skin to test the fragrance, adjusting the blend of essential oils to suit your preference.

TIP

You can use this oil to draw the energy of Venus into your rituals by anointing green, pink, or red candles, applying it to ritual objects such as crystals, or wearing it on the body to attract romance, enhance personal magnetism, and confer abundance and beauty in all of its forms. You can also add it to ritual baths to facilitate self-love and heart healing.

Mars

Mars is the planet of action, aggression, courage, and defense. In herbal magic, Mars-ruled plants are fiery, potent, and often pungent or prickly. They stimulate blood flow, increase energy, and are often used in protective or banishing work. These herbs embody raw power and survival instincts, making them ideal for spellwork involving strength, conflict, sexual drive, and the assertion of will. Spells making use of the energy of Mars are most powerful when performed on a Tuesday.

TIP

Ginger, galangal, tobacco, nettles, red sandalwood, and chili pepper are all examples of Mars-aligned herbs. Their warming, stimulating natures enhance physical vitality and help ward off illness or spiritual intrusion. Mars herbs are also associated with blood purifiers and remedies for injuries, fevers, and immune-related conditions. In magic, they're used to ignite passion, build resilience, and combat harmful influences — perfect allies when swift, decisive action is needed.

You can create a simple ritual oil to incorporate the magic of Mars into your spellwork. You can use this ritual oil immediately because you're making it with essential oils.

TIP

Create this ritual oil on a Tuesday, the day ruled by Mars.

Combine the following ingredients into 30 ml of carrier oil in a glass bottle with a lid: basil essential oil (10 drops), bay leaf essential oil (10 drops), and ginger essential oil (5 drops).

After you blend all ingredients together, you can apply a few drops of the oil to your skin to test the fragrance, adjusting the blend of essential oils to suit your preference.

WARNING

The essential oils associated with Mars are warming and stimulating so it is recommended to test a small amount on the inner wrist to check for any skin sensitivity before applying to other parts of the body or adding to baths.

You can use this oil to draw the fiery energy of Mars into your rituals by anointing red candles, applying it to ritual objects such as crystals, or applying the oil to windows and doorways for protection or to anoint protective objects to hang around the home or in your car. You can also access Mars energy when additional willpower and courage are needed.

Jupiter

Jupiter governs expansion, luck, prosperity, and spiritual authority. Its herbal correspondences bring growth, optimism, and abundance without overstimulation. Jupiterian herbs often warm, nourish, and calm the system, supporting digestion, metabolism, and overall well-being. They help build bodily strength and support overall health, particularly in cases involving depletion, restriction, or malnourishment.

TIP

Herbs like oak, pine, cedar, fennel, benzoin, agrimony, and sage carry Jupiter's expansive and protective qualities. Fruits such as olives, figs, and nuts also align with this benefic planet. In magical work, Jupiter plants aid in rituals for wealth, wisdom, and personal development, particularly where faith, law, or spiritual growth are involved. Spells associated with Jupiter are best performed on Thursdays. Their generous, uplifting energy promotes success, confidence, and harmony in both material and spiritual pursuits.

You can create a simple ritual oil recipe to incorporate the magic of Jupiter into your spellwork. You can use this ritual oil immediately because you're making it with essential oils.

TIP

Create this ritual oil on a Thursday, the day ruled by Jupiter.

Combine the following ingredients into 30 ml of carrier oil in a glass bottle with a lid: cedarwood essential oil (10 drops), sage essential oil (10 drops), magnolia flower essential oil (10 drops), and fennel essential oil (5 drops).

After you blend all ingredients together, you can apply a few drops of the oil to your skin to test the fragrance, adjusting the blend of essential oils to suit your preference. You can use this oil to draw the energy of Jupiter into your rituals for abundance, expansion, and success by anointing purple candles, applying it to ritual objects such as crystals, or applying the oil before any business ventures or in situations that you want to have the upper hand. Jupiter is also associated with the spiritual realm and can be called into rituals to aid in meditation and psychic ability.

Saturn

Saturn represents boundaries, structure, time, discipline, and protection through restriction. Its plants are often slow-growing, shade-loving, or invasive in nature, with cooling, drying, or astringent qualities. Many Saturnian herbs are poisonous or medicinally powerful, making them allies in banishing, binding, or cursing work, as well as in long-term protective magic. Saturday is the appropriate day to perform spells related to the energy of Saturn.

TIP

Saturnian herbs include myrrh, cypress, comfrey, horsetail, belladonna, henbane, and cannabis. These plants often affect the bones, joints, teeth, and aging process, helping to stabilize or constrict runaway energies. In magical herbalism, Saturn plants are used to impose necessary limits, break habits, sever ties, and work within the structure of natural law.

WARNING

Poisonous plants in general fall under the rulership of Saturn. Herbs like belladonna, henbane, and other members of the nightshade family are potent medicinal herbs that are potentially toxic when not used properly. It is necessary to have an understanding of these powerful plants, and I recommend my book *The Poison*

Path Herbal (Park Street Press) for learning more about this fascinating topic and how to safely work with these plants.

You can create a simple ritual oil to incorporate the magic of Saturn into your spellwork. You can use this ritual oil immediately because you're making it with essential oils.

Create this ritual oil on a Saturday, the day ruled by Saturn.

Combine the following ingredients into 30 ml of carrier oil in a glass bottle with a lid: patchouli essential oil (10 drops), cypress essential oil (10 drops), myrrh essential oil (20 drops), and valerian essential oil (5 drops).

After you blend all ingredients together, you can apply a few drops of the oil to your skin to test the fragrance, adjusting the blend of essential oils to suit your preference.

You can use this oil to draw the energy of Saturn into your rituals for strengthening boundaries and spell of protection by anointing black or white candles, applying it to ritual objects such as crystals, or applying the oil to the skin for resilience and perseverance. Saturn is also associated with the material realm and can be called into rituals related to career and manifestation. Saturn is also a strong energy to work with when working toward a long-term goal.

Sun

In magical herbalism, the Sun governs vitality, energy, health, inspiration, creativity, and the power to manifest. Plants associated with the Sun often reflect its radiant, life-giving nature — they bear bright yellow or gold flowers, exhibit *heliotropic behavior* (opening and closing with the sun), and bring warmth and illumination to both body and spirit.

These herbs commonly benefit the heart, eyes, and circulatory system, and their warming, invigorating effects promote optimism and overall wellness. The solar influence in herbal magic is linked with confidence, personal power, and joy, making these herbs ideal for spells related to success, leadership, healing, and creativity. Sunday is ruled by the Sun and the day that spells drawing on its life-giving energy should be performed.

TIP

Examples of solar herbs include calendula, chamomile, centaury, St. John's wort, and frankincense. Their scents are often uplifting and purifying, used to clear stagnation and revitalize the energy field. Clove and citrus fruits enhance clarity and motivation, while mistletoe, though parasitic, has long been linked with solar deities and sacred rites of healing. Working with Sun-aligned herbs helps practitioners harness inner light, radiate positive energy, and cultivate spiritual and physical strength.

You can create a simple ritual oil to incorporate the magic of the Sun into your spellwork. You can use this ritual oil immediately because you're making it with essential oils.

TIP

Create this ritual oil on a Sunday, the day ruled by the Sun.

Combine the following ingredients into 30 ml of carrier oil in a glass bottle with a lid: frankincense essential oil (10 drops), rosemary essential oil (10 drops), and bay laurel essential oil (5 drops).

After you blend all ingredients together, you can apply a few drops of the oil to your skin to test the fragrance, adjusting the blend of essential oils to suit your preference. You can use this oil to draw the energy of the Sun into your rituals for manifestation and creativity by anointing yellow or orange candles, applying it to ritual objects such as crystals and charms, or applying the oil to the skin for extra energy and charisma. The Sun as the center of the solar system and source of all life can be called into rituals for a variety of purposes that require extra energy, from healing magic, to receiving divine inspiration, or illuminating the truth of a situation.

Astrological Correspondences

Based on the 12 signs of the zodiac, the astrological correspondences for herbs are made up of various combinations of planetary and elemental energies. These correspondences can work in combination with astrological timing to create additional layers of energetic and symbolic associations in your rituals. By combining the appropriate herbs along with the right astrological timing, the idea is that you're able to draw in more energy for your ritual and create an intense focus for your intention. These various combinations create more nuanced areas of influence that you can tap into when they're intentionally incorporated into spellwork.

REMEMBER

Some herbs may pop up under more than one category. While all these herbs have traditional and historical associations, the interpretation of those associations is largely subjective.

TIP

The dates provided in this section tell you the time of year that the Sun is in each of the zodiac signs. The Moon moves through each sign approximately every 28 days, which gives you more frequent opportunities to work with the energies of the zodiac. Many websites and apps can tell you what sign the Moon is in at any given moment.

Aries, the Ram

Aries (March 21–April 19) is a sign of dynamic energy and bold initiative. As the first sign of the zodiac, Aries is a natural leader, known for its courage, drive, and competitive spirit. Ruled by Mars, Aries possesses a fiery enthusiasm and a desire to take action, often diving headfirst into challenges. While impulsive at times, Aries is also resilient and determined, always seeking new adventures and experiences.

TIP

Herbs that are associated with Aries are typically spicy, stimulating, energizing, and warming. They're often used to ignite courage, passion, and physical strength. Some herbs associated with the energy of Aries include blackberry, ginger, nettle, pepper, plantain and thistle. Spells that work well with the energy of Aries are spells for protection, courage, boundaries, energy, motivation, and assertiveness.

You can create a ritual oil to call the energy of Aries into your magic for strength and motivation and for starting new projects. Create this formula when either the Sun or the Moon is in the sign of Aries.

During the appropriate magical timing of either the Sun or the Moon, combine stinging nettle, chili pepper, and blackberry leaves in equal parts to a 30 ml glass bottle with a lid and cover with carrier oil allowing it to infuse for 28 days. You can use this oil to anoint red or orange candles or wear it on the body to access the energies associated with Aries.

Leo, the Lion

Leo (July 23–August 22) is radiant, confident, and expressive. Ruled by the Sun, Leo exudes warmth, vitality, and charisma. This Fire sign is drawn to creativity and recognition, often stepping into leadership or performance roles with natural ease. Proud and generous, Leo values loyalty and appreciation, but can become self-centered or dramatic when seeking attention.

TIP

Herbs linked to Leo tend to strengthen the heart and circulatory system, boost confidence and energy, and encourage self-expression and courage. They're often warming, invigorating, and sometimes aromatic. Some herbs associated with the energy of Leo include angelica, bay laurel, calendula, rue, and St. John's wort. Spells that are enhanced by the energy of Leo involve creativity, manifestation, courage, leadership and generosity.

You can create a ritual oil to call the energy of Leo into your magic for gaining courage, expressing leadership qualities, and attracting and displaying generosity. Create this formula when either the Sun or the Moon is in the sign of Leo.

During the appropriate magical timing of either the Sun or the Moon, combine calendula flowers, sunflower petals, and St. John's wort flowers in equal parts in a 30 ml glass bottle with a lid and cover with carrier oil allowing it to infuse for 28 days.

TIP

You can use this oil to access the abundant, creative, and charismatic energies associated with the sign of Leo. You can apply it to yellow or orange candles for extra energy and inspiration in artistic endeavors and for working with other people.

Sagittarius, the Centaur

Sagittarius (November 22–December 20) is adventurous, philosophical, and freedom-loving. Ruled by Jupiter, Sagittarius seeks truth, knowledge, and broad perspectives. This Fire sign loves exploration, whether through travel, study, or spiritual pursuits. Optimistic and open-minded, Sagittarius can sometimes be tactless or restless in its pursuit of expansion.

TIP

Herbs linked to Sagittarius tend to support growth, wisdom, spiritual awareness, travel, and good fortune. Some herbs associated with the energy of Sagittarius include centaury, echinacea, hyssop, licorice, oak, and sage. Spells that are enhanced by the energy of

Sagittarius are spells for creative vision, honesty, travel, truth-seeking, good fortune, study, and spiritual growth.

You can create a ritual oil to call the energy of Sagittarius into your magic for shifting perspectives, new ideas and insight, and protection during travel. Create this formula when either the Sun or the Moon is in the sign of Sagittarius.

During the appropriate magical timing of either the Sun or the Moon, combine the following ingredients in equal parts: centaury herb, oak wood or leaves, sage, and coneflower petals. Add the ingredients to a 30 ml glass bottle with a lid and cover with carrier oil, allowing it to infuse for 28 days.

You can use this oil to connect with the spiritual and philosophical aspects of life associated with the sign of Sagittarius. You can apply it to purple candles for wisdom, spiritual guidance, and clarity. It's also a powerful formula for travel protection that you can wear during any kind of journey or use to anoint protective charms that you can hang in your vehicle.

Gemini, the Twins

Gemini (May 21–June 20) is curious, witty, and adaptable. Ruled by Mercury, Gemini is associated with communication, learning, and mental agility. This Air sign thrives on variety and intellectual stimulation, often juggling multiple interests at once. Energetic and sociable, Geminis are quick thinkers and great conversationalists, though they may struggle with focus or indecision.

TIP

Herbs linked to Gemini typically enhance mental clarity, focus, speech, and breath. Herbs associated with the energy of Gemini include dill, fennel, lavender, lemon balm, mullein, and skullcap. Spellwork involving communication, intellectual power, versatility, and adaptability are enhanced by the energy of Gemini. You can use these herbs in magical workings for communication, study, memory, travel, social interaction, and eloquence.

You can create a ritual oil to connect with the energy of Gemini for shifting intellectual pursuits, facilitating honest communication, and fostering success in business partnerships. Create this formula when either the Sun or the Moon is in the sign of Gemini.

During the appropriate magical timing of either the Sun or the Moon, combine dill, licorice root, and mullein in equal parts in a

30 ml glass bottle with a lid and cover with carrier oil, allowing it to infuse for 28 days.

TIP

You can use this formula to facilitate communication, smooth relationships and promote honest exchange. You can apply it to yellow candles and burn it during meditation in situations that require versatility and adaptability. You can wear this powerful oil formula while studying or before taking exams as it's associated with intellectual ability.

Libra, the Scales

Libra (September 23–October 22) is diplomatic, graceful, and fairness-loving. Ruled by Venus, Libra is concerned with harmony, aesthetics, and social relationships. This Air sign is a natural mediator, often seeking balance and beauty in all aspects of life. Charming and considerate, Libra can struggle with decision-making and may prioritize peace over confrontation.

TIP

Herbs connected to Libra often promote emotional equilibrium and are used in magical work related to love, partnership, aesthetics, and peace. Some herbs that connect with the energy of Libra are bergamot, catnip, lemon verbena, primrose, and yarrow. Spells that are enhanced by the energy of Libra and its associated herbs involve restoring balance, justice, diplomacy and peaceful home rituals. Herbs associated with Libra can help restore harmony, attract love, enhance beauty and diplomacy, and support Libra's quest for peaceful, meaningful connections.

You can create a ritual oil to connect with the energy of Libra for rituals of justice and decision-making and in situations where diplomacy is needed. Create this formula when either the Sun or the Moon is in the sign of Libra.

During the appropriate magical timing of either the Sun or the Moon, combine bergamot herb, rose geranium herb, rose petals, and honeysuckle leaves or flowers in equal parts. Add the ingredients to a 30 ml glass bottle with a lid and cover with carrier oil, allowing it to infuse for 28 days.

TIP

You can use this ritual oil to bring peace to relationships, ensuring both parties are able to communicate and be heard, to promote peace and balance in the home, and to create a sense of harmony. You can apply it to pink candles and burn it during rituals to prevent gossip. You can wear this powerful oil formula to make a good first impression when meeting new people.

Aquarius, the Water-bearer

Aquarius (January 20–February 18) is innovative, independent, and forward-thinking. Ruled by Saturn and Uranus, Aquarius is a visionary sign focused on progress, individuality, and collective ideals. This Air sign embraces uniqueness and often challenges the status quo. Though socially conscious, Aquarius can appear aloof or emotionally detached.

TIP

Herbs associated with Aquarius often affect the nervous system, circulation, and mental clarity and are used in magical practices involving insight, psychic development, communication, and the breaking of old patterns. Some herbs that connect with the energy of Aquarius are anise, clove, lemongrass, marjoram, and valerian. Spells that can be enhanced with the energy of Aquarius include those focused on innovation, community rituals, independence, mental innovation, spiritual awakening, emotional detachment, and visionary leadership.

You can create this ritual oil to connect with the energy of Aquarius for rituals to bring innovative change, when working within ones community, or when a new perspective is needed. Create this formula when either the Sun or the Moon is in the sign of Aquarius.

During the appropriate magical timing of either the Sun or the Moon, combine star anise pods, and valerian root in equal parts and spikenard essential oil (20 drops). Add the ingredients to a 30 ml glass bottle with a lid and cover with carrier oil, allowing it to infuse for 28 days.

TIP

You can use this formula to facilitate community and hold space for others and to help situations where people need to be brought together to work toward a common goal. You can apply it to light-blue or white candles and burn it during rituals to promote solidarity and understanding. You can wear this powerful oil formula when engaging in activism, strengthening one's independence, or beginning new projects.

Cancer, the Crab

Cancer (June 21–July 22) is nurturing, emotional, and deeply intuitive. Ruled by the Moon, Cancer is closely tied to cycles, memory, and the home. This Water sign is protective of loved ones and drawn to emotional connection, often acting as a caretaker or emotional anchor. Though sensitive and empathetic, Cancer can retreat into their shell when hurt or overwhelmed.

Herbs of a Cancerian nature are connected to emotion, intuition, nurturing, home, and the subconscious. In magical herbalism, they're used for dreamwork, protection, healing, intuition, and the creation of emotional or energetic safety. Some herbs that help connect with the energy of Cancer are aloe vera, chamomile honeysuckle, lemon balm, and jasmine. Spells that can benefit from the energy of Cancer and its associated herbs are rituals involving the home, facilitating peace and kindness, keeping secrets, and promoting emotional security.

You can create this ritual oil formula to connect with the watery energy of Cancer for intuitions, dreams, and the psychic realm. It's also an effective formula for protecting the home and promoting peace within it. Create this formula when either the Sun or the Moon is in the sign of Cancer.

During the appropriate magical timing of either the Sun or the Moon, combine jasmine flowers, honeysuckle flowers, lemon balm herb, and mugwort her in equal parts in a 30 ml glass bottle with a lid and cover with carrier oil, allowing it to infuse for 28 days.

Work with the Cancer ritual oil before meditation or divination to connect with the subconscious and the psychic senses. You can use this oil to anoint candles for spells to uncover secrets or to keep things hidden. Use this formula as an anointing oil during times of rest and recuperation to regain your personal energy or when you need to set boundaries that prioritize your own healing.

Scorpio, the Scorpion

Scorpio (October 23–November 21) is intense, passionate, and mysterious. Ruled by Mars and Pluto, Scorpio is a sign of transformation, power, and hidden depth. This Water sign feels everything deeply and values loyalty, truth, and personal evolution. Though private and sometimes secretive, Scorpio is a powerful ally and a formidable force when they've been crossed.

Herbs that connect with the energy of Scorpio are associated with transformation, intensity, sexuality, mystery, death and rebirth, protection, and deep emotional or spiritual healing. Some herbs associated with the energy of Scorpio are basil, bloodroot, myrrh, patchouli, and wormwood. The energy of Scorpio and its associated herbs can add extra power to spells involving increasing psychic power and mysticism, spirit communication, banishing, transformation and vengeance. They support journeys into the self, rituals of release, and reclaiming hidden power.

You can create this ritual oil connect with the mysterious energy of Scorpio for rituals of rebirth, mysticism and shadow work. It's also an effective formula for cutting cords and delving into the depths of the subconscious. Create this formula when either the Sun or the Moon is in the sign of Scorpio.

During the appropriate magical timing of either the Sun or the Moon, combine basil, patchouli, and dragon's blood resin in equal parts in a 30 ml glass bottle with a lid and cover with carrier oil, allowing it to infuse for 28 days.

You can use this formula to connect with the spirit realm and hidden parts of the psyche. You can apply it to black, red, or purple candles and burn it during rituals for binding and banishing, working with sexual energy, and discovering hidden truths. You can wear this powerful oil formula when engaging in rituals that honor the dead and working with otherworldly energies.

Pisces, the Fish

Pisces (February 19–March 20) is compassionate, imaginative, and intuitive. Ruled by Jupiter and Neptune, Pisces is deeply connected to the spiritual and emotional realms. This Water sign is sensitive and empathetic, often absorbing the energy around them. Creative and dreamy, Pisces can blur the line between fantasy and reality, sometimes struggling with boundaries or escapism.

TIP

Piscean herbs are helpful for spellwork involving dreams, intuition, spirituality, empathy, illusion, and transcendence. Herbs associated with Pisces often support psychic awareness, emotional healing, connection with the subconscious, and mysticism. The herbs associated with Pisces include blue lotus, moss, passionflower, sea weed, and water lilies. The watery energy of Pisces can empower spells related psychic work, dream exploration, emotional balance, and connection to the unseen world.

You can create this ritual oil to connect with the dreamy energy of Pisces for rituals associated with dreamwork and emotional depth. It's also an effective formula for working with dreams to inspire creativity and gain new ideas and insights. Create this formula when either the Sun or the Moon is in the sign of Pisces.

During the appropriate magical timing of either the Sun or the Moon, combine passionflower, moss, and orchid in equal parts. Add the ingredients to a 30 ml glass bottle with a lid and cover with carrier oil allowing it to infuse for 28 days.

You can use this formula to connect with the dream realm and the subtle energies of the spirit realm. You can apply it to blue or silver candles and burn it during rituals or add it to baths to connect with the energies associated with Pisces. You can work with this powerful oil formula when going through emotional transitions and supporting self-reflection.

Taurus, the Bull

Taurus (April 20–May 20) is grounded, sensual, and dependable. Ruled by Venus, Taurus is deeply connected to the physical world and appreciates comfort, beauty, and stability. This Earth sign is patient and persistent, often working steadily toward long-term goals. Loyal and reliable, Taurus values routine and security, but may resist change or disruption to their carefully built environment.

TIP

Herbs associated with Taurus are often associated with sensuality, stability, fertility, abundance, beauty, and grounding. They often embody earthy, nourishing, and harmonizing qualities. They support physical comfort, emotional steadiness, and pleasure through the senses. Examples of herbs connected to the energy of Taurus include apple, clover, rose, thyme, and violet. Incorporating the energy of Taurus can be effective for spells involving beauty, patience, fertility, stability, and material security.

You can create this ritual oil to connect with the grounding energy of Taurus for rituals associated with stability, loyalty, and material security. It's also an effective formula for rituals focused on beauty, enjoyment, and self-care. Create this formula when either the Sun or the Moon is in the sign of Taurus.

During the appropriate magical timing of either the Sun or the Moon, combine comfrey root, rose petals, hibiscus flowers, and daisy flowers in equal parts. Add the ingredients to a 30 ml glass bottle with a lid and cover with carrier oil, allowing it to infuse for 28 days.

This formula is effective for rituals of abundance and growth and also stability and grounding. You can apply it to green or pink candles and burn it during rituals for both prosperity and love magic. You can work with this effective oil formula when performing rituals to promote peace and tranquility in the home, as well as for rituals of self-care when you need to slow down and nourish oneself.

Virgo, the Maiden

Virgo (August 23–September 22) is analytical, practical, and detail-oriented. Ruled by Mercury, Virgo excels in organization, critical thinking, and service to others. This Earth sign seeks perfection and often strives to improve themselves and their environment. Though modest and reliable, Virgo can become overly self-critical or concerned with small details.

TIP

Bringing the energy of Virgo into a ritual brings the energy of health, analysis, purification, service, discipline, and attention to detail. The herbs associated with the energy of Virgo include eyebright, lavender, myrtle, peppermint, and verbena. Working with herbs associated with Virgo can help to empower rituals for organization, clarity, study, discernment, and integrity. These herbs are ideal for cleansing, focusing the mind, supporting healing, grounding energy, and promoting inner order and peace.

You can create this ritual oil to connect with the characteristics of Virgo for rituals associated with organization, re-evaluation, and planning. It's also an effective formula for spells that involve discernment and discretion. Create this formula when either the Sun or the Moon is in the sign of Virgo.

During the appropriate magical timing of either the Sun or the Moon, combine cinquefoil, lavender, and peppermint in equal parts. Add the ingredients to a 30 ml glass bottle with a lid and cover with carrier oil, allowing it to infuse for 28 days.

This oil is effective to work with if you're in a profession that involves customer service or work with other people on a regular basis. You can wear the oil on the skin or use it to anoint green or white candles for rituals to facilitate community building and interpersonal interaction, as well as when organizing groups around a common goal. The energy of Virgo helps assist with decision-making when you need to weigh multiple options before determining the best outcome.

Capricorn, the Sea-goat

Capricorn (December 21–January 19) is ambitious, disciplined, and pragmatic. Ruled by Saturn, Capricorn values structure, responsibility, and long-term achievement. This Earth sign is often seen as mature and dependable, working diligently to build lasting success. Though serious and reserved, Capricorn has a dry wit and a deep respect for tradition and legacy.

Herbs connected to Capricorn often reflect its serious, grounded nature and are typically strengthening, protective, and supportive. Some herbs that share an affinity with Capricorn's energy include boneset, comfrey, cypress, horehound, and solomon's seal. These herbs are powerful allies for manifesting goals, enhancing discipline, reinforcing boundaries, and anchoring energy. In ritual, you can use Capricorn's herbs for binding, protecting, connecting to ancestors, crafting spells that require patience, and effecting long-term results.

You can create this ritual oil to draw on the qualities of Capricorn for rituals associated with strength, resilience, and determination. It's also an effective formula for spells that involve material wealth and domestic issues. Create this formula when either the Sun or the Moon is in the sign of Capricorn.

During the appropriate magical timing of either the Sun or the Moon, combine English ivy, valerian, and Solomon's seal root in equal parts. Add the ingredients to a 30 ml glass bottle with a lid and cover with carrier oil, allowing it to infuse for 28 days.

This ritual oil is an effective blend to work with before beginning a long-term project. The stabilizing and grounding energies of Capricorn help set a strong foundation to ensure success. Capricorn is all about planning and perseverance. Apply this oil formula to green or brown candles for grounding, especially during times that are chaotic and uncertain. Working with the energies of Capricorn is also helpful for all workings of protection.

Herbal Magic Correspondences

Creating your own herbal magic correspondences is a deeply personal and intuitive practice that allows you to form a unique and powerful relationship with plants. While traditional correspondences offer valuable guidance, your own experiences, associations, and insights can often lead to even more potent and meaningful magical work. One of the most profound ways to create personal correspondences is by drawing from your own intuition. When you handle an herb, take time to feel its energy, noticing its scent, texture, color, and the way it makes you feel emotionally or physically. These impressions can form the foundation of your personal magical associations, which often reflect a deeper resonance between you and the plant spirit.

Your life experiences and memories can also shape these correspondences. For example, if a certain flower grew in your childhood garden and always brought you comfort, you might associate it with protection, home, or emotional healing, regardless of its traditional magical attributions. In this way, plants become woven into your personal mythos, their meanings colored by your story and relationships. Communicating with plant spirits through meditation, journeying, or simply spending quiet time in their presence can open new channels of understanding, allowing the plants themselves to share how they want to work with you.

As you deepen your practice, exploring folklore, mythology, and traditional uses of herbs adds another layer of richness. Myths and stories are the language of the unconscious and can unlock archetypal meanings that connect your personal associations to a broader magical framework. For example, learning that a certain herb was sacred to a specific deity or used in ancient rites may inspire new ways of working with it or affirm your intuitive connection. Over time, this process of blending intuition, memory, plant communication, and historical context helps you speak the language of herbs fluently, making your magic not only more personalized but often more effective than rigidly adhering to established correspondences.

By working with herbs regularly over time, you begin to develop your own magical associations with the herb. You may also realize that you already have some existing associations that you were unaware of. Through plant spirit communication, you are able to connect with plants on an intimate level, drawing in insight and inspiration.

In the following exercise, you create a living dialogue with the herbs themselves. Instead of relying solely on established lists, you weave your own symbolic tapestry, one that reflects not only tradition but also your personal bond with the green world. The more that you communicate with herbs in this way and incorporate them into your personal practice, the more their spirits will speak to you and share new ways of working with them.

1. **Choose your herb.**

   Select one herb to begin working with. It may be one you already feel drawn to, a plant you encounter often, or an herb that has caught your attention in your magical or everyday life.

2. **Observe and connect through your senses.**

   Sit quietly with the herb, holding it in your hands, if possible. Breathe deeply and take in its scent. Notice its texture, shape, color, and overall form. Ask yourself: What emotions or thoughts does this herb stir within me? Does it feel calming, uplifting, protective, or stimulating? Write down your impressions without judgment.

3. **Reflect on memories and association.**

   Reflect on whether this plant connects to any personal memories, places, or experiences. Was it used in family cooking, or in a healing remedy someone once gave you? These associations can be powerful clues to the plant's personal meaning in your practice.

4. **Communicate with the plant spirit.**

   Close your eyes and take a few slow breaths. Imagine reaching out with your energy to connect with the spirit of the plant. Ask, silently or aloud: What lessons or gifts do you wish to share with me? How would you like to be worked with in my magic? Sit in stillness and notice any images, words, or feelings that arise.

5. **Research the plant's uses, folklore, and correspondences.**

   When you finish, take time to research the plant's traditional uses, folklore, and magical correspondences. Compare what you discovered intuitively with what history and tradition say. Where do they align? Where do they differ? You may be surprised by how closely your intuition reflects an herb's traditional associations.

6. **Record and reflect.**

   Write everything in a journal. Over time, revisit your notes and track how the plant continues to show up in your life and practice. You may notice new patterns, shifts, or deepening insights as your relationship grows.

2 Crafting Spells and Rituals

IN THIS PART . . .

Prepare herbs for magical uses.

Craft spells for protection.

Promote harmony with cleansing herbs.

Cultivate abundance and achieve goals.

Practice healing and wellness.

Open your heart to romance and self-love.

Create personal spells and rituals.

IN THIS CHAPTER

- » Gathering herbs for magic
- » Activating herbal ingredients
- » Getting to the root of things

Chapter 4 Preparing Herbs for Magic

Working with herbs in magical practice is an ancient and sacred art, one that has been woven into the tapestry of human spirituality for thousands of years. The ways in which herbs are prepared determine their potency and energetic alignment, shaping how effectively they serve in ritual and spellwork. From the moment a plant is chosen to the time it's placed upon the altar, each step carries meaning: sourcing reflects intention, harvesting builds relationship, and preparing the herb awakens its spirit.

Ancient magical practitioners understood that plants were not inert substances to be used at will, but conscious allies with whom one forms a reciprocal relationship (see Chapter 12). This chapter explores the methods of preparing herbs for magical practice in depth, from ethical sourcing to awakening their latent energies and infusing them with specific intentions.

Sourcing Herbal Ingredients

The foundation of magical herbalism begins long before the herb is ever placed in your hand. Sourcing high-quality plant materials is the first step in creating potent magical preparations, and it's essential that you approach this process with both discernment and respect. Mindfully sourcing your herbal ingredients is an important way to connect with your herbs energetically and with integrity when not growing them yourself. Today, you can acquire every kind of herb imaginable from the far-flung corners of the globe. While it's impossible to be completely aware of an herb's journey before it makes it to you, keeping in mind the interconnectedness of all things and the sacredness of nature is an important rule to follow when sourcing herbal ingredients.

Ethical and sustainable sourcing

Ethical sourcing ensures that the plants you work with are harvested in ways that preserve the environment and honor the plant's spirit. Look for herbs that are organically grown, ethically wildcrafted, or cultivated through regenerative farming practices. These methods protect biodiversity, maintain soil health, and prevent overharvesting of endangered species.

REMEMBER

Sustainable wildcrafting follows the principle of reciprocity: Take only what you need, leave plenty behind, and ensure the plant population can continue to thrive. Wildcrafting often means following the *one-third rule*, where no more than one-third of a plant or patch is harvested at any time. Some practitioners even take less, depending on the abundance of the plant in that location.

Reputable sources

In modern practice, gathering your own herbs may not always be possible. Fortunately, many reputable suppliers prioritize quality and sustainability. Well-known companies, such as Mountain Rose Herbs, Starwest Botanicals, and Frontier Co-op, are widely respected for their commitment to organic and ethically harvested herbs. Local apothecaries and metaphysical shops are also valuable resources, allowing you to support small businesses and engage with a community of practitioners.

TIP

When sourcing from shops, inquire about their suppliers, whether their herbs are certified organic or sustainably wildcrafted, and how they handle rare or endangered plants.

Responsible sourcing is not only a matter of quality but also of magical ethics: Herbs carry the imprint of how they were grown and gathered, and working with unethically sourced plants may hinder the potency of your work.

Bioregionalism

Bioregionalism in herbal magic emphasizes the use of plants that are native or well-established in the area where the practitioner lives. By working with local herbs, you engage in a form of ecological and spiritual reciprocity, fostering a deeper connection to the land, its cycles, and the spirits that inhabit it. Local plants carry the unique energetic imprint of their environment, the soil, climate, and surrounding ecosystem and therefore respond more readily to your intentions and rituals. Harvesting and using herbs from your own bioregion encourages respect for the natural community, supports sustainable practice, and strengthens your relationship with the local elemental and plant spirits.

While some rituals may call for specific herbal ingredients that come from different parts of the world, you don't always need to obtain every rare and hard-to-find ingredient out there. Learning to listen to the land that you're living on and connect to the local plant spirits will teach you that local plants are available for virtually any magical situation. This practice not only honors the plants themselves, but also attunes the practitioner to seasonal cycles, regional energies, and the subtle nuances of the local landscape, deepening the magical resonance of any work performed.

Your own herb garden

For the most direct and personal connection, consider growing your own magical herbs. Even a small garden of basil, rosemary, sage, or mint can provide a steady supply of fresh materials while fostering a deep bond with the plants themselves. Tending to your own magical garden allows you to participate in every step of the process, infusing your herbs with your energy from the very beginning. For more on growing your own garden, see Chapter 11.

Practicing Magical Harvesting

Harvesting herbs for magical use is not just a simple act of collection; it's a ritual exchange between the practitioner and the plant spirit. Traditional magical systems and folk practices place great importance on when and how herbs are harvested because these factors influence their potency and alignment. You may harvest herbs based on the phase of the Moon, the day of the week, or on special day such as Midsummer (June 21st) for extra magical potency.

REMEMBER

First and foremost, magical harvesting should be sustainable. Always seek abundant plant populations, avoid endangered species, and never harvest from polluted or chemically treated areas. Be mindful of the environment and the ecosystem; your actions should nurture, not deplete, the land.

Harvesting herbs ritually

In many traditions, harvesting for magical purposes differs from harvesting for medicine. It was believed that medicinal herbs should be collected with the right hand, symbolizing the giving hand, while magical herbs were plucked with the left hand, the receiving hand, to draw in their spiritual properties.

Tools also hold significance. Practitioners traditionally avoided iron in magical harvesting, as it was believed to disrupt or drive away spirits. Instead, to preserve the plant's spiritual essence, practitioners used ritual blades made of copper, bronze, or other nonferrous materials or harvested by hand.

Harvesting times: Days of the week

The timing of the harvest was historically guided by planetary correspondences. Each day of the week carries distinct energies based on its traditional planetary ruler, as shown in Table 4-1.

TABLE 4-1 Harvesting Times

Day	Planet	Energies
Monday	Moon	Intuition, emotions, psychic work, dreams
Tuesday	Mars	Courage, protection, banishing, energy
Wednesday	Mercury	Intellect, communication, travel, divination
Thursday	Jupiter	Prosperity, luck, expansion, spiritual growth
Friday	Venus	Love, beauty, fertility, friendship
Saturday	Saturn	Protection, boundaries, endings, banishment
Sunday	Sun	Healing, vitality, success, illumination

TIP

Harvesting on the day that aligns with your magical intention can enhance the potency of the herbs.

Factoring in lunar phases

The influence of the Moon and its phases can be seen in agricultural practices around the world. Today, many modern farmers still observe the influence of the phases of the Moon. You also see this in magical practice where lunar cycles have always played an important role in magical herbcraft. Table 4-2 lists which lunar cycles work well with herbs gathered during that time. (For more information on moon phases in spellwork, see Chapter 10.)

TABLE 4-2 Lunar Cycles

Cycle	Timing	During this phase. . .
New moon	A time of beginnings and potential	Herbs gathered are suited for setting intentions and planting seeds for future work
Waxing moon	A period of growth and attraction	Herbs harvested aid in drawing energy toward you
Full moon	The height of power	Herbs are most potent for manifestation, empowerment, and celebration
Waning/dark moon	A time of release and reduction	Herbs collected now are ideal for banishing, protection, and endings

Magical harvesting was traditionally performed before dawn or under moonlight, when the veil between realms was thought to be thinner, and the plant's spiritual energies were at their most potent. In some traditions, practitioners also worked with the lunar *mansions*, specific segments of the moon's path through the zodiac, to select the most auspicious times for harvesting.

TIP

The Moon moves through each of the 12 signs of the zodiac every 2.5 days. You can easily find the lunar mansion for any given time online.

TIP

You can work with lunar mansions to combine the additional qualities of the 12 signs of the zodiac with the phases of the Moon.

Offerings to the plants

An essential part of magical harvesting is the act of making offerings. This reciprocal gesture honors the plant spirit and thanks it for its gift. Offerings may include honey, fresh water, milk, crystals, incense smoke, or a simple prayer of gratitude. In many folk traditions, a pinch of tobacco, a strand of hair, or even a song was considered a fair exchange. The act of giving creates a sacred bond and ensures that the plant's spirit remains connected with the harvested material.

Harvesting your herbs

Harvesting herbs is another way to infuse your herbal ingredients with magical energy. When you're ready to harvest, you need to do a little planning:

- Identify abundant, clean stands away from roadsides, sprayed lawns, and pet traffic. Pack breathable bags (paper or cloth), labels, twine, pruning shears, ritual blade, and a harvesting basket.
- Choose the right moment. Harvest in the morning after the dew has fully dried and before midday heat.
  - *Leaves:* Pick just before flowering when oils peak.
  - *Flowers:* Harvest as buds open.
  - *Seeds:* Collect when fully mature and dry on the plant.
- Use a clean, sharp nonferrous blade (copper/bronze) or scissors dedicated to plant work.
- Wash hands; wear gloves for resinous or prickly plants. Bring alcohol wipes to sanitize between species.
- Harvest with care. Cut above a node or side branch to encourage regrowth. Take only the top-third of soft growth. Avoid bruising and do not compact plants in your bag. Keep species separated and labeled at the point of harvest.

Drying and Preserving Harvested Herbs

The way you handle herbs between harvesting and storing determines how much color, aroma, and magical energy is maintained. The goals are simple: Keep them cool, keep them dry, keep them dark, and keep the air moving, all while protecting against pests and mold.

The following practices maintain magical energy when drying and preserving harvested herbs. You will notice that many of these techniques blend practical knowledge for optimum quality with folk beliefs regarding magical harvesting techniques:

- **Handle carefully:** Keep cut material shaded and ventilated immediately. Never leave bags in a hot car. If insects are present, gently shake the bundle over the patch to return hitchhikers.
- **Preclean and prewilt:** If dusty, give a quick rinse and then thoroughly pat dry. Spread in a single layer 30 to 60 minutes to prewilt and shed surface moisture, which reduces mold risk.
- **Set up a drying space:** Choose a cool (60 to 75°F/16 to 24°C), dark room with low humidity. Avoid kitchens and bathrooms, which are typically more humid. Use a fan for gentle airflow that circulates the room but doesn't blow directly on the herbs. In humid climates, run a dehumidifier.

Choosing a drying method

When you're ready to dry the herbs, you need to choose a drying method. You have several options:

- **Hanging bundles (stems and leafy herbs):** Gather small bundles ½ to 1-inch thick and tie with twine. Invert the bundle into a paper bag with vent holes to block dust and sun and deter pests. Hang in darkness.
- **Using screens or racks (delicate leaves & flowers):** Lay in a single, loose layer on mesh or window-screen frames and elevate for airflow. Turn daily. You can make a tent with muslin or cheesecloth to keep off the insects.
- **Dehydrating (for humid weather or thick parts):** Set the temperature to 95 to 110°F (35 to 43°C) for leaves and flowers and 110 to 120°F (43 to 49°C) for peels and seeds. Keep trays uncrowded and check frequently.

WARNING

Avoid ovens or microwaves for aromatic herbs as heat drives off volatile oils and can cook the plant material.

Monitoring daily

No matter which drying method you choose, look for even color, crisp texture, and no musty odor. Remove any piece that shows gray fuzz or dark, wet spots. These pieces have mold and should be discarded immediately.

You also should conduct dryness tests. When the following happens, you know the herbs are ready:

- Leaves crumble to flakes; stems snap, not bend.
- Flowers feel papery and rattle when rubbed.
- Seeds are hard and brittle; they shatter, not dent.
- Citrus peel snaps cleanly; no tackiness on the inner side.

Freezing, curing, and storing

Seal dried herbs in bags or jars and freeze 48 to 72 hours to kill insect eggs or larvae. Return to room temperature before opening to prevent condensation.

To cure, place dried herbs loosely in an airtight glass for 3 to 7 days. Burp daily by opening the lid for a minute and feeling the texture. If you see moisture on the glass or herbs soften, return them to the drying rack 12 to 24 hours and resume curing.

Once the herbs are cured, you're ready for long-term storage. Keep the following pointers in mind:

- Use amber glass jars with tight lids.
- Fill the jars no more than ¾ full to avoid crushing.
- Add a food-safe desiccant packet.
- Label with plant, part, location, and date.
- Store in a cool, dark, dry place.

WARNING

Avoid plastic bags for long storage.

TIP

For ongoing protection from humidity and pests, inspect the herbs monthly. If the herbs feel limp, redry them briefly. Keep storage shelves clean and place bay leaves or whole cloves on the shelf (not inside the jars) to deter pantry moths.

Table 4-3 lists the suggested shelf life of herbs for maximum freshness.

TABLE 4-3 Suggested Shelf Life for Maximum Freshness

Type	Shelf life
Leaves/flower	About 12 months
Seeds/barks	18 to 24 months
Citrus peels/resinous aromatics	12 to 24 months

TIP

Refresh when the aroma fades noticeably.

TIP

Remove older plant material from your container before filling with freshly dried plant material. Then replace the older plant material on top so that it gets used first.

Awakening Herbs for Ritual Use

Once harvested or purchased, herbs often rest in a dormant state, especially when dried. Before you can use them for magical purposes, they must be spiritually awakened. *Awakening* an herb is the process of inviting its spirit to become active and cooperative in your work. Awakening herbs can be as simple as a spoken invocation or as elaborate as a full ritual. An *invocation* is a spoken statement or chant that calls upon the energy or spirit of something to be present. The goal is to recognize the plant as a conscious ally and to stir its energy to life.

Here's a ritual for awakening herbs:

1. **Prepare the space.**

   Cleanse the area with incense or essential oils in a diffuser. A general incense blend or aromatic resin works fine, or you can choose an incense or essential oil that aligns with your intention.

2. **Present the herb.**

   Hold the herb in your hands or place it upon your altar.

3. **Make an offering.**

   Waft incense smoke over the herb or place a small offering of honey, water, or milk nearby.

4. **Speak to the spirit.**

   Whisper or chant, inviting the plant's essence to awaken. State your purpose clearly: "I call upon the spirit of rosemary to awaken and lend your power of protection to this work."

5. **Visualize the energy.**

   Imagine the herb glowing, its energy stirring, connecting with your own.

Infusing Herbs with Your Intention

Awakened herbs are receptive to your magical purpose, but intention is the spark that directs their power. Infusing herbs with your intention ensures that their natural properties align with your desired outcome.

To infuse the herbs with your intention:

1. **Hold the herb between your hands or hover your palms over it.**
2. **Focus your mind on your specific goal: love, prosperity, protection, healing.**
3. **Visualize your intention as a colored light or flowing energy streaming into the herb.**

   Some practitioners whisper prayers, chant incantations, or trace symbols in the air above the plant. Others use their breath, gently exhaling onto the herb to "breathe" life into it.

REMEMBER

Infusing herbs with your intention step is often performed immediately before crafting spell bags, incense blends, ritual oils, or offerings. The clearer and more focused your intention, the more effectively the herb will carry it forward.

ROOTWORK

The term *rootwork* originates from Hoodoo, a traditional African American folk magic system where roots were employed for their spiritual potency in charms, mojo bags, and workings of protection, prosperity, and love.

In Ancient Greece, a *rhizotomos* was a skilled root-gatherer, herbalist, or root-cutter, a practical practitioner of traditional medicine who harvested plants for their pharmacological properties. This is where the term *rhizome,* which refers to a plant's root system. This historical perspective is a reminder that the practice of gathering roots was once seen as both an art and a science, blending practical healing with the mystical reverence for plant spirits.

Working with Roots

Roots hold a special place in magical practice. They're considered the seat of a plant's soul, housing its deepest reserves of life force. In many traditions, roots are treated as sentient beings deserving respect and reverence. They're often given offerings, such as anointing oils or incense smoke, acknowledging their power before they're incorporated into spellwork or healing practices.

Following is a list of magical roots and their uses:

- **Adam and Eve roots** (*Aplectrum hyemale*) come from a species of orchid growing in the eastern United States and Canada and are traditionally used in potent love spells to strengthen bonds between partners or to attract true, lasting affection. These roots are commonly carried in pairs to harmonize romantic relationships and ensure fidelity. The roots are worked with in pairs because one is believed to be of a masculine nature and the other feminine.
- **Angelica root** (*Angelica archangelica*) is a protective and healing root, especially favored by women for spiritual defense, inner strength, and warding off negativity. In Traditional Chinese Medicine, *Angelica sinensis* (dong quai) is used to nourish the blood, regulate menstrual cycles, alleviate cramps, and support overall female reproductive health. Angelica root is associated with divine protection and

helps to connect with guardian spirits of a celestial nature. You can carry pieces of angelica root in charm bags for good luck and protection during travel or keep whole roots in the home to confer protection to all who dwell inside.

- **Black cohosh** (*Actaea racemosa* or *Cimicifuga racemosa*) is an herb that grows natively in North America. Black cohosh offers strong protection and is traditionally used to repel unwanted spirits or harmful influences. Medicinally, Black cohosh has been traditionally used in Indigenous plant medicine to support women's health, especially for easing symptoms of menopause, regulating menstrual cycles, and alleviating cramps. It has also been applied for its anti-inflammatory properties and to relieve muscular pain.
- **Calamus** (*Acorus calamus*) is known for its commanding and controlling properties and is often included in court case spells, domination work, and rituals where influence over situations or people is desired. Calamus, also known as Sweet Flag, has been used to aid digestion, soothe stomach ailments, and strengthen as a mild stimulant. In the Indigenous plant medicine traditions of North America, the root was chewed for energy and clarity and to ward off illness. Calamus root was carried for protection and believed to break jinxes, while some folk practices held that placing it across doorways would repel evil spirits.
- **Devil's shoestring** (*Tephrosia virginiana*) grows natively in the central and eastern United states and is known for its long stringy roots from which it gets its name. Devil's shoestring is used in folk magic in both protection magic and binding spells to "tie up" enemies and prevent them from working against you. Devil's shoestring can be made into bundles or added to charm bags and carried for good luck as well as defensive magic. It offers strong protection and is frequently used for securing court case victories and attracting employment or job opportunities.
- **High John the Conqueror root,** also called High John root (*Ipomoea jalapa*), is native to the southeastern United States and is one of the important "*master*" roots in Hoodoo folk practices. Symbolizing the cleverness, strength, and enduring spirit of the legendary folk hero, this root is a powerful staple for gaining personal power, drawing luck, and overcoming challenges. It is especially associated with men seeking strength, respect, and success.

HIGH JOHN ROOT

High John root is of particular importance to African-American practitioners. According to the legend, High John was an African prince enslaved in the Americas who outwitted his oppressors through cunning, humor, and magical prowess. Though enslaved, his spirit could not be bound, and he became a trickster-hero who uplifted his people with courage and wit. Carrying or working with this root is believed to invoke his enduring power for gaining personal strength, drawing luck, overcoming challenges, and achieving success.

- Lucky hand root, *Dactylorhiza* spp., is a variety of marsh orchids, commonly named for the resemblance of their roots to tiny hands. Lucky hand root is carried as a charm to attract good luck and success, specifically in gambling and games of chance. Due to its hand-like shape lucky hand root helps to bring success and achievement in any area especially when it involves working with the hands.
- Orris root (*Iris germanica*), also sometimes referred to as Queen Elizabeth root, can be used whole or in powdered form. It is sometimes used in perfumery as a scent fixative and makes a good addition to herbal powders for love, attraction, and influence. Associated with feminine empowerment and love-drawing rituals, this root enhances attraction and is commonly used in spells for love, beauty, and influence. Orris root is also an ingredient in formulas for same-sex love and romance magic.
- Yellow dock (*Rumex crispus*), traditionally used to attract wealth and prosperity, is also valued for its cleansing and purifying energy, which helps remove blockages that hinder personal or financial growth. In folk practice, it is carried to draw steady income or sprinkled in the home to encourage abundance. Magically, it is linked to grounding and renewal, and offerings of coins or grain were sometimes made to the plant spirit to encourage fruitful harvests and fortune.

Preparing roots for magical use

When working with roots in magical practice, it's essential to treat them as living vessels of the plant's spirit and energy. Before use, roots should always be ritually cleansed to remove any residual or stagnant energy they may have absorbed during harvest, storage, or transport. Common methods include passing the root through purifying incense smoke (such as frankincense, copal, or cedar), sprinkling it lightly with blessed or spring water, or briefly exposing it to the cleansing rays of the sun or the illuminating glow of the moon. Each method carries its own energetic signature — incense for air and spirit, water for emotional cleansing, sunlight for vitality, and moonlight for intuitive and magical attunement.

After cleansing, roots are often prepared for magical work through anointment with ritual oils, fumigation with incense, or consecration through ritual used to dedicate the root to a specific purpose. Fumigating with incense further awakens the plant spirit and aligns it with your purpose. The root is then wrapped in cloth or kept in a charm bag or wooden box. In many traditions, offerings such as a few drops of honey, coins placed near the root, a splash of rum, or whispered prayers are given to "feed" the root and strengthen its spirit for the work at hand.

Once prepared, roots can be used in various ways depending on their magical correspondences. You can carry them in mojo or charm bags to draw their influence to a specific place or person, bury them near thresholds or property lines to protect and bless the home, or place them upon altars where they receive regular attention and offerings.

REMEMBER

Because roots concentrate the life force of the plant, even a small piece can exert powerful influence maintaining its connection to the plant spirit that inhabits it.

Offerings to roots

Roots, as the seat of a plant's spirit, respond well to consistent care and offerings. Just as one would maintain a relationship with a familiar or guardian spirit, regular offerings keep the root "alive" and cooperative in your magical workings. Common offerings include smoke from incense, a few drops of ritual oil or alcohol, honey, fresh water, or even words of heartfelt gratitude.

In Hoodoo rootwork traditions, an offering is often referred to as "feeding the root," ensuring its spirit remains nourished, strong, and aligned with your goals. (See Chapter 1 for more information on rootwork.) Some practitioners speak or sing to their roots, sharing their intentions and thanking them for their ongoing assistance, reinforcing the bond between human and plant spirit.

IN THIS CHAPTER

» Defending your castle

» Claiming your space

» Rallying plants for protection

» Weaving magical boundaries

Chapter 5
Protecting Yourself and Setting Boundaries

Protection magic is quite possibly one of the oldest and most extensive forms of magic. Every culture throughout history has its protective charms, ranging from simple to complex. These objects are used as talismans and amulets and are carried to protect against negativity and misfortune. Simple rituals and folk practices to avert bad luck and negative energy have become ingrained in the human psyche. Certain taboos, like spilt salt, broken mirrors, and black cats, are rooted in protective practices.

There is perhaps no larger category of plants in magical practice than those with protective properties. Protection manifests itself in a number of different ways. Plants with protective properties display their powers based on their defensive traits, such as thorns, burrs, poisons, and other evolutionary characteristics.

You can approach spells for protection from different directions depending on the need demanded by the circumstances. They can have preventative measures, such as carrying protective herbs to attract good luck and promote positive vibrations. They can also involve more active spellwork to protect against something specific that is more defensive in nature or be spells that go on the offensive for more serious circumstances.

This chapter introduces you to protection magic. In this chapter, discover different approaches to protecting yourself and your home from unwanted energies and influences. You find a variety of herbs that are known for their protective properties, as well as formulas and rituals for maintaining the safety and sanctity of your personal space.

Enforcing Safe Spaces

Everyone deserves to feel safe and secure — at work, at home, and while out going about their lives. Safety and security look and feel different to everyone, but it all comes down to boundaries. Personal boundaries help define what is and is not acceptable to your own sense of safety and well-being. Protection magic helps you to define and enforce those boundaries physically and spiritually.

REMEMBER

When you're clear about the energies and influences that you don't want in your life, you're more open to receive the things that you do want. By cultivating safe spaces and protecting yourself from harmful, unhealthy, and unwanted influences, you're able to live your life more fully. Through the use of herbal magic, you can take a more active role in the people and energies that you allow into your personal sphere and empower yourself to draw clear lines between what is and is not acceptable.

Defining defensive operations

Defensive operations are essential components of any spiritual or magical practice, serving to protect the practitioner, their space, and their workings from intrusion, harm, or interference. These techniques form a layered system of defense, ranging from energetic wards and clearly defined boundaries to spiritual alliances and empowered objects. Whether enacted through the creation of psychic fortifications, physical symbols of protection, or the invocation of spiritual allies, these practices help maintain sovereignty over one's environment and energy. Practitioners establish protection through warding, boundary-setting, and divine or magical reinforcement.

Warding

Warding is a kind of spiritual alarm system that is programmed to react to specific environmental factors, including undesirable forces and individuals. You can program wards to detect specific persons, entities, or forces or to act as a general sentry. You can create these semiconscious programmed energy forms to serve a specific function, such as preventing a specific individual from entering or remaining in your space. You can make wards last indefinitely or dissipate them after a predetermined period of time.

Boundaries

Boundaries are part of all healthy relationships, both physical and ethereal. Boundaries keep you from feeling vulnerable and give you dominion over your environments. Developing healthy boundaries in your relationships, both physical and spiritual, makes both parties aware of the terms of the relationship, while also keeping toxic people and spirits away.

Physical boundaries are tangible parameters where protection is cast around a specific person, place, or object. They take the form of *protective circles* — a continuous marking of a boundary or multiple points that, when connected, create geometric shapes.

Psychic boundaries strengthen the aura and energy centers while keeping them clear of blockages. Psychic boundaries are like strengthening the immune system to protect the body from disease. Strong and healthy boundaries are achieved by regular cleansing, energy work, and shielding (see Chapter 6).

Divine, spiritual, and magical protection

By petitioning protective deities, guardian spirits, and familiars to actively patrol and protect a person, place, or object, you can bestow protection in return for regular offerings for the entity's intervention. By gaining the protection of a spirit with greater power than the one sent against you, you can command the offending spirit to cease and desist. *Hierarchical spirits* (those that rule over specific area) or those of a contrasting influence can be set against one another for protective purposes.

REMEMBER

A focal point, such as an altar, spirit house, or statue, can serve as an anchor for the entity in a particular area. These spirits can also be tied to the land itself, either to particular objects or to organic matter, such as wood or bones. These objects are the physical representations of the spirit in question and should be treated with reverence. This type of *magical agreement* — a pact between you and the entity — is continually renewed via ritual offerings.

A witch or magician can employ their own spiritual power through visualization and willpower to place a protective aura around a person, place, or object. The will of the witch is directed through concentration and ritual, with some physical representation of the spell, such as an object or talisman bearing symbols of protection, usually serving as the focal point.

Launching offensive operations

The forms of protection I describe in this section, such as binding, banishing, and return to sender spells, actively seek out the perpetrator when harm is coming from a specific source, whether known or unknown. Hexing and cursing can also be considered a form of offensive versus defensive protection, used to neutralize the threat posed by a perpetrator or distract them by creating strife and discord. *Hexing* and *cursing* are forms of harmful magic that are used to create a deleterious effect on the target.

REMEMBER

The more aggressive forms of protection magic are considered taboo by those practitioners who follow the maxim of "harm none." However, some situations, such as toxic relationships or situations with individuals that have harmful intentions, call for such drastic measures.

Deflection and return to sender spells

Deflection spells are preventative in the sense that they bounce back negative forces directed at the practitioner before they can hit their target. *Return to sender spells* are done in retaliation to spells that have already been cast when the sender is known.

Both spells combine defensive measures with offensive maneuvers. When harmful energy, intent, spells, or spirits are detected, they're returned to their source.

Witch bottles and other magical containers, such as boxes lined with mirrors, are some of the protective objects kept in or near the home to protect from harm and return the energy to the sender. (See the section "Working with Witch bottles," later in this chapter, for instructions on creating a witch bottle.)

Binding and banishing spells

Also used in times when protection is needed, binding and banishing spells are a more assertive protection measure.

Binding is used to restrict the actions of would-be perpetrators before such perpetrators can do harm. You can also use binding to protect others and even from themselves.

Through a physical binding, a photo or other symbolic representation of the target is bound with cord and nailed to a piece of wood or tied down. Sympathetic magic is enacted, which cuts the target off from their energy and prevents them from manifesting harm.

Banishing is the forcible removal of harmful forces and malevolent energy or entities, which can then be returned to the sender or neutralized in some fashion. Banishing requires the concerted will of the practitioner, who is free of fear and doubt.

Banishing has different levels, depending on the severity involved.

TIP

You can perform simple banishing rituals on a regular basis to remove any unwanted energies as part of your regular devotional practice. When you banish what does not benefit you, you make room for what does.

Exploring Herbs of Protection

Herbs associated with protection is possibly one of the largest categories of plant correspondence because protection is an important topic and often a priority for many. You can use herbs to confer protection in many different ways, and the intention and the way that the herb is being used is what brings out its protective properties.

In this section, I cover some general protective herbs as well as some that are particularly helpful for protection magic.

REMEMBER

I don't include many general protection herbs in my general discussion here. You may also find that you have some of your own personal herbal associations for protection magic, such as a specific herb from your childhood that brings back good memories and a sense of safety. These personal associations are just as powerful as traditional herbal correspondences, if not more so.

Herbs used in protective magic are often spicy, fragrant, or thorned, with each one exhibiting their protective qualities in a different way. The following list highlights some of those qualities:

- Agrimony
- Anise
- Basil
- Bay
- Betony
- Birch
- Blackberry
- Broom
- Burdock
- Carnation
- Clove
- Cumin
- Damiana
- Dill
- Fennel
- Fern
- Frankincense
- Garlic
- Hawthorn
- Holly
- Ivy
- Lilac
- Mugwort
- Mullein
- Orris
- Parsley
- Rosemary
- Sage
- Vervain
- White heather
- Woodruff

REMEMBER

When selecting your herbs for protection, ask yourself what you're protecting yourself against and what kind of energy will best bring you the protection that you need.

Herbs of the Sun

Herbs of the Sun bring in light and raise the vibrations of an area. They illuminate the shadows and create an energy that wards off dark, stagnant, and low vibration energies. Herbs like angelica, cedar frankincense, mistletoe, and St. John's Wort are associated with the energy of the Sun.

Angelica

Angelica (*Angelica archangelica*) is a member of the carrot family and is a powerful ally of protection. often associated with the Archangel Michael and other protective, celestial energies, angelica helps keep away harmful spirits and removes negative influences from the body and home. You can use angelica in rituals to call upon divine protection.

You can place pieces of angelica root in charm bags or use them in ritual baths (see Chapter 2) to bring positive energy and light to any situation. You can buy whole angelica roots, although the plant is easy to grow.

You can anoint angelica roots with protective oils and carry them as amulets or keep them in the home to confer their protective vibrations. *Amulets* refer to objects, such as a piece of jewelry, specifically related to protection. Angelica is also a powerful herb to work with for warding off evil and returning any harmful thoughts, energies, or spells sent your way by other people rebounding back to them.

Frankincense

Frankincense (*Boswellia sacra*) is a sacred resin renowned for its powerful magical properties, particularly in protection, purification, and spiritual elevation. Burned as incense, frankincense clears negative energies from people, places, and ritual tools, creating a purified space suitable for sacred work.

Deeply connected to the energy of the Sun, frankincense carries a radiant, golden vibration that aligns with solar qualities of clarity, illumination, and divine authority. Its uplifting scent is said to raise energetic frequencies, making it ideal for meditation, invoking higher spiritual realms, and enhancing the effectiveness of spells and rituals.

Often used in offerings and anointing blends, frankincense serves as a bridge between the physical and spiritual worlds, illuminating the path for deeper insight and divine protection.

St. John's Wort

St. John's Wort (*Hypericum perforatum*) is a powerful protective herb long associated with the energy of the Sun and used in magical practices to ward off negativity, banish evil spirits, and bring light into dark spaces. Traditionally harvested around the Summer Solstice, when solar energy is at its peak, the plant is believed to capture and store the Sun's power, making it especially potent for protection, purification, and uplifting spells.

You can carry St. John's wort as an amulet, hang it above doorways, or burn it as incense to dispel harmful energies and restore spiritual vitality. In magical workings, St. John's wort also serves as a remedy for emotional darkness.

Herbs of Mars

Herbs associated with Mars are hot and fiery and often have thorns, which shows their aggressive nature. Herbs like blackthorn, dragon's blood resin, rue, stinging nettle, yarrow, and wormwood are associated with the energy of Mars and used in defensive and offensive protection and magical warfare.

Dragon's blood resin

Dragon's blood resin (*Daemonorops draco*) is secreted by a variety of trees and can be burned as an incense. When the resin melts, it has the color and consistency of blood. Some varieties of dragon's blood resin come in liquid form, depending on its source.

REMEMBER

Dragon's blood resin is a powerful ingredient for any spell and can add power and potency to spell or ritual. You can use dragon's blood resin for a variety of magical purposes, including luck, love, exorcism, and empowerment. One of its primary uses is in protection magic. Red is a protective color and also indicates the fiery nature of this plant ally.

TIP

You can burn dragon's blood resin on charcoal disks to free the home of any negative energy and erect a protective boundary. You can also add pieces of the resin to charm bags and carry them for protection. Dragon's blood resin can also be powdered and infused into carrier oil to anoint candles, wear on the body, or to trace protective boundaries around windows and doorways. (For more on carrier oils, see Chapter 2.)

Rue

Rue (*Ruta graveolens*) is a powerful plant to work with in protective magic and is used in both Italian and Mexican folk magic to protect against (and remove) the evil eye. Rue has a powerful reputation for being able to remove negative energies and parasitic entities that may be draining your energy. Used in counter magic to break the effects of harmful spells cast against you, rue can be used as an herb of exorcism as well as an herb for banishing bad luck, ill intentions, and energetic blockages.

WARNING

Rue is a plant with potent chemistry, so be careful when you work with it. Fresh rue can cause skin irritation and blistering when the juices get on the skin and are exposed to sunlight. Anyone who is pregnant or trying to get pregnant should not consume it internally because it can also be an *abortifacient* (causing the termination of pregnancy).

TIP

You can carry rue in charm bags and work it into talismans for protection. You can also hang dry sprigs of rue in the home near windows and doorways to guard against unwanted influences and energies.

Yarrow

Yarrow (*Achillea millefolium*) is a warrior's herb, named for the hero Achilles. Roman soldiers carried yarrow, which is also known as warrior's woundwort, to staunch bleeding when they were wounded. Yarrow brings courage and protection, among other things, and is a powerful ally for establishing and strengthening boundaries. Yarrow also helps with psychic protection, working to prevent energy drain and stave off unwanted influences.

REMEMBER

Yarrow is a supportive and helpful herbal ally that is easy to grow. You can incorporate yarrow into charm bags, work it into amulets, and burn it as an ingredient in incense blends to protect both the body and home. Yarrow supports energetic health and keeps energy moving while acting as a filter to keep out heavy energies. (See Chapter 8 for more information on yarrow and energetic wellness.) You can harvest yarrow leaves, wrap them into smoke bundles, and burn them in cleansing and protection rituals.

Wormwood

A member of the artemisia family, wormwood (*Artemisia absinthium*) is a wonderful plant ally to work with for all types of protective workings. Wormwood is a fiery and bitter herb that you can use for banishing unwanted influences. It was once used expel intestinal parasites, which makes it a powerful herb for removing unwanted entities and keeping the energy field clean.

You can work with wormwood you need to purge stubborn energies. You can add wormwood to incense for smoke-cleansing with powerful effects. You can also powder wormwood and sprinkle it around the outside of the home and across doorways to create protective barriers. You can also carry wormwood in charm bags, work it into amulets, and use it in incense blends.

TIP

Wormwood is easy to grow, and keeping a live plant near your front door will help to keep away unwanted energies and persons.

WARNING

Take care when working with wormwood internally or as an essential oil. Although it's used as an ingredient in the liquor absinthe, wormwood can be mildly toxic when not handled properly.

Herbs of Saturn

Saturnian herbs are those with heavy, earthy vibrations. They're used in binding, banishing, and setting strong boundaries. These plants may also be used to protect things by hiding them from view — for example, when someone is walking home alone in the dark or entering a potentially hostile environment. Herbs that are associated with Saturn include comfrey, mullein, nightshade, and valerian.

Mullein

Mullein (*Verbascum thapsus*) is a potent herb in protective spellwork, valued for its strong, grounding energy and its ability to ward off harmful influences. Traditionally used to drive away evil spirits and baneful energies, mullein can be carried as a protective charm, placed in the home, or burned as an incense to create a spiritual shield.

Its tall, torch-like stalk and soft, velvety leaves are symbolic of inner strength and resilience, making it an ideal ally for guarding against psychic attack, fear, and negativity. In folk magic, herbal practitioners have used mullein to strengthen courage and resolve, helping practitioners stand firm in the face of adversity.

Valerian root

Valerian (*Valeriana officinalis*) is a powerful herb in defensive magic, prized for its ability to banish unwanted energies and protect against spiritual intrusion. Though often known for its calming effects, valerian holds a fierce, grounding energy in spellwork that makes it effective for warding off hostile forces and breaking hexes or curses. Its strong, pungent scent was traditionally believed to repel evil spirits and malicious entities, and it can be burned, scattered, or carried in a charm for personal protection.

In banishing rituals, valerian serves as a potent force to drive out negativity, sever toxic energetic ties, and establish firm boundaries. Its deep roots mirror its magical ability to anchor the practitioner and create a strong defensive barrier against psychic or emotional attack.

Creating Formulas for Defense

You can create protection formulas in varying forms, including powders, incense, salt, and oil.

Fiery Wall of Protection Powder

This Fiery Wall of Protection Powder formula is based on the classic Hoodoo (see Chapter 1) formula and can be sprinkled around the home, mixed with salt and kept in a dish by the front door, or added to carrier oil (see Chapter 3) and used to anoint windows and doorways to protect the home. You can also sprinkle this powder in charm bags with other protective herbs and carry it to bring protection with you.

Mix equal parts of powdered myrrh, frankincense, dragon's blood resin, red sandalwood, and cayenne pepper. To turn this formula into a banishing formula, add black pepper, mustard seed, and graveyard dirt.

Hot Foot Powder

Hot Foot Powder is a classic Hoodoo formula used for protection and, more specifically, the removal of unwanted people. Blend equal parts of powdered cayenne pepper, red pepper flakes, black pepper, graveyard dirt, and sulfur. While you're powdering and mixing the ingredients, focus on your intention to infuse the formula with your energy.

TIP

Sprinkle Hot Foot Powder in your home's doorways and room corners to create an energy of protection. Alternatively, if you're concerned about unwanted people, sprinkle Hot Foot Powder in any location that you want to remove them from or keep them away from. (Traditionally, you'd sprinkle the powder on the floor where that unwanted person would walk.)

Protection Incense

To make Protection Incense, take equal parts of dragon's blood resin and frankincense resin and mix them with equal parts dried patchouli and rosemary. Burn on charcoal in a firesafe dish to call upon the protective powers of these herbs.

TIP

Burn in the home during a waxing Moon to strengthen protective boundaries or burn during a waning Moon to remove unwanted energies.

Black Salt

Black Salt is a modern adaptation of a classic formula used for banishing and protection. You can sprinkle black salt around the home, carry it in charm bags, and use it to draw protective symbols to banish negativity. You can sprinkle Black Salt in the shape of a cross at your front door to protect the home from any unwanted visitors. After you sprinkle the salt and set your intention for protection, you can cover the cross with a doormat or sweep the salt away from the front door.

To create this formula, take table salt or sea salt and add ashes, activated charcoal, and/or iron shavings until the salt takes on a black/gray color. The ashes can be from anywhere — for example, from a fireplace, incense burner, burning herbs, and so on.

TIP

Instead of iron shavings, you can also scrape the rust off of a nail or other rusty object and add that to the salt. Optionally, you can add powdered valerian root, wormwood, comfrey root, and/or mullein.

Protection Oil

On a Sunday or Tuesday when the Moon is waxing, combine dried yarrow, wormwood, stinging nettle, valerian root, and salt with carrier oil in a sealable glass jar. (See Chapter 3 for more on carrier oils.) Allow this mixture to infuse for 28 days to let the lunar cycle completes itself. Shake the bottle when you remember to do so, keeping it in a sunny location during the day and storing it near the front door at night.

After the 28 days have passed, strain out the ingredients and use the oil to anoint candles to burn for protection, wear the oil on your skin for personal protection, or use the oil to anoint window frames and doorways to protect the home.

Casting Spells of Protection

Protection magic is one of the oldest and most essential forms of spellwork, practiced across cultures and traditions to guard the self, the home, and sacred space from harm. These spells act as energetic boundaries, barriers that deflect negativity, prevent spiritual intrusion, and strengthen the practitioner's inner and outer defenses. Protective spellcraft often combines physical materials, such as herbs, salts, oils, and symbolic tools, with intention, incantation, and ritual timing to generate a powerful shield of spiritual security. Whether you're safeguarding your energy from toxic influences or anchoring your home in protective force, these spells help establish a stable foundation for all other magical work.

This section provides a variety of protective rituals and formulas designed to meet different needs and lifestyles. From quick candle spells for personal shielding to more elaborate home protection rites, each working channels natural energies — herbal, elemental, and planetary — to build a strong magical defense.

REMEMBER

The timing and materials of each spell are carefully chosen to amplify their potency: Tuesdays and Sundays for strength and divine support, waxing and full moons for growth and empowerment, red and white candles for courage and clarity, and solar-aligned herbs and resins for illumination and purification.

These spells aren't only rituals of defense, but they're also declarations of sovereignty. As you move through these workings, remember that protection is both a magical act and a sacred responsibility. When cast with clarity and conviction, these spells become living wards, anchoring protective energy wherever they're placed and woven into your everyday life.

Candle spell for protection

Cast this particular spell on a Tuesday, Thursday, or Sunday during the waxing or full moon.

For this spell, you need one red candle (for strength, courage, and protection) and Protection Oil. (See the formula in the preceding section or craft your own formula.) You may also want a pin or blade to carve symbols into the candle.

After you gather the necessary materials, do the following:

1. **Anoint the candle with protection oil, moving from base to wick, saying:**

   "Oil of ward and warrior's will,
   With sacred flame my space I fill."

2. **Carve into the candle (if desired) a symbol of protection.**
3. **Light the candle and speak:**

   "By flame of red and moon above,
   I call upon the powers of love,
   Of shield, of strength, of fire and might,
   Surround me now in sacred light."

4. **Sit with the flame for a few moments, visualizing a strong, glowing barrier surrounding you and your space.**
5. **Let the candle burn safely down or snuff it out to relight on the next appropriate day until the candle is fully spent.**

Home protection with herbal salt bowls

This spell makes use of the protective and purifying qualities of salt combined with protective herbs to help cleanse the home of unwanted energies and also to prevent any harmful or low vibration influences from collecting in the home.

For this spell, you need a small dish or bowl for each location (front door, back door, kitchen, and living room). Then gather the following: sea salt or kosher salt, dried bay leaves, dried fennel seeds or sprigs, dried sage, and dried rosemary. You also have the option of including other protective herbs, such as lavender, basil, mugwort, or thyme.

Then follow these steps:

1. **In each small dish, combine a generous pinch of sea salt or kosher salt, crushed bay leaves, a sprinkle of dried fennel seeds or sprigs, crumbled dried sage and rosemary, and any other protective herbs, such as lavender, basil, mugwort, or thyme, that you feel called to include.**
2. **As you mix the herbs and salt, speak aloud:**

*"Salt of Earth and herbs of grace,
Guard this home, protect this space.
From door to hearth, from wall to wall,
Let no harm or shadow fall."*

3. **Place one dish each at the front door, the back door, in the kitchen, and in the living room, repeating the following as you place each dish:**

   *"By leaf and root, by stone and flame,
   I seal this threshold in protection's name."*

   Let them sit undisturbed to absorb and neutralize any unwanted energy.

TIP

If you're interested in carrying out a monthly cleansing and recharging, gather the contents of all four dishes at each full moon and combine them in a large bowl. While combining the mixtures, say the following:

"Four corners joined in circle round,
Purified where light is found.
Let moonlight cleanse, renew, restore,
Protection strong forevermore."

Place the large bowl under the full moonlight overnight — outside, if possible, or on a windowsill if not. The next morning, redistribute the mixture back into the four dishes and repeat the placement incantation if desired.

Home protection ritual

You can repeat this simple ritual on a regular basis to keep one's home protected. On a Sunday or Tuesday when the Moon is waxing to full, take some of your finished Protection Oil (see the formula earlier in this chapter) and hold it while focusing on your intention of protecting the home. If you work with any spirits, deities, or ancestors, you can also pray to them during this ritual to ask for their protection; otherwise, just ask the plant spirits for their help.

To perform the ritual, follow these steps:

1. **Starting at the point of the house that is farthest from the front door (upstairs, at a back-facing window if it's a**

two-story house), anoint the window frames and doorways in each room.**

Take some of your oil and apply it to your fingers, starting with the bottom-left corner of the window or door and trace around it in a clockwise direction until you've connected to your starting point. (For bedrooms or other rooms where the doorways don't connect to the outside, you'll do this from inside each room.)

2. **Repeat this process for every window and doorway as you work your way finally to the front door while focusing on your intention.**
3. **When you reach the front door, repeat this process three times on both the inside and outside of the door to seal the home with protective energy.**

Charm bag for protection

For this simple ritual, you construct a protective charm bag that you can carry around with you wherever you go. You can make these charm bags for loved ones, carry them yourself, or keep them in your car.

TIP

Perform the ritual on a Sunday or Tuesday when the Moon is waxing to full.

Gather the following:

- White candle
- Small red or black drawstring bag or a square of fabric that you can tie a string around to make a small pouch
- Angelica root pieces
- Nine rose thorns
- 1 tablespoon yarrow
- A pinch of dragon's blood resin
- Incense burner and charcoal disk

After you gather all your ingredients, do the following:

1. **Lay everything out and light the white candle and the charcoal disk.**

2. **Burn the dragon's blood resin on the charcoal, passing each of your ingredients through the smoke of the incense while focusing on your intention before adding them to your bag or pouch.**
3. **Pass each of the rose thorns through the smoke individually and then place them in your bag or pouch.**

   If you're working with small pieces of angelica root or ground yarrow herb, you can hold all pieces in your hand and hold it over the incense smoke all at once before placing them in your bag or pouch.
4. **After adding all the ingredients to the charm bag you created, tie it shut and pass the entire bag through the incense smoke.**
5. **Set the completed charm bag in front of the candle and either allow the candle to burn out completely or, if you're using a larger candle, let it burn until you go to bed.**

TIP

You can recharge the charm bag every full Moon by smoking it in more dragon's blood resin and burning a candle next to it.

Witch bottles

Witch bottles are a form of protective charm that consists of burying a protective object on one's property to act as a decoy for harmful spirits and witchcraft cast against the household. Witch bottles were common in England and parts of Europe starting in the 16th and 17th centuries, and they could also be found in America dating as late as the 19th century.

Originally, witch bottles would have been filled with all sorts of sharp objects, as well as the hair and urine of the person making the witch bottle. These personal components would serve as the means of absorbing any spiritual attacks that may be directed at the person who created the witch bottle.

For the following ritual, I've adapted some ingredients as well as added some herbs for extra protection.

Gather the following:

- Empty glass or clay container with a lid
- Protection Oil (see earlier formula)

- Thirteen pins
- A pinch of Iron shavings
- 1 tablespoon stinging nettle
- Vinegar

Choose a Saturday or Tuesday during a waning moon as the day to construct your witch bottle. Be sure to have all the ingredients ready.

Here's what the process for making a witch bottle looks like:

1. **Anoint each pin with Protection Oil while focusing on your intention.**

   Say something like "I am protected from all harm that is directed at me physically and spiritually."

2. **Add the iron shavings and the stinging nettle, while repeating your intention for each ingredient.**
3. **After adding the dry ingredients, fill the bottle with vinegar and seal it with the lid, shaking the ingredients together.**
4. **Bury your witch bottle upside down near the front door or hidden under the front doorstep.**

   If you can't bury the bottle in one of these locations, hide it somewhere in the house where it will not be disturbed, such as the back of a closet.

IN THIS CHAPTER

» Cleaning up your energy

» Removing obstacles

» Breaking attachments

Chapter 6
Cleansing, Purifying, and Banishing with Herbs

Every day, you come into contact with a broad spectrum of energies and influences. Some of them are naturally present in your environment, while others come from the individuals around you. Places hold energy, and every place that a person inhabits has its own unique vibration based on the energies that are present. For example, walking into a busy bar on a Saturday night is going to have a much different energy compared to taking a Sunday afternoon stroll through a tranquil garden.

This chapter focuses on those energies, how they affect you on a day-to-day basis, and how to remove them when they become overwhelming. You discover the subtle distinctions between cleansing, purifying, and banishing practices for good energetic hygiene, including how to maintain healthy energetic boundaries through personal cleansing practices for you and your space.

Practicing Energetic Hygiene

You can pick up on energies based on the input of your physical senses, but you're also picking up a nonphysical element. You mingle your own energy with the places that you frequent, and the hope is that you leave the space energetically better than before your arrival.

REMEMBER

Not only do you leave your own energetic signature, but you also take a little bit of the place's energy with you, especially if the energy is intense. If you've ever walked into a room where two people are fighting, you can literally feel the tense energy in the air, even if they're no longer in the room.

Certain places and people leave you feeling energized and energetically lighter, while other people and places can leave you feeling energetically drained or depressed. Places that are especially sacred have their own energetic characteristics. On the other hand, places where terrible things have happened over a long period of time have left the energy of that place unbalanced.

Your personal energetic health and the energetic health of the places that you spend the most time in can have a huge impact on your mood, sense of wellbeing, and overall wellness. *Energetic hygiene* is important and is a foundational skill for all magical practitioners, especially when you come into contact with so many different energies.

TIP

Energetic hygiene is like brushing your teeth, running the vacuum, or doing your laundry. Energetic hygiene can become a simple daily habit. While your life doesn't depend on you taking a shower or doing the dishes, it sure makes life easier (and smell better). Picking up simple practices that contribute to your energetic hygiene will make a huge difference, not only in how you feel, but how effective your magic is. While you can't always claim dominion over the energetics of the places that you visit, you can control your own personal energy and your energetic imprint on the world around you.

To maintain energetic hygiene for the magical practitioner, you'll want to know a few techniques: cleansing, purifying, and banishing.

Cleansing

Spiritual cleansing is simple, general practices that you can perform on a daily or regular basis and that maintain the overall energetic health of your space and your person. Cleansing can involve burning herbs and resins or applying a perfume that lifts your energetic frequency.

REMEMBER

Cleansing is probably one of the most fundamental and important magical practices because it keeps everything moving smoothly. You can compare ritual cleansing to cleaning up the kitchen after you finish cooking or taking out the trash every day. It's a generalized cleansing that keeps the overall environment in good working order. Of course, you can also perform cleansing practices on yourself.

TIP

With cleansing practices, you help to keep the beneficial energy coming in while helping any energy or influences that have become stagnant or unnecessary to move on. Cleansing practices keep the energy of the place or person intact, raising the vibration and promoting harmony without removing desirable energy along with undesirable energy.

Purification

You can use purification rituals and practices when you need more than general cleansing practices. While some techniques associated with cleansing are also used in rites of purification, purification rituals and practices are typically performed over a longer period of time and have a more profound effect. For example, when a person is going through a difficult transition or healing from trauma, their own energy may be depleted, or it may leave room for unbalanced energy to collect, causing a change in mood or sense of well-being. Purification practices are like deep spring-cleaning — moving the furniture to clean out all the cobwebs and throwing out things that are no longer needed.

REMEMBER

Purification is more than just energetic maintenance and can take various forms, such as taking a ritual bath for nine nights in a row or drinking an herbal tea blend that helps detoxify the physical body as well as the spirit.

Banishing

Banishing can be compared to calling the exterminator when you have cockroaches. You can use banishing to forcibly remove harmful or unhealthy energies that are influencing people, and having a deleterious effect on the energetic health of people or places.

Banishing rituals make use of powerful herbs that have purging effects when used in ritual baths, charms, or incense. These herbs can remove specific targets from the environment, whether they want to leave or not.

Exploring Herbs of Energetic Hygiene

You can use a wide variety of herbs for cleansing, purification, and banishing. While all the herbs listed in this section support energetic hygiene and the removal of unwanted or unhealthy vibrations, they work in slightly different ways.

Some herbs in this section have an overpowering odor, while others are extremely bitter. Other herbs have a clean citrus scent and are both physically and energetically cleansing. Depending on your type of work, you can choose from these herbal allies for cleansing the home, purifying the body, and removing any unwanted or unhealthy energies or influences.

Be sure to take precautions before working with any new herbs and consider your individual health and sensitivity, any contraindications, and potential interactions, especially before ingesting anything or applying it to your skin.

Angelica root

Angelica root (*Angelica archangelica*) holds a long-standing reputation as both a medicinal herb and a powerful magical ally. In traditional medicine, particularly in European and Asian systems, angelica was valued for its ability to strengthen the body, aid digestion, and stimulate circulation. In Traditional Chinese Medicine, the variety *Angelica sinensis* (dong quai) is a famous tonic for the blood, used to regulate menstruation and support overall female reproductive health. Its warming and invigorating qualities made it a trusted remedy for colds, sluggish digestion, and general weakness. Beyond its physical uses, angelica has been regarded for centuries as a plant of high vibration, associated with purity, health, and divine presence.

Folklore surrounds angelica with themes of divine protection and holiness. Angelica was believed to have been revealed by an angel during the plague, giving the plant its name and sanctified reputation. European folk practices often hung angelica in homes to ward off disease and evil spirits, and it was burned as incense in exorcisms and blessings.

TIP

As a magical herb, angelica is considered one of the most powerful guardians and cleansers. It can be used to break hexes, repel malicious spirits, and provide an energetic shield against harmful magic. Its bright, uplifting energy not only removes negativity but also invites blessings, healing, and good fortune into one's life.

In practical magic, angelica root is highly versatile. Infusing it into a ritual bath can wash away harmful magic and unhealthy energy, making it an excellent preparation before any major spiritual working. Carrying a piece of angelica root provides strong protection against curses and spiritual attack, acting as a constant barrier of positive force. For home cleansing, you can sprinkle powdered or ground angelica root mixed with salt around the perimeter of a property to purify and guard its energy. In rituals of exorcism, angelica is invoked to banish malevolent entities and to seal spaces with divine light.

Angelica's role as both a cleanser and a magnet for beneficial energies makes angelica a staple herb in the arsenal of any practitioner seeking purification, protection, and blessings.

Asafoetida

Asafoetida (*Ferula foetida*), also known as devil's dung for its intense and overpowering odor, is a resin obtained from the root of *Ferula* species native to Iran and Afghanistan and later cultivated in parts of India. Historically, asafoetida has been used for over a thousand years in both culinary and medicinal practices. In Ayurveda and traditional Persian medicine, it was valued as a digestive aid, an antispasmodic, and a treatment for respiratory ailments. Despite its pungent smell, when asafoetida is cooked, it transforms into a savory flavoring used in Indian cuisine. This dual nature mirrors its magical qualities as a powerful substance for repelling negativity while inviting cleansing energy.

Magically, asafoetida has long been recognized as a potent herb of banishment and exorcism. Its acrid scent is said to drive away harmful spirits, stubborn energies, and malicious magic. In purification rituals, only the smallest pinch of this resin is burned as incense or placed in protective charms because its odor is both its strength and its warning. Folk traditions across the Middle East, South Asia, and later European occult practices adopted asafoetida for its ability to ward off evil and protect against enemies. Its intense aroma can create a strong energetic boundary, ensuring that malevolent forces are repelled and kept at bay.

Because of its powerful and pervasive nature, a tiny amount of asafoetida goes a long way. In banishing and protective workings, practitioners often add a minute pinch to spell bottles, sachets, or floor washes to remove unwanted influences.

Use asafoetida with caution, as its scent can drive away not only harmful spirits but also people who are sensitive to its odor.

Asafoetida makes an excellent ally when you want to clear a space of unwelcome guests or lingering negative energy. Asafoetida exemplifies the principle that some of the most potent magical tools are those that work through their sheer force of presence.

Eucalyptus

Eucalyptus (*Eucalytpus* spp.), native to Australia and widely cultivated across the world today, has long been revered for its potent medicinal and spiritual qualities. For thousands of years, Indigenous Australian peoples applied eucalyptus leaves and oils to wounds, used them in steam inhalations to clear respiratory ailments, and burned them to cleanse and protect sacred spaces. Its reputation as a purifying and healing plant spread globally in the 18th and 19th centuries as European settlers and herbalists recognized its powerful antiseptic and germicidal properties.

Medicinally, eucalyptus oil is renowned for its antibacterial, antiviral, and germicidal properties, making it a cornerstone in natural remedies for colds, coughs, and respiratory congestion. It helps prevent the spread of disease, mirroring its spiritual role as a cleanser of stagnant or harmful energies. The invigorating aroma of eucalyptus has an uplifting and revitalizing effect on the mind and body, clearing mental fog and promoting a sense of renewal and freshness.

Magically, eucalyptus is considered a powerful herb for cleansing, purification, and protection. You can incorporate dried eucalyptus into ritual formulas, sachets, or incense to banish negativity and refresh the energy of a space. You can hang bundles of eucalyptus in the shower, where the steam releases its purifying essence, or add its leaves to ritual baths to wash away heavy or unhealthy energy.

Eucalyptus essential oil, with its sharp, clean fragrance, is a powerful ingredient in cleansing oil blends used to anoint doors, windows, or ritual tools. Whether used as a physical disinfectant or a spiritual purifier, eucalyptus restores balance and clarity.

Hyssop

Hyssop (*Hyssopus officinalis*) is a revered herb with deep historical and spiritual significance, particularly within the Mediterranean and Middle Eastern regions where it has been cultivated since ancient times. Hyssop is mentioned several times in the Bible, most notably in Psalm 51:7 "Purge me with hyssop, and I shall be clean" where it symbolizes spiritual cleansing and purification. In biblical times, hyssop was used in ritual sprinklings and offerings to cleanse lepers, sanctify homes, and ward off plague. Its enduring presence in scripture and ancient ritual practices cemented its reputation as a sacred herb for blessing, purification, and the removal of spiritual impurities.

Folklore and magical traditions continue to uphold hyssop as a powerful herb for cleansing and protection. Hyssop is often used in ritual baths to wash away negative energies, in incense to bless sacred spaces, and in floor washes to cleanse the home. Hyssop's light, herbaceous fragrance is believed to uplift the spirit, banish sin or negativity, and invite divine favor. Many practitioners include hyssop in exorcism rites and blessing rituals to remove harmful influences and to create a barrier of spiritual purity around people or places.

TIP

Medicinally, hyssop has been valued for its expectorant and antiseptic properties. Traditionally, it has been used to soothe respiratory conditions, such as coughs, colds, and congestion, as well as to support digestion and circulation. Its slightly bitter, aromatic nature stimulates the system and promotes overall vitality.

Juniper

Juniper (*Juniperus communis*) has a long history of use in both medicine and magic, revered by cultures across Europe, Asia, and North America. Known for its sharp pine-like aroma with earthy undertones, juniper was traditionally burned as an incense to ward off plague, disease, and malevolent spirits. Its berries have been used in folk medicine for centuries as a digestive aid, diuretic, and detoxifying agent, helping to cleanse the urinary tract and support kidney function. The antiseptic qualities of juniper make it both physically and energetically cleansing, mirroring its spiritual associations with purification and protection.

In magical practice, juniper is highly valued for its ability to banish negativity and attract positive, healthful energy. The wood, leaves, and berries are commonly used in ritual baths, incense blends, and protective charms. Burning juniper has long been a practice for clearing spaces of stagnant or harmful energy, and it is often included in rituals designed to break spells, prevent theft, or shield against unwanted influences. When added to ritual baths, juniper assists in detoxifying the body and restoring vitality, making it a powerful ally in rites of renewal and energetic cleansing.

Folklore also depicts juniper as a guardian herb that invites good spirits while repelling evil. In some European traditions, sprigs of juniper were hung above doorways to safeguard the home and its inhabitants, while in others, its berries were carried as charms to ensure safety and success on travels. Its enduring reputation as a protector and purifier has made juniper a staple in magical and spiritual traditions.

Lemongrass

Lemongrass (*Cymbopogon citratus*) is a fragrant, citrus-scented grass native to Southeast Asia, where it has been cultivated for centuries both as a culinary herb and a medicinal plant. Traditionally used in Thai, Indian, and Indonesian cuisines, lemongrass is valued not only for its refreshing flavor in teas and soups but also for its ability to reduce fever, aid digestion, and support the immune system. In folk medicine, it has long been employed as an antifungal, antibacterial, and anti-inflammatory herb, making it a natural remedy for infections, stomach upset, and general malaise.

Spiritually, lemongrass is known for its vibrant, citrus aroma, which is strongly associated with cleanliness, freshness, and renewal. Lemongrass is a key ingredient in formulas for spiritual healing and energetic cleansing, where its uplifting scent helps to remove stagnant or negative energy. Beyond cleansing, lemongrass is also known to attract blessings, including good luck, abundance, and joy, making it an herb of both purification and prosperity.

TIP

In ritual practice, you can use lemongrass in multiple forms. You can add its dried leaves to spiritual baths to refresh the body and mind, lifting fatigue and easing depression, while its essential oil is often used in anointing oils, room sprays, or diffusers to clear heavy or oppressive energy. Lemongrass is also a common ingredient in ritual floor washes, where its purifying properties not only cleanse the physical surfaces of a home but also impart a bright, protective energy throughout the space.

Mugwort

Mugwort (*Artemisia vulgaris*) has a long and storied history as a sacred herb of protection and cleansing and for creating sacred space. Native to Europe and Asia, mugwort has been used since ancient times in both medicine and magic. In traditional European folk practices, mugwort was considered a powerful warding herb, hung in doorways or woven into midsummer garlands to repel evil spirits, guard against the plague, and protect travelers. Mugwort was often associated with the goddess Artemis, from whom its botanical name is derived, and was revered as a plant of vision and dreamwork.

Medicinally, mugwort has been used to stimulate digestion, regulate menstruation, and support the nervous system. In Traditional Chinese Medicine, mugwort is prized for its warming and invigorating properties and is burned on specific locations of the body to stimulate energy and circulation in the practice known as *moxibustion*.

WARNING

To avoid injury, only trained professionals should perform moxibustion.

In magical practice, mugwort is highly valued for its cleansing and purifying abilities. It's often burned as incense or in bundles to cleanse ritual spaces, remove stagnant energy, and prepare sacred tools for magical work. Its smoke is believed to dispel negative influences and create a clear, spiritually attuned atmosphere. You can also add mugwort to ritual baths to cleanse both the body and the spirit before spellcasting or divination. The essential oil, though potent and to be used sparingly, may be incorporated into anointing oils for purification of magical implements or worn lightly to shield the aura during spiritual work.

WARNING

Avoid consuming mugwort or using its essential oil if you're pregnant or trying to get pregnant.

Beyond its cleansing qualities, mugwort is known to heighten intuition and open the mind to visions, making it a favorite for dream pillows and rituals of psychic protection. (For more on dream pillows, see Chapter 2.) In many traditions, practitioners burn mugwort to consecrate their magical tools.

Rosemary

Rosemary (*Salvia rosmarinus*), native to the Mediterranean region, has been cherished for thousands of years for its medicinal, culinary, and spiritual properties. The ancient Greeks and Romans regarded rosemary as a sacred plant associated with remembrance and loyalty, often using it in religious ceremonies and as a symbol of fidelity in weddings and funerals. Throughout history, rosemary has been burned in sickrooms and temples to purify the air and ward off illness, reflecting its strong connection to healing and protection. Its invigorating aroma and evergreen nature made it a symbol of vitality and resilience in many folk traditions.

TIP

Medicinally, rosemary is known for its stimulating and restorative qualities. Taken as a tea, it helps revitalize the energy system, rejuvenate exhausted nerves, and sharpen the mind, making it a traditional aid for fatigue, poor circulation, and low mood. Rosemary is also rich in antioxidants and has been used to support digestion and boost the immune system.

Spiritually, rosemary is a powerful herb of purification and healing. You can incorporate rosemary into smoke bundles or burn it loose on charcoal to cleanse people, objects, and spaces of stagnant or harmful energy. You can hang fresh sprigs of rosemary in the shower to release their cleansing steam, while the essential oil is a key component in bath blends designed to invigorate the senses, enhance memory, and stimulate psychic ability.

Rue

Rue (*Ruta graveolens*), often called the Herb of Grace, has a long and storied history stretching back to ancient Mediterranean civilizations. Native to southern Europe, rue was highly regarded by the Romans and Greeks for its medicinal and protective qualities, often planted near homes and temples to ward off ill fortune and malevolent forces. In medieval Europe, rue was a common ingredient in protective charms. During blessings and exorcisms, priests dipped fresh sprigs of rue in holy water and used them to *asperge*, or sprinkle, the water over people, objects or places, which gave rise to rue's enduring association with purification and spiritual defense.

TIP

Rue is an herb of healing, purification, and protection, long employed in rituals of exorcism and banishing. Rue is particularly effective in breaking spells cast against a person and removing unwanted attachments or influences that may have been placed upon gifts or objects of uncertain origin. You can burn the herb as incense to drive away harmful energies or brew it into a hot water infusion for cleansing baths, washes, or ritual cleansings of spaces and tools. Its strong, somewhat acrid aroma has been traditionally believed to repel the evil eye, curses, and envy, creating a shield of spiritual defense around those who carry or use it.

Beyond its protective virtues, rue is also said to bring blessings of health and happiness. Rue helps cleanse the aura, strengthen the *life force* (the vital energy that sustains all life), and lift the weight of spiritual or energetic fatigue. In folk medicine, it was once used to ease ailments, such as headaches, digestive troubles, and nervous tension, though it must be handled carefully as it can be irritating to the skin in large quantities. Magically, rue reinvigorates the spirit, lifts depression related to energy depletion, and restores a sense of vitality and clarity, making it a powerful ally for both spiritual and physical renewal.

WARNING

The essential oils found in rue can cause *photosensitivity*, or blistering when exposed to sunlight. When working with fresh rue or its essential oil, wear gloves and wash your hands or any areas that may have been exposed to the fresh oils while handling.

Sage

Sage (*Salvia officinalis*), or garden sage, has a long and storied history in European herbalism, medicine, and folklore. Native to the Mediterranean, it was cultivated by the ancient Greeks and Romans not only as a culinary herb but also as a medicinal plant for strengthening the body and preserving health. Its very name, sage, derives from the Latin *salvare*, meaning to heal or to save, reflecting its reputation as a panacea for ailments ranging from digestive issues to sore throats. Medieval herbalists praised sage as a tonic for longevity, while monastic gardens throughout Europe ensured its presence as both a sacred and practical plant.

TIP

In ritual and magical practice, garden sage is regarded as an herb of purification, protection, and wisdom. Like its relative white sage (*Salvia apiana*), it can be burned to cleanse spaces, objects, and people, dispelling stagnant or negative energy. However, garden sage offers a more accessible and sustainable alternative. Unlike white sage, which has faced issues of overharvesting and carries deep cultural significance in Indigenous North American traditions, garden sage is easily grown in home gardens or pots, allowing practitioners to work with its cleansing smoke without ethical or environmental concerns. This distinction makes garden sage an excellent substitute for ritual use, while still carrying the purifying qualities attributed to sage in general.

Folklore surrounding garden sage ties it to clarity of mind, longevity, and protection from evil. In some traditions, it was believed that sage growing strongly in a garden signified a prosperous household, while cutting sage improperly might bring bad luck. In ritual work, you can add sage leaves to charm bags, infuse them in baths, or burn them as incense to invoke purification and wisdom.

Valerian root

Valerian root (*Valeriana officinalis*) has been used for centuries in both medicine and magic. Native to Europe and parts of Asia, valerian root was highly regarded by the ancient Greeks and Romans, who prescribed it for a variety of ailments, particularly those affecting sleep and the nervous system. During the Middle Ages, valerian root was a common remedy for hysteria, anxiety, and seizures, while later herbalists recommended it as a gentle sedative and aid for insomnia. Today, valerian root is still widely used in herbal medicine to calm the nerves, ease restlessness, and promote deep, restorative sleep, making it one of the most enduring herbal allies for mental and emotional balance.

In folklore and magical practice, valerian root has long been associated with protection, purification, and banishment. Its earthy, pungent odor, though often considered unpleasant, is part of its power — it's grounding, heavy, and effective at creating a protective barrier against unwanted energies or influences. You can carry the root in charms or sachets to ward off negativity or burn it as incense in protective rituals. Valerian root has been used in spells to banish unwanted visitors and to sever harmful attachments, ensuring that the practitioner's space and energy remain their own.

Wormwood

Wormwood (*Artemisia absinthium*) has a long and fascinating history as both a medicinal and magical herb. Native to Europe, Asia, and North Africa, wormwood was well known in the ancient world — used by the Egyptians, Greeks, and Romans for its powerful bitter qualities. Its name reflects its primary medicinal role: As a *vermifuge* to keep away pests like insects and rodents, wormwood was a traditional remedy for expelling intestinal worms and other parasites. The intense bitterness of the plant also made it valuable for stimulating digestion, cleansing the liver, and purging the body of toxins. It later gained notoriety in the 19th century as the key ingredient in *absinthe,* the infamous green fairy liqueur prized by artists and poets.

In folklore and magical practice, wormwood is recognized as a potent herb of banishing and protection. Its strong, acrid nature makes it ideal for driving away unwanted influences, both physical and spiritual. Just as it rids the body of pests and disease, wormwood is believed to purge parasitic entities and stagnant energies from the aura or home. You can burn wormwood as incense, scatter it around thresholds, or carry it in sachets to repel negativity and ward off hostile forces. Wormwood is often combined with its close relative, mugwort (*Artemisia vulgaris*), to increase potency, especially in workings of spirit contact or exorcism. (For more on mugwort, see the section earlier in this chapter.)

Wormwood also has a deep association with the spirit world. Folklore holds that wormwood can aid wandering spirits in moving on, serving as a guide herb to clear blockages and release attachments. This quality makes wormwood useful in rituals of purification, ancestral rites, or in the cleansing of haunted spaces. Whether used to banish harmful energies, assist the dead in crossing over, or cleanse the body of toxins, wormwood embodies the archetype of the fierce protector and purifier.

Wormwood contains the chemical compound thujone, which is potentially harmful in extremely large doses. To err on the side of caution, don't consume wormwood internally or apply it to skin.

Creating Herbal Formulas for Energetic Hygiene

You can create a variety of formulas for magical cleanliness. You can create formulas that help you keep your overall energy healthy on a regular basis, purify yourself before important workings, and remove unhealthy and unwanted influences from your life.

For the formulas in this section, you will need a mortar and pestle.

Cleansing Incense

You can create a general all-purpose cleansing formula that you can use on a regular basis to raise a space's vibration, keep a healthy energetic environment, and perform personal cleansing rituals.

To create this Cleansing Incense, use a mortar and pestle to grind 1 tablespoon each of sage, eucalyptus, and copal resin until they reach a uniform consistency. Store the finished incense in a sealed container.

TIP

Burn small amounts on incense charcoal before and after any ritual to set and cleanse the space. You can also burn small amounts after bathing to cleanse your energy after work or going out in public.

Removal Bath Blend

You can create a Removal Bath Blend to remove unwanted energy, break unhealthy attachments or patterns, or sever outside influences. Using a mortar and pestle, grind 1 tablespoon each of stinging nettle, lemongrass, angelica root, and sage until they reach a fine consistency. In a jar or container, mix the herbs with 1 cup Epsom salt and 1 teaspoon activated charcoal. Add the blend to a cloth drawstring bag or pour directly into bath water.

TIP

For additional power, take this bath during the waning moon. Bathe on Saturdays to strengthen boundaries and on Sundays or Tuesdays to break away from resistant habits or patterns of behavior.

Banishing Incense

You can create this Banishing Incense to drive away negative energies or influences.

Using a mortar and pestle, grind up a pinch of asafoetida and 1 tablespoon each of frankincense resin, wormwood, rosemary, rue, and bay leaf until they reach a uniform consistency. While grinding up the ingredients, focus on your intentions of banishing. Store the finished incense blend in a sealed container.

TIP

Burn small amounts of incense on charcoal in an incense burner and carefully carry it throughout your living space while stating your command for whatever is you want to banish to leave. Depending on the energies or influences that you're banishing, you may have to do this on a regular basis to ensure that the banishing is complete.

Flying Devil Oil

You can make Flying Devil Oil to protect against individuals with bad intentions. The red pepper flakes that float in the oil represent the little devils flying away.

TIP

Make this oil on a Tuesday when the Moon is waning.

In a glass bottle, combine 1 teaspoon each of black pepper, cayenne pepper, red pepper flakes, and St. John's wort with 60 ml carrier oil. Infuse for an entire lunar cycle (28 days). Shake the bottle at least once a week while focusing on your intention.

Once blended, you can use Flying Devil Oil in a variety of ways:

- Anoint the frame of your front and back doors to keep unwanted persons away.
- Apply the oil to furniture, desks, door knobs, and so on in your office, workspace or bedroom to keep unwanted people out.
- Anoint red or black candles and burn for protection on Tuesdays or Saturdays.

Uncrossing Oil

You can also make Uncrossing Oil. Make this oil on the day after the full moon when the Moon begins to wane.

To make Uncrossing Oil, combine a pinch of salt, 1 teaspoon rue, 1 teaspoon angelica root, 20 drops lemongrass essential oil and 60 ml olive oil in a glass bottle and cover with a lid. Allow the ingredients to infuse until the day before the new moon, taking advantage of the entire waning period of this moon cycle. Shake the bottle at least once a week while focusing on your intention.

Once blended, you can use Uncrossing Oil in a variety of ways:

- Wear the oil to remove obstacles and blockages that may be impeding success.
- Use the oil to anoint four chime candles and burn them while taking a ritual bath.
- Anoint an old key with uncrossing oil and carry it as a charm to open the doors to new opportunities.

Florida Water

Florida Water is a classic American cologne that emerged in New York in 1808, created by perfumer Robert I. Murray and later popularized under the Murray & Lanman brand. Inspired by European eau de cologne yet tilted toward bright citrus with spice, its name nods both to floral notes and to the fabled Fountain of Youth in Florida.

Beyond its use as a fragrance, Florida Water took on a strong role in spiritual practice across folk traditions in North America, African diasporic traditions, and traditions in Central and South America. Florida Water is sold around the world today and is one of the most popular formulas for spiritual cleansing and purification.

Florida Water is used in a variety of ways for general cleansing, purification, and banishing of unwanted energies. You can rub a small amount in the palms of your hands and inhale its scent to shift energy and focus the mind, add it to ritual baths for extra cleansing power, and use it as a fragrance after ritual bathing. You can also add Florida Water to house-cleaning products or use it on its own to anoint windows and doorways to attract beneficial energies.

WARNING

While storebought Florida Water, is effective, it's made from completely synthetic ingredients and is very different from its original formula.

The following formula for Florida Water has many variations. For this easy formula, you'll need a mason jar or other dark glass container with a lid. To make you own Florida Water:

1. **Break up three cinnamon sticks and tear the petals from one to two fresh roses and fresh orange and lemon peels into smaller pieces so that they release their scent.**
2. **Add the cinnamon, rose petals, citrus peels, cloves, vanilla bean (whole or crushed), 1 tablespoon fresh lavender buds, and 1 teaspoon fresh rosemary to the jar.**
3. **Cover the herbal ingredients with 2 cups spiced rum and add 2 to 3 tablespoons rose water and ¼ cup distilled water.**
4. **Allow everything to infuse for 14 to 28 days in a cool, dark place; shake regularly.**
5. **After infusing, strain through a cheesecloth and then a coffee filter for extra clarity.**

You can store the Florida Water in a dark bottle. Don't forget to add a label and date.

TIP

Florida Water is best when used within 6 to 12 months.

Casting Cleansing Spells

You can perform an all-purpose cleansing ritual that will simultaneously cleanse and purify your home as well as your own energy field. You can perform a home and self-cleansing ritual on a regular basis as a monthly cleansing ritual for energetic maintenance that can be timed to coincide with the full moon. For this home and self-cleaning ritual, you can create your own Florida Water and Cleansing Incense using the formulas earlier in this chapter. Gather the following:

- Bouquet of fresh flowers
- Vase for flowers
- Bell
- Florida Water (storebought or homemade)
- Small dish

- Spring water
- White candle
- Cleansing incense
- Metal tongs
- Incense burner and charcoal

Then follow these steps:

1. **Prepare your space.**

   Gather all the necessary items. Place your fresh flowers and white candle in the kitchen or living room.

   TIP

   Having fresh flowers in the space helps invite new energy into the space. Light the candle. Open at least one window.

2. **Fumigate with incense.**

   Using your metal tongs, light the charcoal for your incense burner. Add a pinch of cleansing incense and carefully walk room to room allowing the smoke to fill the room, adding more incense as needed.

3. **Wash with Florida Water.**

   Add some Florida Water and spring water to the small dish. Go from room to room, dipping your fingers in the water and tracing the trim of every door and window. (Optional: Use your fingers to also sprinkle the water in each corner of the room and across the thresholds of any doors leading outside.)

4. **Ring the bell.**

   In each room of the house, stand in the center of the room (or as close as possible) and ring the bell three times. Do this step in every room and also at the front door.

5. **Bring your incense burner, dish of Florida Water, and bell to the flowers.**

6. **Fumigate yourself.**

   Add more incense to the charcoal as needed and fumigate yourself with the incense smoke by allowing it to pass over your arms, legs, front, and back.

   TIP

   The easiest way to fumigate yourself is to place the incense burner on the floor and stand over it. Just make sure that the incense burner is on a firesafe surface.

7. **Anoint yourself.**

   Dip your fingers in the Florida Water, rub it between your hands, and apply it in a downward movement on both of your arms and legs. Dip your fingers in the Florida Water again and apply it to your heart and forehead.

8. **Ring the bell.**

   Standing in front of the flowers and the candle, ring the bell three times.

After you complete these steps, clean up all supplies. You can let the candle burn down for the rest of the evening or blow it out and save it for next time. Remember to close your windows.

Performing a Banishment Ritual

You can perform a banishing ritual end toxic relationships, remove the influence of people who do not have your best interests in mind, or break unhealthy cycles to allow for your energy to shift in new and more productive ways.

Perform this ritual on a Saturday during the waning moon. You can repeat this ritual weekly for serious situations that require breaking through lots of attachments, or you can perform it on a monthly basis after the initial ritual for maintenance.

If you're performing this ritual on a weekly basis for more intense energy removal, the moon phase will change. Continue performing the ritual every Saturday for three to four weeks.

I provide all the formulas for the formulas used in this ritual in this chapter. Depending on the urgency of the situation, you may not have all the formulas on hand, so you can make substitutions. Sometimes a situation requires you to work with what you have to get the job done. Omitting ingredients from formulas or substituting other herbs from this chapter will still be effective. If you're unable to recreate the following formulas, you can still make the ritual work using olive oil, Epsom salt, and stick incense if that is all you have.

Perform this ritual during a time when you won't be disturbed for the entire ritual.

For this banishment ritual, gather the following:

- Black chime or taper candle
- Uncrossing Oil (see earlier formula)
- Removal Bath Blend (see earlier formula)
- Banishing Incense (see earlier formula)
- Small piece of paper
- Something to write with
- Firesafe dish
- Metal tongs

TIP

If you plan to perform this ritual more than once, you can use a glass-encased seven day candle.

1. **Prepare your space.**

   Bring together all your ingredients in the bathroom.

2. **Remove your clothing and draw your bath.**

   While the bath water is running, take your candle and rub it over the surface of your skin from head to toe while focusing on what it is you're banishing.

3. **Light your incense and pass your candle through the incense smoke.**

   Ignite the charcoal and begin burning your banishing incense. Pass the candle through the incense smoke.

4. **Anoint and light the candle.**

   Apply the uncrossing oil to your candle from the base toward the wick to send the energy away and then light the candle.

5. **Write it down.**

   Take your piece of paper and write down the name of the person, situation, or energy that you're banishing.

6. **Fumigate and burn the paper.**

   Hold the paper over your incense burner, allowing it to be consumed by smoke as your project all your willpower toward pushing away whatever it is you wrote down. Then, using your metal tongs, light the paper on fire using the flame of your candle. Allow the paper to burn in the fire-safe dish, saving the ashes.

By this point the bathtub should be finished filling.

7. **Add your removal bath blend to the water and put some more incense on the charcoal before getting in the bath.**

8. **Soak in the bath, preferably until your candle burns out.**

   If you're used a seven-day candle, make sure that you blow out the candle when you're finished in the bath.

9. **Dry off and anoint with oil.**

   When you finish your bath and dry off, anoint yourself with some of the Uncrossing Oil, applying it to your feet, wrists, chest and forehead.

10. **Clean up and dispose of the ashes outdoors.**

    You can bury them away from your home, sprinkle them at a crossroads, take them to the ocean and let them blow away in the wind, or deposit them at the base of a tree.

WARNING

However you choose to dispose of the ashes is up to you, but don't keep them and don't dispose of them on your property.

You can dispose of the ashes the next day or at a convenient time.

IN THIS CHAPTER

» Claiming abundance and prosperity

» Reaching the end of the rainbow

» Sharing the wealth

Chapter 7 Attracting Abundance and Prosperity

In this chapter, you find out how to define what abundance and prosperity mean to you. By truly understanding your goals and motivations, you are better able to tailor your spells and formulas to exactly what it is you're trying to achieve. You discover a variety of herbs used in formulas for prosperity and abundance and how to incorporate them into formulas for money magic, customer attraction, and good luck.

Cultivating an Abundance and Prosperity Mindset

Abundance is a state of having more than enough. It is used to describe a bountiful harvest, whether literally or metaphorically. Abundance is the result. It's the reaping of what you sow and can include everything from fruits and vegetables, to people and opportunities. Abundance is the energy of potential and having multiple options and creating growth and expansion.

Prosperity is the ability to flow in a way that creates a state of abundance. It's the ability to succeed in your efforts and to flourish.

Many things contribute to a sense of prosperity: money, state of mind, beneficial connections and the ability to uplift others.

Abundance and prosperity magic starts with defining what abundance and prosperity mean to you. For some, wealth is numbers in an account; for others, it's time, freedom, stable housing, good health, creative flow, or the ability to travel and learn. Prosperity might look like dependable clients, but it can also mean a quiet mind and a stocked pantry.

TIP

Before you begin any spell, define your desired outcome in plain language naming the feeling (security, joy, freedom), the form (steady income, debt paid, time off). While money may play a role in achieving these things, it's a means to a deeper goal. Aiming for your true goal opens your magic to more possibilities, instead of focusing on the means to an end.

For example, perhaps you have a dream of living in a swanky downtown apartment in a big city, but can't afford the ever-increasing rent. Instead of focusing on doing spellwork for more money, aim for the actual desire: the apartment. This more precise goal gives your spell more to work with. Perhaps you get a new job that transfers you to a different city and puts you up in a corporate apartment. Or maybe you meet a new friend that is looking to rent out their top floor condo for a really good deal so they can relocate on short notice. The possibilities are endless when you give the universe something to aim for.

A helpful foundation is the worldview that the universe is infinitely abundant. It's a field of possibilities rather than a closed system. Cultivating a perspective of universal abundance reminds you that opportunities, allies, and resources can arrive through many channels.

TIP

Daily practices, such as creating gratitude lists, blessing what you already have, and celebrating small wins, train your attention toward availability rather than lack. In energetic terms, these practices tune your frequency to an energy of abundance, which ultimately attracts more of the same. You want to cultivate this type of energy when performing rituals for abundance and prosperity, conjuring a feeling of abundance can be difficult when you're just trying to pay the electric bill!

By contrast, *scarcity mindset* is the belief that there's not enough money, time, clients, or luck and that others' gains diminish your own. It breeds fear, hoarding, comparison, and self-sabotage, which can choke the flow of energy your spellwork is trying to invite. Before engaging in prosperity magic, gently shift this stance: Release limiting beliefs, dissolve shame around not having money, and align action with your intention by putting in the physical effort to match your magic. With mindset, intention, and behavior pointed in the same direction, your workings amplify infinitely, calling in the form of abundance that truly fits your life.

Exploring Herbs of Abundance and Prosperity

Just as prosperity and abundance have different definitions, different herbal ingredients allow you to take different approaches to achieving abundance and prosperity. Fiery and solar herbs like bay, basil, cinnamon, and allspice are warming, bright, and energizing. They spark momentum, lift confidence, and bring vital energy to any endeavor. Fiery herbs are the herbs of victory wreaths, open doors, and golden hours; they clarify vision, and galvanize will.

Balancing that heat are the earthy and green allies: patchouli, vetiver, oakmoss, mint, thyme, and cinquefoil. They root wealth, protect gains, and cultivate steady growth. Their energies are fertile, grounding, and lush like the energy of the Earth. They sweeten transactions, stabilize cash flow, strengthen boundaries, soothe money anxiety, and help goals grow to their full potential. Combined, Fire sets things in motion, while Earth builds a strong and lasting foundation, using fiery herbs to ignite the work and earthy herbs to sustain it.

In this section, I explore herbs from both of these categories that you can use in herbal magic for all forms of prosperity, success, and abundance magic.

Allspice

Allspice (*Pimenta dioica*), the dried berry of a Caribbean myrtle, entered European trade in the 16th century and was prized for tasting like a warming blend of cinnamon, clove, and nutmeg in one. Historically, healers used allspice as a *carminative* to soothe the stomach, ease gas, and stimulate sluggish digestion. Its warming nature also made it a traditional aid for cold, achy muscles when prepared as a rub or poultice. In the kitchen and apothecary alike, allspice was valued for gently stimulating circulation and activating the body's systems, qualities that later informed its magical reputation.

In folklore and ritual work, allspice carries a bright, fiery energy that's ideal for manifestation. Its warming, stimulating properties are said to open the way to opportunities and set intentions in motion, making it a favorite for abundance rites and money magic. Practitioners add whole berries to money bowls, cash drawers, or prosperity jars to attract wealth and steady business; ground allspice can be blended into incense or sachets to draw luck and customers. Anointing a green or gold candle with a prosperity oil and then rolling it lightly in crushed allspice is a classic way to heat up money-drawing spells.

Allspice is an easy everyday ally for building momentum toward financial goals. Use it in charm bags with bay leaf and cinnamon for business luck, sprinkle a pinch into ledger books, apply the essential oil on price tags to increase sales, or burn a small amount of crushed allspice as a prosperity incense before opening hours. Its steady, warming presence supports focus and confidence for turning intention into income.

Basil

Basil (*Ocimum basilicum*) has ancient roots across the Mediterranean and South Asia. In Greek, basil's name means royal, hinting at a long association with sovereignty, dignity, and good fortune. Traditional herbalists use basil as a warming carminative to ease digestion, lift low spirits, and freshen the breath. Its aromatic oils are also valued for general cleansing and household protection. In folk magic, basil is added to door garlands, set on shop counters, and tended in courtyard pots to invite blessings while keeping ill will away. Basil also helps to protect against jealousy.

In magical practice, basil is a classic prosperity herb, attracting abundance, drawing money, and bringing luck in business. It carries a fiery, vital current that heats intention and strengthens personal magnetism, especially helpful for those in leadership roles who need decisiveness and presence. Add basil to success oils and charm bags to protect and grow wealth; tuck a few leaves into your wallet or cash drawer; or fix a green candle with basil and a money-drawing oil for career advancement. You can lightly sprinkle powdered basil around a storefront threshold or counter to attract customers and sweeten transactions, while a living basil plant kept near the entry or in the kitchen acts as a steady beacon for prosperity, safeguarding what comes in and encouraging more to follow.

Because it blends protection with prosperity, basil is ideal for building and guarding the gate of success. Use it to fortify confidence before negotiations, bless invoices and contracts, or anchor weekly money-bowl work with a pinch of dried leaf. Its bright, spicy spirit helps clear hesitation, focus will, and keep your endeavors moving, drawing opportunity while shielding your growing harvest.

Bay leaf

Bay laurel (*Laurus nobilis*) is the classical laurel tree of Greece and Rome, whose evergreen wreath crowned poets, victors, and emperors. Bay laurel is the tree that bay leaves come from. Dedicated to Apollo, bay laurel became an emblem of triumph, clear sight, and inspired counsel. Bay laurel is associated with the Oracle at Delphi, whose prophesies shaped ancient society. In the household, it was equally valued: a warming, aromatic leaf used to flavor food and, in traditional herbalism, taken as a gentle carminative to settle the stomach, ease gas, and support respiratory comfort in steams.

Magically, bay leaf is a versatile powerhouse for success, prosperity, and protection because it's aligned with elemental Fire and the Sun's bright, victorious energy. Bay leaf is a classic in money-drawing charms, prosperity jars, and business sachets. You can slip a leaf into a wallet or cash drawer, add it to a money bowl, or steep it in a floor wash to activate a space for good fortune and steady customers. Many practitioners write an intention on a single leaf and burn it to release their intention, or they anoint and fix a green or gold candle with crumbled bay for abundance workings. Because laurel symbolizes victory, it's also associated with legal success making it useful for court cases, contract negotiations, and career advancement where clarity, confidence, and favorable outcomes are needed.

TIP

Working on Sundays, particularly during a waxing moon, amplifies bay's success magic. Combine bay leaf with cinnamon for speedy results, basil for wealth attraction and protection, or frankincense for elevating prosperity and attracting blessings. Whether you need a spark of courage, a shield for your gains, or a steady wind at your back in business, bay leaf carries forward its ancient promise of triumph, prosperity, and the momentum to see endeavors through.

Chamomile

Chamomile (*Matricaria chamomilla*) has been cherished since antiquity: It was honored by Ancient Egyptians, Greeks, and Romans for its sunny fragrance and gentle healing. In traditional herbalism, chamomile is a classic calming nervine and carminative — a tea to soothe the nerves, settle the stomach, and ease tension after long days. Topically, chamomile infusions have been used in compresses and baths to comfort irritated skin and tired muscles, underscoring the plant's reputation as a reliable restorative ally.

In folklore, chamomile's bright, solar nature links it to luck, success, and steady prosperity. Gamblers' lore speaks of washing hands in chamomile tea to sweeten the odds, and shopkeepers have tucked the flowers into cash drawers or swept floors with chamomile infused water to draw customers.

TIP

In prosperity work today, chamomile strengthens money charms, and you can add it to any spell meant to ensure success — for example, you can dress green or gold candles with chamomile, tuck a pinch into a money bowl, or include it in sachets with bay and cinnamon to warm and amplify abundance.

Chamomile also protects what it helps attract. Use it in charms to keep money safe, guard against theft or financial leaks, and support better habits when overspending is an issue. A simple ritual rinse of chamomile tea over your hands before budgeting invites calm, wise choices, and carrying a small sachet of chamomile with a coin can serve as a reminder to spend intentionally. Gentle but effective, chamomile assists at clearing worry, brightening outlook, and encouraging the prosperous results your work is aimed toward.

Cinnamon

Cinnamon (*Cinnamomum* spp.) has traveled trade routes for millennia, prized in ancient Egypt, classical Greece and Rome, and throughout Asia for its fragrance, flavor, and medicinal value. In traditional herbalism cinnamon is a warming carminative used to stimulate digestion, ease gas, and support healthy circulation. Its aromatic oils also make it a classic ingredient in steams and rubs for cold, heavy winters.

In prosperity magic, cinnamon raises the vibration and adds energetic heat to any spell, charm, or formula it touches. Cinnamon is used to bring good fortune in business and money matters, from anointing green or gold candles to tucking chips of bark into cash drawers and money bowls.

A simple trick is to mix cinnamon with powdered sugar and lightly sprinkle it near a storefront threshold or register to attract customers and sweeten transactions. Blended into floor washes or incense, cinnamon helps clear stagnation, draw attention, and keep revenue flowing.

Because it's also famous in love spells, cinnamon's magnetic, fiery quality easily translates to other forms of passion, such as galvanizing support for projects, attracting long-time customers, and even helping to influence investors by boosting charisma and confidence. Pair cinnamon with bay for legal and career success, basil for protection and steady growth, or allspice for fast manifestation.

Cinquefoil

Cinquefoil (*Potentilla* spp.), often called five-finger grass, has been known in European and North American folk traditions for centuries. Its name and virtue are linked to its distinctive five-lobed leaf shape, seen as a living talisman shaped like a hand. Medieval herbals praised cinquefoil forwarding ill fortune and for blessings. Because its leaf-shape echoes the human hand, practitioners came to say it aids "anything the five fingers can do," tying the plant to craft, trade, and skillful works of all kinds.

In prosperity and success magic, cinquefoil is a favorite for victory, attraction, and good outcomes. It's used to sweeten negotiations, open doors, and secure help from those in positions of authority, giving eloquence and influence to those that carry this herb so that requests and petitions are heard. Carried in a sachet or added to a money bowl, cinquefoil supports endeavors involving handling money, business transactions, and even games of chance. Creators, artisans, and anyone who works with their hands often keep it nearby to enhance their craft.

Versatile and cooperative, cinquefoil blends beautifully into manifestation formulas of all kinds, including oils, incenses, and charm packets aimed at calling in what is desired. Whether you're seeking steady customers, a granted favor, or a winning edge, five-finger grass embodies the gesture of the open hand that is reaching, receiving, and skillfully shaping success.

Mint

Mint (*Mentha* spp.) has a long, lively history from the ancient Mediterranean to the medieval market stall. Greeks crowned tables with mint and rubbed it into surfaces to freshen rooms for guests. Romans infused it in wines and wore it for clear thought. Later, European households used it as a strewing herb to deodorize and cheer a space. This heritage of brightness and welcome underpins mint's modern reputation in folk magic as a purifier for business and work environments. Mint's crisp scent clears stale energy and sets a hospitable, money-friendly tone.

As a prosperity ally, mint is used to protect and attract wealth. Tuck a few leaves (fresh or dried) into a wallet or cash drawer, add them to a money bowl, or craft an anointing oil to lightly dress cash, ledgers, and receipt books. In floor washes, sprays, or incense, mint helps neutralize negativity, encourage repeat customers, and keep transactions smooth. Mint also fits neatly into rituals aimed at good fortune.

Astrologically, mint is a Mercurial herb, ruled by Mercury, the swift god of commerce, communication, and trade, which makes it ideal for negotiations, marketing, and sales.

Time mint workings for Wednesday, which is ruled by Mercury, especially during a waxing moon, to amplify attraction and enhance the flow of prosperous energies. Whether you're refreshing a storefront, sealing a deal, or calling in clients, mint's quick-to-the-point energy creates a clean and open space for prosperity to cross your threshold.

Oakmoss

Oakmoss (*Evernia prunastri*) is a lichen that grows on oaks and other trees across Europe, long gathered by foragers and perfumers for its deep, forest-floor aroma. In folklore, anything taken from the oak carried the tree's virtues of strength, longevity, and steady increase. Mosses and lichens were sometimes tucked into household charms to fix prosperity and protect stored goods. Oakmoss embodies that slow, dependable growth, an emblem of wealth that accumulates over time rather than in a flash.

In fragrance, oakmoss is legendary. Its fragrance lends perfumes an earthy, mossy, slightly leathery base that reads as cool shade and damp bark. The smell of the fertile forest brings this energy of abundance to any formula. Even in modern formulas where usage may be limited, oakmoss (or its accords) remains the signature note that suggests old-world luxury and velvet greens.

TIP

Magically, oakmoss is worked with to anchor and stabilize one's prosperity. It grounds intention, protects earnings, and encourages steady, sustainable abundance. Add a pinch to money bowls and business sachets to hold wealth and blend it with other herbs and resins to create a balanced prosperity incense. Its earthy scent purifies and settles a workspace, creating a calm, welcoming atmosphere for clients and good deals.

Patchouli

Patchouli (*Pogostemon cablin*) is a tropical mint native to South and Southeast Asia, long valued for its unmistakable aroma: earthy, musky, woody-sweet, like damp soil after rain. In the 1800s, Indian and Indonesian merchants scented fine textiles with patchouli leaves to signal authenticity along the trade routes to Europe and the Middle East. By the 20th century, patchouli was a staple in perfumery and counterculture alike. That history helped cement its association with luxury goods, sensuality, and the slow, steady magnetism of the Earth element.

TIP

In magic, patchouli is a classic prosperity ally linked to wealth and abundance. Its grounding scent roots intentions so that they grow and endure, making patchouli a favorite in money bowls, prosperity oils, and incense. Dress green or gold candles with patchouli-infused oil for business success, sprinkle a pinch in a cash drawer or ledger to bless income, or add it to floor washes to set a warm, welcoming tone for clients. Because it's also common in love-drawing formulas (see Chapter 9), patchouli's sensual pull can be redirected to other forms of attraction: drawing customers, favorable terms, or supportive partners to your work.

For business and sales, patchouli creates a subtly luxurious atmosphere that encourages lingering and spending. Used with intention and moderation, patchouli's rich, earthy scent helps anchor deals, stabilize cash flow, and monetize opportunities into tangible wealth.

Thyme

Thyme (*Thymus vulgaris*), a small Mediterranean shrub with a big aroma, is a popular culinary herb that is full of magic. The Greeks burned thyme to purify temples and associated its scent with courage and spirit. Roman households used it to cleanse spaces and flavor food, while medieval lore linked thyme with fairies and the dream world. In traditional herbcraft, thyme is used in steams and tonics for general resilience and to freshen the home.

In magical practice, thyme is a reliable ally for abundance and prosperity. Its clarifying fragrance helps clear mental clutter and worry, bringing peace of mind around money matters so that plans can take root. Add thyme to money bowls and prosperity sachets to increase and protect money, dress green candles with a pinch of dried leaf for business luck, or steep it into a light floor wash to refresh a shop, office, or studio and invite supportive clients. Because thyme is purifying and promotes strength and fortitude, it's especially helpful when launching new ventures by clearing doubts, strengthening resolve, and signaling that your work is ready to meet the world.

TIP

Practical ways to work with thyme include tucking a sprig into your ledger or cash drawer to guard earnings, combining it with basil and bay for success charms, or burning a small amount while working on book keeping or before negotiations to energize but keep calm and focused. Whether you're opening your first storefront or building a side business from home, thyme's bright, confident spirit supports clear decisions, steady growth, and the grounded optimism that prosperity loves.

Vetiver

Vetiver (*Chrysopogon zizanioides*) is a deeply rooted tropical grass, related to lemongrass and citronella, native to South Asia. For centuries its fragrant roots have been woven into cooling mats, fans, and sachets, and their distilled essence has anchored perfumery as a classic base note and fixative with a scent that is earthy, smoky-green, and quietly enduring. In folk tradition, vetiver's extensive root system became a symbol of stability, protection, and wealth that accumulates slowly but surely, making it a favored ally where steadiness and material support are needed.

In prosperity magic, vetiver is used to attract good luck, increase one's fortune, and keep earnings grounded rather than fleeting. Its strong roots point to its ability to bring security. Vetiver is ideal for money bowls, business sachets, and anointing oils for steadying cash flow, encouraging loyal clientele, and preventing losses. You can add a drop or two of vetiver essential oil to prosperity oil formulas, floor washes, or the corners of a storefront to draw customers and create a subtle atmosphere of dependable abundance, a little goes a long way. (See the next section for a formula for Prosperity Oil.)

TIP

Vetiver pairs beautifully with other earthy prosperity herbs, especially patchouli to attract and retain customers. Blend vetiver with cinnamon for momentum, bay for victory, and basil for guarded growth. Dress green or gold candles with a light touch of vetiver oil for business success or tuck a small root chip into a wallet or cash drawer to anchor wealth. Grounding yet attractive, vetiver helps you build prosperity that lasts.

Creating Herbal Formulas for Prosperity and Abundance

Crafting formulas for abundance, prosperity, and success is an act of alignment with the energetic currents of growth, opportunity, and achievement. Whether the aim is to open roads for new income, draw steady clients, strengthen a venture, secure fair outcomes, or cultivate the confidence and clarity that success requires, these formulas are intended to help support success in all forms.

The formulas in the following sections offer foundational blends you can tailor to your goals bringing in speed, stability, visibility, protection of gains, or long-term growth.

Prosperity Oil

This all-purpose Prosperity Oil attracts success and abundance in all forms. Whether you're casting a money spell, looking for a new job or beginning a new project, this Prosperity Oil can help attract what you're working toward. Wear it on the skin as a fragrance or use it to anoint money for savings or spending to ensure its return.

For this formula, you will need 20 drops orange essential oil, 20 drops of bay leaf essential oil, 10 drops lemongrass essential oil, 10 allspice berries (crushed), ½ teaspoon cinnamon powder, and 60 ml carrier oil.

During a waxing moon, add the essential oils and dry ingredients to your glass bottle and fill it with the carrier oil. Cover with a lid and allow the oil to infuse for at least two weeks before using.

TIP

Blend the oil on a Wednesday for business-related matters, such as attracting customers and increasing revenue. Blend the oil on a Sunday for general manifestation related to career and self-image. Blend the oil on a Friday for attracting new professional relationships, networking, and influencing potential business partners.

Money-Drawing Powder

Money-drawing powders are a popular form of application for money magic because you can use them easily and discreetly in a variety of ways. You can use money-drawing powder to dress candles for use in prosperity magic or sprinkle it on money charms to feed them. You can also dust the powder around a business or office space before opening. Alternately, use money powder to dust your hands before making any sales agreements or handling any cash transactions.

During a full moon, blend 1 teaspoon powdered orange peel with 1 teaspoon each of the following finely ground herbs: bay leaves, patchouli leaves, and oakmoss. When finished, mix with 1 cup cornstarch and 1 teaspoon mica powder (optional).

TIP

Using a coffee grinder helps create a more uniform, powdery consistency when mixing the herbal ingredients with the cornstarch. The consistency of the final powder is a matter of preference. If you're using a mortar and pestle instead of an electric coffee grinder, you may not get the herbal ingredients to powder as finely, but it won't diminish the effectiveness of the formula.

Success Incense

You can burn Success Incense to promote all forms of success and achievement. You can use it in manifestation rituals of to attain goals, advance professionally, attract wealth, and create it. Success comes in many different forms and isn't always related to finances.

On a waxing or full moon that falls on a Sunday, blend ½ teaspoon powdered orange peel with 1 teaspoon each of powdered frankincense resin, powdered benzoin resin, calamus root powder, and powdered sandalwood.

TIP

Burn small amounts in an incense burner with charcoal when studying, working on proposals, or during the creative process.

Good Luck Oil

You can use this anointing oil to attract good luck and good fortune for any endeavor. Use this Good Luck Oil to anoint coins before spending or donating or to anoint lucky charms or pieces of jewelry to attract general good luck. You can also wear this oil as a personal fragrance or use it to anoint green candles before burning to attract good luck.

In a glass bottle or jar with a lid, combine the following ingredients on a Wednesday when the Moon is waxing or full: 60 ml of carrier oil, 20 drops peppermint essential oil, 10 drops fennel essential oil, 10 drops bergamot essential oil, 1 teaspoon dried clover, 1 teaspoon dried cinquefoil, and angelica root pieces.

Allow the carrier oil to infuse for an entire moon cycle (four weeks) before using.

Blockbuster Ritual Bath

This Blockbuster Ritual Bath blend is a formula for *road opening*, meaning that you can use it to break stagnancy, remove blockages, and clear the way for new opportunities.

In a jar or container, mix 1 tablespoon each of marigold flowers, lemongrass, epazote, five-finger grass, and barberry root into 1 cup Epsom salt and add to your bathwater on the night of a new moon.

TIP

For the additional effects of aromatherapy, you can also add essential oils, such as lemongrass, mint, or bergamot, to the Epsom salt before adding to the bath.

Fancy Business Oil

Create this Fancy Business Oil when the Moon is waxing or full on a Friday to draw upon the abundant power of Venus's day, but also because Friday is when checks are cut and money is counted.

Combine all following herbal ingredients and essential oils in a bottle or storage jar and cover with 60 ml carrier oil: one dried orchid flower, one piece of dried ginseng root, two vanilla beans (crushed) or ½ teaspoon vanilla bean powder, 20 drops orange blossom essential oil, 10 drops bergamot essential oil, and 5 drops clove essential oil. Allow to infuse for an entire moon phase (28 days) before using.

TIP

Use this oil to anoint orange candles to burn when planning a new business venture. Apply the oil as a personal fragrance and wear during marketing campaigns and business meetings. You can also use this oil to create new opportunities at your job or to attract new customers through referrals when used to anoint your workspace.

Customer-Attraction Incense

To attract customers, burn this Customer-Attraction Incense formula on charcoal in a firesafe incense burner inside of the business before opening to customers. Alternatively, use this incense blend to fumigate business cards or other marketing materials before distributing them. If you're unable to burn incense at your office or place of business, you can also use this formula as a powder that you sprinkle around the workspace or outside the front of the business.

Using a mortar and pestle, grind 1 tablespoon each of benzoin resin, cinnamon powder or chips, and powdered patchouli to a uniform consistency. Store the finished incense in a sealed container.

Casting Spells for Prosperity and Abundance

Success and abundance come in many shapes, with many ways to manifest prosperity in its different forms. In this section, I look at three commonly employed spells and rituals for money magic, prosperity, and general good fortune.

You can perform these rituals on their own or add them as part of a larger working. All rituals make use of herbs of abundance and prosperity as their backbone. Whether you're creating a money bowl, a prosperity candle, or a charm bag to carry, each object is enlivened by the herbal components through anointing with oil, fumigating with incense, and blessing with herb-infused water.

Money bowl

Creating and maintaining a money bowl is an easy way to create a focal point for manifesting abundance and prosperity. Your money bowl can be simple and discreet, or you can create a larger prosperity altar for it, including images of your goals and other symbolic items representative of success and abundance.

REMEMBER

When properly maintained the money bowl is constantly circulating the energy of prosperity, sending it out into the world and bringing more back with it.

To make a money bowl, gather the following:

- Bowl (simple or ornate)
- Physical currency (coins and paper money)
- Good luck charms
- Money-Drawing Powder (see earlier formula)
- Prosperity Oil (see earlier formula)

1. **Prepare your bowl by anointing the inside of the bowl with Prosperity Oil and sprinkling the Money-Drawing Powder inside the bowl.**
2. **Add the physical currency to the bowl.**

The currency can be whatever cash or coins you may have. You can also use currency from other countries and other symbols of wealth, including play money.

3. **Add offerings.**

   Place any good luck charms you want to add inside or around the bowl. You can add herbal ingredients, such as allspice berries or bay leaves, or use them as future offerings.

4. **Maintain the money bowl.**

   Continue adding any loose change or money that you find to the money bowl.

   Any time you have an extra dollar, I make an effort to add it to the money bowl.

5. **Charge the money bowl.**

   Burning a green candle and some Money-Drawing Incense near the money bowl on the full moon will recharge its energy.

6. **Circulate the prosperity.**

   The money that is accumulated in the money bowl is then sprinkled with Money-Drawing Powder and spent.

TIP

The idea of circulating the prosperity is that it goes out into the world to bring back more prosperity. I use this money for mundane tasks, such as paying for laundry, and tipping. Another great way to work with the money from the money bowl is to give it away to someone who needs it.

Prosperity Spell Candle

Candle dressing is a way of ritually preparing candles for spellwork using oils, herbs, and other ingredients to infuse your intention into the candle before burning it. Candle dressing is a simple but effective way to add layers of magical intention to your workings.

You need a green glass encased 7-day candle, herbal tea made from mint, thyme, and patchouli, a permanent marker, five bay leaves, a firesafe dish, and matches or a lighter. Then follow these steps to create a Prosperity Spell Candle:

1. **Hold the candle while focusing on your intention.**

   See the energy of your intention fill the candle with a green light.

2. **Wash the candle with the tea.**

   Rub a small amount of the herbal tea between your hands and use it to wash the candle's glass container.

3. **Allow the tea to dry while burning bay leaves.**

   Light each bay leaf on fire one at a time, allowing it to burn in the firesafe dish while holding the candle in its smoke. As the bay leaves are consumed by the fire, imagine your goal coming to fruition.

4. **Write your petition.**

   Fill the outside of the glass candle with your goal or intention in permanent marker — for example, "to find a new job" or just money signs ($) over and over. Whatever you decide to write, completely cover the outside of the candle. While you are writing, focus on your intention and what it is you desire.

5. **Burn the candle.**

   Place the candle on a prosperity altar or near your money bowl while burning.

TIP

Burn the candle everyday while spending at least 10 to 15 minutes to sit with the candle and focus on your intention.

A charm for good fortune

For this ritual, you construct a simple good fortune charm that you can carry in your pocket or keep on a prosperity altar to attract success, abundance, and good fortune. Perform this ritual on the night of the full moon for the most potency.

Gather the following: 3-x-3-inch square of green fabric, red string, plate, three green chime candles, Prosperity Oil (see earlier formula), Success Incense (see earlier formula), incense burner and charcoal, nine cloves, and pinch each of frankincense resin, cinquefoil, and patchouli. Then follow these steps to create a charm for good fortune:

1. **Set your intention and prepare all your tools.**

   Place the plate at your altar or on your workspace surrounded by the three green candles in the shape of an upward-pointing triangle. Anoint the candles with Prosperity Oil before placing them around the plate.

2. **Burn the incense and fumigate your charm components.**

   Pass the green fabric and red string through the incense smoke while focusing on your intention. Place them on the plate in front of you.

3. **Awaken and add the herbal components.**

   Take each of the herbal ingredients individually and awaken them by stating your intention and blowing on each ingredient three times. Pass the herb through the incense smoke, adding more incense if needed before placing the ingredient on the center of the green fabric.

4. **Light the candles.**

   While the candles are burning, add a few drops of Prosperity Oil to the pile of herbal ingredients at the center of the green fabric.

5. **Tie up the charm to seal your intention.**

   Take all the corners of the fabric together, twisting them to make a tiny pouch. Use the red thread to securely tie the bag shut and anchor your intention.

6. **Fumigate and charge the charm.**

   Take the newly created charm bag and hold it in the incense smoke one final time before placing it back on the plate at the center of the candles.

7. **Allow the candles to burn down.**

   While the candles are burning, you may choose to incorporate other spells or rituals that may go along with your working, or you may sit in front of the workspace and focus on directing energy towards your goal.

8. **Maintain the charm.**

   Carry the charm with you whenever you need to attract extra good luck and fortune. Recharge the charm every full moon by feeding it smoke from the Success Incense Blend and a few drops of Prosperity Oil.

IN THIS CHAPTER

» Cultivating healing spaces

» Removing unhealthy energy

» Caring for your loved ones

Chapter 8
Supporting the Healing of Body and Spirit

In this chapter, you discover the important connection between physical and spiritual wellness. You find herbs that are specifically helpful for supporting the overall wellbeing of both the physical and spiritual bodies. The herbs I include in this chapter have been some of the most foundational and important healing herbs for millennia. In addition to learning about these gentle, yet powerful herbs of healing, you also find formulas for promoting a healthy environment, sending healing energy, and supporting overall well-being.

Approaching Spiritual Healing Practices

Traditional healing practices have survived around the world for millennia, and even today, 80 percent of the world's population relies on these practices and herbal medicine as their primary source of preventing and treating disease and maintaining overall health. Traditional healing practices recognize that health isn't just physical, but the result of living in balance physically, mentally, emotionally, and spiritually. Illness and disease are often the result of these aspects being out of balance. Modern medicine is something that is finally beginning to recognize, that healing isn't just about treating individual symptoms but looking at each person as a whole organism composed of both physical and non-physical parts.

While modern clinical herbalism in the West does take a more treatment-based approach by looking at individual symptoms and treating them with the appropriate chemical compounds contained in herbs, it still has remnants of more holistic and traditional concepts. Herbal energetics and correspondence are examples of how you can come to understand how the physical and nonphysical aspects of herbs come into play when it comes to healing practices.

This balanced approach to health and wellness has benefits for a variety of reasons, including connecting with healing herbs on both a physical and spiritual level, as well as forming a deeper connection with the natural world. All these components facilitate deeper and more profound healing.

WARNING

However, the herbs and practices I cover in this chapter aren't magical cure-alls and aren't meant to replace modern medical advice. This information isn't intended to treat any diseases or illnesses or be taken as a prescription of treatment. When used in combination with a healthy lifestyle and modern medicine (when needed), they're part of a balanced system that can promote overall wellness not only physically, but spiritually, mentally, and emotionally.

Exploring Herbs of Healing and Support

Every herb has some sort of healing action or medicinal property because every herb contains chemical constituents that affect the body. However, not every herb has become a staple in the herbalist's medicine cabinet. Some herbs outshine others in a physical healing capacity and in supporting overall wellness, and they also support health and healing on a spiritual level. The herbs in this section are great examples of the master-healers of the plant kingdom.

While each herb has its own unique properties when it comes to its medicinal effects on a physical level, you can incorporate all these herbs into rituals and spellwork for health, vitality, wellness, and restoration. Each herb is full of beneficial healing energy and is willing to help those in need.

All-heal

All-heal (*Prunella vulgaris*), also known as self-heal, is a humble mint-family wildflower with a reputation far grander than its size. Native across Europe, Asia, and North America, all-heal threaded through cottage gardens and field margins alike, earning names such as heal-all and woundwort for its long use on cuts, bruises, and sore throats. Traditional Western herbals describe all-heal as a cooling, gently astringent *vulnerary* (used for healing wounds); folk herbalists chewed or crushed the fresh leaves to apply to minor wounds and to create brewed teas or gargles for mouth and throat irritation.

As a wellness ally, all-heal is often taken as a light, everyday tea to support resilience, soothing inflamed tissues, easing minor digestive upset, and lending a steadying, restorative tone to the system. Externally, herbalists use simple washes or salves for chapped skin and small scrapes, reflecting the herb's old reputation for knitting things back together — skin, nerves, and spirits. While it's no panacea, the name all-heal points to something herbalists still value as a tonic herb: a reliable, gentle plant that meets common complaints and that can be taken on a regular basis to support overall wellness.

In folklore and magic, all-heal carries themes of repair, protection, and reconciliation. All-heal is tucked into healing charms, added to bath blends for recovery after illness or heartbreak, and sprinkled in the home to mend frayed dynamics and invite peace. Because all-heal grows readily and bounces back after cutting, practitioners read it as a sign of self-renewal, an herb to strengthen the aura, close energetic wounds, and encourage the will to heal.

TIP

Use all-heal in candles or sachets dedicated to wellness, pair it with rose for comfort of the heart or chamomile for soothing sleep, and let this modest wayside plant stand as a reminder that steady, everyday care is powerful magic.

Blessed thistle

Blessed thistle (*Cnicus benedictus*), also called holy thistle, is a spiky Mediterranean herb whose very name *benedictus* means blessed — a testament to its reputation in medieval Europe as a plant of protection and mercy. Monastic gardens kept blessed thistle on hand as a household remedy and safeguard, and early herbalists praised its strong, clean bitterness. Traditionally, blessed thistle was prepared as a digestive bitter to kindle appetite, wake a sluggish stomach, and support digestion; it also found its way into old-style tonics and bitters formulas.

In magical lore, blessed thistle is a well-attested banishing and blessing herb. Often aligned with elemental Fire and planetary Mars (and sometimes the Sun), bless thistle is used to burn away malaise, fortify boundaries, and restore courage during convalescence or low spirits.

TIP

Tuck a pinch of blessed thistle into a charm bag for protection and recovery, add it to bath blends or floor washes to clear stagnant energies from a home, or include a trace in healing incense to cut through heaviness. Blessed thistle's sharp, aromatic bitterness is read as a signature of resolve, an herb that reminds the body to kindle its inner flame and the spirit to keep faith with the work of healing.

For wellness-focused rituals, pair blessed thistle with chamomile to soothe while you strengthen or with rosemary for purification and uplifting energy. Write a simple petition for renewed health, dress a white or gold candle with a tiny sprinkle of the herb, and speak your intention for cleansing, courage, and steady improvement. As with all thistles, a little goes a long way, as the plant teaches you to take space for your healing.

Lady's mantle

Lady's mantle (*Alchemilla* spp.) is a softly scalloped, dew-catching herb long cherished in European folk medicine and lore. Medieval healers prized its strong astringency for toning tissues. Lady's mantle was brewed as tea or used as a wash for minor wounds, mouth and throat irritation, and skin care. In women's herbcraft, Lady's mantle was traditionally used to support menstrual regularity, ease heavy bleeding, and heal and strengthen after birth. Externally, simple poultices and rinses helped calm puffy, irritated skin, reflecting the plant's reputation for gentle containment and repair.

Its very name nods to old beliefs: Lady's mantle evokes the Virgin Mary's protective cloak, while *Alchemilla* means little alchemist and refers to the glittering beads of dew that pool on its leaves, once gathered by alchemists as celestial water. In magic, the plant carries themes of protection, healing, and grace. The leaf's cloak-like shape makes it a favorite for shielding rituals, recovering after illness, and strengthening emotional boundaries.

Add dried leaf to healing sachets, bath blends, or honeyed teas for comfort and restoration. Use the dawn dew or a sprinkle of fresh water from the leaves in beauty and glamour rites to bless the skin and self-image.

Lavender

Lavender (*Lavandula* spp.) is a Mediterranean native whose name comes from *lavare,* meaning to wash, which provides a clue to its long history in cleansing due to its antimicrobial properties. Romans scented baths and linens with lavender, and medieval and Renaissance households used lavender as a *strewing herb* to be laid upon the floor in sickrooms to prevent the spread of illness. In traditional herbcraft, lavender is gentle and calming and is sipped as tea to settle the nerves and stomach or inhaled to ease stress and anxiety. Externally, herbal practitioners use lavender water and salves to freshen and soothe the skin, while the essential oil's aroma is widely relied upon for relaxation and sleep support.

In folklore and magic, lavender is associated with purification, peace, and protection — a calm, bright presence that clears heaviness without harshness. Lavender is a classic in sleep pillows and healing sachets, burned or diffused to cleanse a room, and added to ritual baths to release grief, calm anxiety, and invite restorative rest.

Many traditions also value lavender not only for its ability to heal the body and spirit but to create a peaceful environment in which healing can take place where it sweetens hot tempers, restores harmony, and blesses the home.

TIP

As a wellness ally, lavender is ideal for convalescence and stress-related tension: A few blossoms in tea, a lightly anointed candle, or a scented compress can help the body and spirit be at ease so healing can take hold.

Life everlasting

Life everlasting is a name given to several dryable wildflowers whose blooms keep their color almost indefinitely, most commonly sweet everlasting (*Pseudognaphalium obtusifolium*, also called rabbit tobacco) in North American folk practice, and pearly everlasting (*Anaphalis margaritacea*), with Old World cousins in the Helichrysum clan. Their durability, honeyed straw-scent, and long-lasting bloom made the plant a favorite in cottage garlands and graveyard wreaths, and earned it a place in charms for longevity, vitality, and remembrance. In traditional herbcraft, life everlasting was brewed as a gentle, aromatic tea or steam for seasonal discomforts, soothing irritated throats and easing tight chests, and used as a mild astringent wash for tender skin.

In folk magic, life everlasting is worked as an herb of healing, endurance, and ancestral blessing. Because the flowers seem to defy decay, they're added to recovery sachets, convalescent bath blends, and household incenses to promote wellness. In African-American conjure practices, life everlasting appears in healing and peace formulas. The dried flowers are burned to calm a room, carried to steady the heart after grief, or included in spiritual baths to renew strength and invite protective guardianship from the ancestors. On the altar, a small dried sprig honors continuity between worlds, supporting work of remembrance and healing grief while encouraging the living body to knit and restore through its nourishing properties.

Purple coneflower

Purple coneflower (*Echinacea purpurea*), commonly known as echinacea, is a North American prairie native that is an important herb in Indigenous plant medicine. Plains peoples, including the Lakota, Kiowa, and Cheyenne, used echinacea for a wide range of complaints, from soothing sore throats and coughs to easing stings and minor wounds. Early Euro-American eclectic physicians adopted echinacea enthusiastically in the late 19th to early 20th centuries as a cleansing, balancing tonic. Today, echinacea remains one of the most popular herbs in Western herbalism, typically prepared as tincture or tea at the first sign of seasonal challenges, and used topically in washes or salves for uncomplicated skin irritations.

As a healing ally, echinacea is often framed as a plant of defense and renewal. Its traditional use centers on helping the body rally by supporting resilience during the onset of colds, encouraging healthy lymphatic flow, and lending a steadying presence to recovery. The sturdy stems and armored seed cone mirror that signature: upright posture, strong boundaries, and clear signaling to the body to organize its resources. Gardeners prize echinacea not just for medicine but for its ability to draw pollinators and return year after year, another metaphor for its energy of recovery and persistence.

TIP

In folklore and magical practice, purple coneflower is known for its energetic potency and is worked to fortify the aura, strengthen defenses, and speed recovery. Add a few petals or a pinch of root to healing sachets and bath blends after illness; dress a white or green candle with echinacea to call upon its healing spirit and safeguard the home; or place a dried cone on the altar as a talisman for stamina, protection, and steady comeback energy.

Plantain

Plantain (*Plantago major*), most often broadleaf plantain and ribwort/English plantain (*P. lanceolata*), is a humble wayside herb naturalized across Europe, Asia, and the Americas. Old English sources call plantain *waybread*, the mother of herbs, praised in the Anglo-Saxon poem *Nine Herbs Charm*, recorded in the tenth century CE, for its power to still pain and heal wounds. Long before apothecaries bottled remedies, travelers and fieldworkers chewed a fresh plantain leaf and laid it on stings, bites, splinters, and scrapes — a quick, green poultice always at hand.

In traditional herbcraft, plantain is gently astringent, cooling, and soothing. Herbal practitioners used teas and washes for hot, irritated tissues and compresses to calm minor skin flare-ups. The leaves were applied to the skin to draw out splinters and soothe nettle stings.

TIP

As a wellness ally, plantain's gifts are steady and practical. You can use a simple infusion as a mouth rinse for tender gums or a skin wash for small, inflamed areas. Salves and oils made from the fresh leaf are household staples for everyday bumps and scratches.

In folklore and magic, plantain is an herb of mending and protection especially for travelers. Travelers carried plantain when on the road to prevent blisters and injury. You can add plantain to healing sachets, bath blends, and floor washes to cool inflammation both physically and energetically and to draw out what doesn't belong. You can also use a fresh leaf charm over the heart to quiet agitation; place dried leaves in a household healing jar with lavender and chamomile; or dress a white or green candle with a pinch of plantain to draw pain away and hasten recovery. Because it thrives underfoot and bounces back after cutting, plantain teaches resilience and perseverance.

Poplar

Poplar (*Populus* spp.), including balsam poplar, cottonwood, aspen, and white poplar, threads through Old and New World herbal traditions. In classical lore, the white poplar was sacred to the underworld, a place within the Earth where people would journey for rest and healing, just like the plants that die back in the winter only to return in spring. The underworld was a place of renewal and ancestral wisdom. Poplar represents this quality of endurance and rebirth. Across North America, Indigenous plant medicine practitioners and herbalists alike prized the resinous spring buds of balsam poplar/cottonwood, whose warm-sweet scent and preservative resins became a household staple.

Medicinally, poplar's buds and young bark were prepared as teas, tinctures, and especially infused oils known as the famous balm of Gilead, made by steeping sticky buds in oil and then used in salves and liniments. In traditional practice, these preparations soothed wind-chapped skin, minor aches after hard work, and the roughness of winter lungs when used as chest rubs. The plant's natural aromatics and mild salicylates explain much of its comforting reputation. *Salicylates,* used in aspirin, are compounds with pain-relieving properties found in some plants. Beyond the body, the buds' scent, warm and sweet like vanilla, was thought to strengthen the weary and mark the turn from illness toward recovery.

WARNING

Individuals who are allergic to aspirin have a salicylate sensitivity and should avoid ingesting plants containing these compounds.

TIP

In folk magic, poplar is employed for protection, transition, and deep healing. The tree that bends and sings in the wind is called upon to carry away grief and stagnant pain, to breathe through stuck places, and to guard the threshold while healing takes hold. A pinch of dried bud in a white candle dressing, a few leaves in a wellness sachet with lavender and chamomile, or a light anointing with bud-infused oil can anchor rites for convalescence, easing sorrow and encouraging steady return of strength.

Skullcap

Skullcap (*Scutellaria lateriflora*), a member of the mint-family plant native to North America, gets its name from the small helmet-like flowers. Skullcap entered Euro-American herbal practice through Indigenous knowledge (like so many herbs native to North America) and became a favorite of 18th to 19th-century eclectic physicians as a calming nervine, used for frazzled nerves, restlessness, irritability, and trouble sleeping. Teas and tinctures remain the classic preparations for gently calming down an overstimulated nervous system, while simple pillow sachets show up in older household lore for easing nightmares. This affinity to the nervous system is a characteristic quality of herbs ruled by Mercury.

As a wellness ally, skullcap is prized for rest and recovery, the process of rebuilding through sustained support that helps the body settle after stress so that repair can take hold. Herbalists often pair skullcap with chamomile, lavender, or milky oats in evening teas; a few drops of tincture before bed or after an agitating day can help take the edge off, release tension, and invite deeper sleep. This ability to calm and quiet the mind made skullcap a go-to in convalescence and for people rebuilding from burnout, grief, or long periods of overwork, when the nervous system is overworked and thrown out of balance.

In folklore and magic, skullcap carries themes of peace, protection of the mind, and boundary repair. The plant's cap is an example of the Doctrine of Signatures (see Chapter 3) for shielding the head, useful in rituals that guard the aura, quiet intrusive thoughts, and seal up energetic weak spots.

Add a pinch to sleep sachets and healing baths, dress a blue or white candle for tranquility, or include it in spells for grounding and self-preservation, particularly after heartbreak or shock. Skullcap helps create a sanctuary of thought and feeling, conferring the sense of safety necessary for healing to occur.

St. John's wort

St. John's wort (*Hypericum perforatum*) is a bright, midsummer-blooming herb. It's named for St. John the Baptist because it flowers around his feast day (June 24), which coincides closely with the summer solstice. St. John's wort is traditionally gathered at dawn, hung over doors, or woven into charms to ward off ill luck and wandering spirits. Its bright-yellow flowers and perforated leaves are indications of this plant's spiritual light. Associated with the light of the Sun, folk names like chase-devil echo its long reputation for protection and for lifting heavy moods. The crimson pigment released from the crushed buds was read as the

Sun's power sealed in the plant, symbolic of blood and vitality. St. John's wort is associated with courage and recovery.

In traditional herbcraft, St. John's wort is a valued ally for nerves and wounds. A red infused oil of the fresh flowers is used topically in folk practice to comfort minor burns, bruises, muscle aches, and nerve tenderness. Teas and tinctures have been used historically to support low spirits and ease restlessness.

Taking St. John's wort internally can interact with certain medications and using the plant topically can cause sensitivity when exposed to sunlight in some individuals, so it is important to work with this plant with understanding.

Magically, St. John's wort carries a solar energy, making it one of the most powerful allies for clearing heaviness, protecting the home, and rekindling hope.

Add a pinch to healing sachets or bath blends after illness, anoint a white or gold candle with a drop of the infused oil to bless recovery, or place a sprig on the altar at Midsummer to invite vitality and good spirits for the year ahead. Worked gently and with respect, this energetically bright herb supports wellness on all fronts, helping to bring perseverance and lift morale, especially during long and difficult healing processes.

Vervain

Vervain (*Verbena officinalis*) and its North American cousin *V. hastata*, or blue vervain, are old-world sacred herbs with a long history in both medicine and magic. Romans reputedly swept altars with vervain and offered it to their deities. Medieval herbals list it among the holy plants used to purify spaces and tools. In folk medicine, vervain earned a place for relieving headaches, lifting low spirits, and reducing fevers and as a classic bitter tonic to kindle appetite and gently support the liver. Herbalists especially remember blue vervain as a cooling nervine for tense, overstimulated nervous systems, helping release shoulder and neck tightness and quiet the mind when stuck in fight-or-flight mode.

In folk magic practices, vervain is a plant of consecration, protection, and clarity. Vervain is sprinkled to cleanse thresholds, added to baths to lift lingering gloom after illness, and burned or infused to dedicate tools and altars to healing work. Vervain helps to soothe anxiety, brighten outlook, and recenter the spirit.

Vervain is especially helpful for recovery, boundary repair, and post-stress recalibration. A pinch of vervain is added to candle dressing for white or gold candles to promote healing. Vervain is also infused into water to wash the hands before healing work or added to a sachet to promote peace and well-being.

Vervain also carries a reputation for peace-making and reconciliation and is used in rituals for harmonizing strained relations within a home or within the self. Pair vervain with chamomile for comfort, rose for heart-healing, or lemon balm for an uplifting effect.

Yarrow

Yarrow (*Achillea millefolium*) carries a long lineage from battlefield herb to household healer. Its genus name honors Achilles, the legendary warrior who is said to have used yarrow to staunch soldiers' wounds, giving the plant folk names like soldier's woundwort and nosebleed plant. In Western herbalism, yarrow is a *styptic* (stops bleeding) and *astringent* (contacts tissue) for minor cuts and scrapes, a *diaphoretic* (causes sweating) tea used at the onset of colds to sweat out a fever, and a tonic for general resilience. Yarrow's finely divided thousand leaves signal a talent for knitting and toning tissues, inside and out. These leaves also reflect the herb's energetic properties, which help to seal any holes in the energy system that may be the result of illness or trauma. Yarrow helps to seal the aura, while still keeping it permeable so energy can move through freely.

In folklore and magic, yarrow is a guardian of thresholds and boundaries, and part of the healing process may require a strengthening of one's boundaries both physically (the immune system) and energetically. Healers have long added yarrow to cleansing baths and floor washes to seal the aura after illness or grief, while a pinch in incense or anointing blends helps close energetic leaks and restore coherence.

TIP

As a wellness ally, yarrow supports both repair and regulation. Yarrow inspires resiliency and a warrior's spirit, and you can use it in ritual for physical support but also to support morale and positive outlook. Use light infusions or rinses in ritual recuperation to help the body recalibrate itself or dress a white or gold candle with an anointing oil containing yarrow to call in protection during recovery.

Yarrow is a powerful ally of healing support. Not only does it help support the one healing, but yarrow is also a supportive ally for caretakers. Yarrow helps end the healing process on a strong note with boundaries restored, vitality returned, and the threshold guarded as you step back into daily life.

Creating Herbal Formulas for Wellness

You can create a variety of multipurpose healing formulas to bring healing to yourself and to others. Healing comes in many forms, including the compassion and support of others, and offering that support can have profound effects on the healing process. All the formulas in this section are made with the endless compassion and support of your herbal allies so that you can heal and support the ones you love.

REMEMBER

While all the herbs mentioned in this section have unique and important medicinal properties, these formulas are intended for ritual use and not as literal medicines.

See Chapter 2 for instructions regarding general preparation and safety for creating formulas.

Healing Oil

You can create your own healing oil and use it in the following ways:

- As an anointing oil for candles burned during healing spells and ritual baths. Anoint the candles in a downward motion from the wick to the base to attract healing energy.
- As an anointing oil for talismans, amulets, or charms to charge them with healing vibrations.
- As addition to ritual baths for healing and to guard against unhealthy energies.

TIP

Craft the following Healing Oil on a Monday when the Moon is waxing or full.

In a bottle, combine 1 teaspoon each of yarrow, holy basil, plantain, pine needles, and camphor crystals and cover with 60 ml of carrier oil. Cover the bottle with a lid and allow the oil to infuse for one full lunar cycle (28 days). Shake the oil regularly to help it infuse. When the oil is finished infusing, you may choose to strain out the herbal ingredients or leave them in the bottle to continue infusing.

Healing Incense

You can burn an all-purpose Healing Incense blend to send healing energy to those who need it, cleanse spaces to promote healing and recovery, and call upon the healing power of your herbal allies.

TIP

Make this incense on a Wednesday (ruled by Mercury) when the Moon is waxing or full.

Use a mortar and pestle to grind the following ingredients until they're a uniform consistency: 1 tablespoon copal resin and 1 teaspoon each of lavender flowers, licorice root, eucalyptus leaves, and purple coneflower (echinacea).

Burn small amounts on charcoal in an incense burner during healing rituals.

Renewing Floor Wash

To create this Renewing Floor Wash, you will need a bucket, towels and gloves for cleaning, a saucepan, and strainer. Then follow these steps:

1. **Make a hot water infusion.**

   Fill a saucepan with water and bring it to a medium-high temperature. Add peels from one orange and one lemon, a handful of fresh pine needles, ½ cup of lavender flowers, and a few sprigs of fresh rosemary.

2. **While the infusion is simmering for 5 minutes with the lid on, fill your bucket with hot water.**

3. **Add pine-scented cleaning solution (or your preferred cleaning solution) to the bucket.**

   REMEMBER

   Leave room to add the hot water infusion from the saucepan.

4. **Strain the herbal infusion directly into the bucket.**

   After the herbs have finished infusing in the sauce pan, take the sauce pan and strainer and carefully strain the liquid directly into the bucket.

5. **Add 20 drops lemongrass essential oil to the water in the bucket.**

You can use this Renewal Floor Wash to clean your home prior to the winter months to keep the energy of the home healthy and keep it from becoming stagnant. If someone in the home is recovering from illness, use this floor wash to help remove the energy of illness from the home to accelerate their healing. You can also use Renewing Floor Wash to clean counters and other hard surfaces in the home.

Avoid using the Renewing Floor Wash on natural wood surfaces.

Golden Healing Salve

This Golden Healing Salve formula is inspired by the *unguentum populeon*, a popular medicinal preparation that has been around since the Middle Ages, making use of the soothing and healing powers of poplar. This warm smelling, golden-colored salve is great for healing scrapes and bruises and soothing minor aches and pains. Energetically, it carries the virtues of the Sun and is healing, purifying, protective, and uplifting.

The formula is good for your skin, and has a sweet-warm vanilla like smell so it can also be worn as a personal anointing oil on a regular basis. Use this salve whenever you need to access the warm-healing energy of the Sun. Apply it to the skin and enjoy its rich fragrance or use it to heal cuts and abrasions. You can also use this formula as an anointing oil, applying it to candles or charms as part of a larger healing ritual.

For this formula, you may want to use small tins or containers for portioning.

This salve formula requires you to first infuse the oil and then create the salve. If you want, you can skip the salve-making steps and create a Golden Healing Oil.

1. **Grind 25 grams dried poplar buds in a mortar and pestle (they will get sticky) to help release their sap.**
2. **Infuse the oil.**

   Add the poplar buds and 10 grams dried calendula flowers to a mason jar with 250 ml carrier oil.

3. **Put a lid on the mason jar and place it in a sunny spot.**

   The jar should be in a spot that will receive direct sunlight for part of the day.

4. **Allow the oil to infuse with the ingredients for 2 to 4 weeks.**

   The heat and light will help with the infusion process and also take the energy of the Sun into the oil.

5. **In a saucepan filled with water, heat the oil on medium heat for two to three hours.**

   Take the lid off of the mason jar, leaving the plant material in the oil. Place the entire jar in a saucepan. Add water to the saucepan until the one-half to three-fourths of the outside of the mason jar is covered. Avoid getting any water inside the jar. Heat on medium temperature for 2 to 3 hours, monitoring the water level, making sure that the water does not boil over or evaporate.

6. **Strain the oil after it cools and is safe to handle.**

   After the oil cools and is safe to handle, use a cheesecloth to strain out the poplar buds and calendula flower. Take a square of cheese cloth and place it over a second mason jar or other glass container. Pour the oil over the cheesecloth, allowing the oil to pass through and leave the plant material in the cheesecloth.

7. **Transfer the strained oil back to the original mason jar.**
8. **Add 4 tablespoons beeswax or carnauba wax to the strained oil.**
9. **Repeat Step 5, heating the oil until the wax is completely melted and stirring at regular intervals to ensure the wax is evenly distributed.**
10. **Using a towel to protect your hands, carefully remove the hot mason jar from the saucepan.**
11. **Add 2 tablespoons benzoin resinoid and mix thoroughly.**

TIP

Benzoin resinoid is sold as an essential oil but has a thicker, sticky consistency.

As the mixture begins to cool, the wax will solidify into a salve consistency. If you're portioning into smaller containers, pour the contents of the mason jar into your containers before the wax sets.

Purify and Revitalize Bath Blend

This Purify and Revitalize Bath Blend has a bright and uplifting energy that combines the healing, purifying, and balancing properties of a variety of supportive flowers. You can use this bath blend on a regular basis as part of your own energetic hygiene routine, but it's especially helpful when recovering from illness or pulling yourself out of difficult mental/emotional spaces.

TIP

You can take this bath any day of the week, but its effectiveness is multiplied when used during the full moon or new moon.

Add 1 tablespoon Himalayan salt and 1 cup Epsom salt to a jar. Using a mortar and pestle, grind 1 tablespoon each of the following until they've reached a uniform consistency: calendula flowers, cornflower, rose petals, lavender flowers, lemongrass, and hibiscus. Add the herbal ingredients and 10 drops each of lemongrass and lavender essential oils.

You can add this blend directly to bath water or use a cloth drawstring bag to allow all ingredients to infuse in the water before bathing.

TIP

If you're creating this Purify and Revitalize Bath Blend for later use, put a lid on the jar and shake well to let all the ingredients marry.

TIP

If taking a bath isn't possible, you can use this bath blend as a steam or a foot soak by filling a large bowl or tub with hot water and adding the bath blend to it. You can soak your feet in the water for relaxation and rejuvenation or place the bowl on a table and breath in the fumes. You can also take a wash cloth and use the water to cleanse your body without having to get in the bathtub.

Casting Spells of Healing and Wellness

The burning of aromatic herbs to promote healing and wellness is common throughout history and still practiced in many places today. Many of the herbs in these smoking blends contain essential oils that have antimicrobial and antiseptic properties, which reflects their energetic ability to cleanse a space of unhealthy energy and promote overall well-being.

Smoke Bundle for Healing

You can create a Smoke Bundle for Healing that you can use on a regular basis as part of your practice, or you can reserve them for future use in the event that you feel an illness coming on.

For the following formula, you will need natural cotton twine (undyed) or hemp cord, scissors, and a small bowl for clippings. Also, gather two 6- to 10-inch cuttings of the following: fresh lavender, rosemary, garden sage, and mugwort. Then follow these steps:

1. **Set your intention.**

   Hold each herb individually and hold your intention in mind while connecting with each plant's spirit.

2. **Prep the cuttings.**

   Strip the lower leaves and flowers from the bottom 1 to 2 inches of each stem. Keep the tops intact for a neat tip.

3. **Arrange the herbs.**

   Place all the cuttings together to create a bundle. Hold the bundle in both hands, gently packing the herbs together while calling upon their healing energies.

4. **Align the stems.**

   Make the base even so that it ties cleanly. Aim for a bundle about 1 to 1.5-inch thick.

5. **Tie-off the base.**

   Cut approximately 3 to 4 feet of twine. Knot firmly at the base, leaving a 3 to 4-inch tail.

6. **Spiral wrap the entire bundle.**

   Wind the twine upward in a gentle spiral, compressing but not choking the herbs. At the tip, cross over and spiral back down, catching any loose bits.

7. **Finish and dry.**

   Tie off at the base with the tail. Snip stray leaves for a tidy shape. Dry thoroughly.

8. **Hang upside down in a warm, airy, shaded place for 10 to 21 days, until stems snap and bundle feels crisp.**

   Proper drying prevents mold and ensures an even smolder.

9. **Cure and store.**

   After drying, rest bundles 3 to 7 days in a paper bag or box. Store in a cool, dry spot.

To use the smoke bundle, light the tip, blow to a smolder, and waft smoke with a firesafe dish beneath. For personal healing, circle the smoke around the body from feet upward, focusing on heart, throat, and crown. For rooms, trace doorways and windows working counterclockwise around the room to draw unwanted energy out.

TIP

When finished, snuff on sand or in a heatproof bowl. Don't use water unless you're finished with the bundle.

Healing Energy Ritual

You can work a simple but effective ritual that sends healing energy to people over long distances or offers continued energetic support to those who need it. You can repeat this Healing Energy Ritual or maintain it by replacing the candle as it burns out, keeping the ritual going for as long as needed.

TIP

Begin this ritual during the first phases of the waxing Moon, unless the situation calls for more urgent attention, in which case perform the ritual when necessary.

Gather the following items: white 7-day glass-encased candle, Healing Oil (see formula earlier in this chapter), pen and paper, and a heat-tray or plate. You also need a link to the person, such as a photo, a small belonging, or their full name written on paper. Then follow these steps to perform a healing energy ritual:

1. **Cleanse and center.**

   Wash your hands and take a few deep breaths. Use a few drops of healing oil to wipe the candle glass from the base of the candle to the top (an upward and outward direction to send the energy).

2. **Set the altar and name the recipient.**

   Place the tray and then the candle in its center. Put the link to the person beneath the candle or directly in front of it. Hold the link at heart level and clearly state their full name, location (if known), and your intention of sending them healing energy.

3. **Anoint the candle.**

   Add 3 drops of healing oil to the top of the wax. With your fingertip, trace a small clockwise circle around the top of the candle as you say something like *"With this light, may healing grow."*

4. **Create a petition.**

   On the paper, write a brief, specific blessing for the person. Fold the paper away from you three times and place it under the candle.

5. **Light the candle and focus.**

   For 5 to 15 minutes, breathe steadily and visualize the person surrounded by soft, white-gold light. See comfort increasing, pain/stress easing, and so on.

6. **Say the following blessing.**

   > *"By growing moon and steadfast flame,*
   > *may strength return and ease remain.*
   > *Surrounded, supported, restored, made whole —*
   > *blessings to [Name], in body and soul."*

7. **Tend the candle daily for seven days (or longer).**

   Anoint the candle again with healing oil and relight the candle. Restate the blessing in Step 6 each day and focus on your intention for 5 to 15 minutes.

8. **Offer gratitude.**

   Thank all helpers, seen and unseen, such as caregivers, medicine, and their own will to heal.

A charm for health

You can construct a simple health and wellness charm that you can carry in your pocket or keep on a healing altar to attract healing, growth, and overall wellness. Perform this ritual on the night of the full moon for the most potency. (For more on charms, see Chapter 2.)

For this ritual, you need a 3-×-3-inch square of white fabric, white string, plate, three white chime candles, Healing Oil and Healing Incense (see earlier formulas), and an incense burner and charcoal. You also need one clove of dry garlic and a pinch each of blessed thistle, vervain, and St. John's wort.

1. **Set your intention and prepare all your tools.**

   Place the plate at your altar or on your workspace surrounded by the three white candles in the shape of a downward-pointing triangle. Anoint the candles with Healing Oil before placing them around the plate.

2. **Burn the incense and fumigate your charm components.**

   Pass the white fabric and string through the incense smoke while focusing on your intention. Place them on the plate in front of you.

3. **Awaken and add the herbal components.**

   Take each herbal ingredient individually and awaken them by stating your intention and blowing on each ingredient three times. Pass the herb through the incense smoke, adding more incense if needed before placing the ingredient on the center of the green fabric.

4. **Light the candles.**

   While the candles are burning, add a few drops of Healing Oil to the pile of herbal ingredients at the center of the green fabric.

5. **Tie up the charm to seal your intention.**

   Take all corners of the fabric together, twisting them to make a tiny pouch. Use the white thread to securely tie the bag shut and anchor your intention.

6. **Fumigate and charge the charm.**

   Take the newly created charm bag and hold it in the incense smoke one final time before placing it back on the plate at the center of the candles.

7. **Allow the candles to burn down.**

   While the candles are burning, you may choose to incorporate other spells or rituals that may go along with your working, or you may sit in front of the workspace and focus on directing energy toward your goal.

8. **Maintain the charm.**

   Carry the charm with you whenever you need to channel healing energy for yourself or for others. Recharge the charm every full moon by feeding it smoke from the Healing Incense Blend and a few drops of Healing Oil.

IN THIS CHAPTER

» Tending to the garden of the heart

» Allowing love to flourish

» Going beyond romance

Chapter 9 Cultivating Love and Sensuality

Love magic conjures images of flickering candlelight, rose petals scattered across silk sheets, and sultry whispers cast beneath a full moon, but as love can be a tangled, intoxicating force, love magic — like love itself — can be messy and complicated. Beneath the sensual surface of love magic lies a deeper current of emotional alchemy: the power to heal heartbreak, ignite passion, awaken pleasure, and magnetize the kind of love that nourishes the soul and stirs the body.

Love magic invites us to revel in our own desirability, to reclaim our sensuality and strength, and to open ourselves fully and fearlessly to new connections. Whether you're drawing in a lover, deepening intimacy, or simply falling in love with yourself, this chapter on love and sensuality offers spellwork that radiates with heat and heart.

Understanding the Ethics of "Love" Magic

Love magic consists of a variety of practices that can range from innocent to manipulative, depending on the intention. Historically, the line was crossed by love potions that contained psychoactive and potentially dangerous ingredients that were both taken recreationally and also given to people unsuspectingly to make them more receptive to one's romantic advances.

Psychoactive love potions aside, the ethics of love magic are complex and deeply personal, hinging on intention, consent, and respect for the free will of others. While drawing love generally or enhancing one's personal magnetism can be empowering and affirming, attempts to manipulate or bind the affections of a specific person without their knowledge can raise serious ethical concerns. Such practices may cross boundaries and create imbalanced or unhealthy relationships.

At the heart of ethical love magic is the principle of self-love — the foundation from which all other love should flow. Cultivating self-worth, confidence, and emotional healing not only attracts healthier connections but also ensures that magic is used in a way that honors both oneself and others. When rooted in self-love, acceptance, and compassion, love magic becomes a path of empowerment, healing, and authentic connection. The innocent, or ethical, forms of love magic work on the self and open one to the various romantic possibilities that may be available.

One common form of love magic is general *love-drawing magic*, which is used to attract new love or invite a romantic presence. Instead of trying to manipulate a specific person, this form of love magic leaves things open to all potential possibilities.

Another form of magic often used to attract romantic attention is the practice of glamour magic. *Glamour magic* starts with the self and is meant to enhance a person's *aura* (their energetic influence), charm, and charisma to make them more appealing in the eyes of others. This form of enchantment often involves ritual baths, oils, perfumes, and beautification practices, helping the practitioner project an irresistible image. Enchanted jewelry or garments may also be worn as talismans, imbuing the wearer with magnetic allure. While you can also use glamour magic for other intentions, ranging from protection to concealment, it is a practice that is well-suited to projecting confidence and attracting romantic attention.

On the more manipulative end of the spectrum is *coercive love magic*, which seeks to influence the will of a specific individual, stirring desire or affection where it may not naturally arise.

Fidelity magic, meanwhile, is used to maintain devotion and loyalty, whether by keeping a lover faithful, drawing back a straying partner, or binding their affections more tightly.

Aphrodisiacs can be used to combine both the magical and therapeutic properties of herbs in love magic. Working with aphrodisiacs involves the use of botanicals, elixirs, or rituals to awaken desire, restore sexual vitality, and enhance pleasure. Herbs with aphrodisiac properties work on both a physical and spiritual level and can help support love-drawing magic by enhancing overall health, reducing anxiety, and creating a sense of well-being. Aphrodisiacs have taken a variety of forms and served numerous functions for centuries. Such practices may be employed to gain a lover's attention, rekindle lost passion, or improve intimacy within a relationship. By working with aphrodisiacs, you can also reconnect to your own sense of passion and intimacy when it comes to healing after heartbreak and learning to love again.

Love magic, in all its forms, reflects a deep human longing for connection, for beauty, for passion, and for control over the unpredictable forces of the heart.

REMEMBER

Starting love magic with the self — by working on self-love, heart healing and opening oneself to romantic energies — is always better than trying to control a specific person. Manipulative love magic often ends in unhealthy relationships and heartbreak.

Exploring Herbs of Love and Sensuality

Love magic falls under the planetary rulership of Venus, named for the Roman goddess of love and beauty. Working with Venus, the goddess and planetary force of love, beauty, and attraction, can involve incorporating the colors red, green, and pink, as well as the copper, the planetary metal associated with Venus and that is often used in charms and magical tools dedicated to her. Venusian energy is gentle yet potent, associated with pleasure, harmony, and the magnetic pull of desire. Herbs ruled by Venus tend to be fragrant, flowering, beautifying, and healing, often promoting skin health and emotional well-being.

For love-drawing magic, you can use a wide array of herbs, such as jasmine, rose, lavender, basil, clove, and High John the Conqueror root, which each bringing unique qualities to the work. To incite lust and deepen physical attraction, stimulating and aromatic botanicals, such as cinnamon, damiana, ginseng, vanilla, and patchouli, are favored. In contrast, fidelity magic may call on chili pepper, licorice root, rosemary, or skullcap to maintain loyalty and bind a partner's affections.

On the more shadowy side of Venusian magic, herbs can also be used to suppress or destroy romantic and sexual desire. Camphor, vervain, and witch hazel are believed to cool lustful urges, while lemon and lotus may be used to end emotional bonds or sever attachments entirely. Whether seeking to attract love, inspire passion, encourage devotion, or banish affection, the magical currents of Venus offer a nuanced and powerful framework for working with the many moods of the heart.

Herbs for All Matters of the Heart

Many of the herbs used in love magic have a fragrant and rich aroma. They are also general tonic herbs that support the body's overall health. *Tonic herbs,* which often fall under the realm of Venus, are herbs that are generally safe to use for long periods of time, by the majority of the population. These herbs, such as lavender, lemon balm, and mint, are often found in tea blends sold at the grocery store and are accessible to anyone.

Many herbs, known as aphrodisiacs, work in different ways than you would expect, as opposed to actually generating feelings of arousal. *Adaptogens,* herbs which lower stress and improve the body's overall function and wellness, are considered aphrodisiacs.

The following sections cover a variety of helpful and versatile herbs that can be incorporated into love magic for a variety of purposes, whether the intention is for romantic love magic or personal heart healing.

Cardamom

Cardamom (*Elettaria cardamomum*), a warm and aromatic spice with a sweet, slightly citrusy flavor, is widely used in culinary traditions around the world, from Indian chai to Middle Eastern desserts and Scandinavian pastries. Cardamom's rich, exotic fragrance makes it a favorite not only in the kitchen but also in magical practices, especially those related to love and sensuality.

In love magic, cardamom is prized for its ability to attract romantic attention, draw in sexual partners, and spice up an existing love life. Often included in formulas for lust, attraction, and passion, cardamom brings a fiery and invigorating energy that stimulates both the senses and the heart. It is also considered a lucky charm in matters of romance, believed to help ensure success in love affairs and deepen emotional bonds. Whether added to a charm bag, a ritual bath, or a magical oil blend, cardamom amplifies desire and infuses spellwork with warmth, pleasure, and undeniable attraction.

Cinnamon

Cinnamon (*Cinnamomum aromaticum*) is a versatile and powerful herb in love magic, known for bringing spice, warmth, and vibrant energy to any magical formula. Its fiery nature makes it especially effective in spells meant to spark passion, attract lovers, and ignite romantic desire. Beyond its lust-inspiring qualities, cinnamon also enhances communication, making it a valuable ally in strengthening emotional connection and intimacy between partners.

As a warming and stimulating herb, you can carry cinnamon sticks in charm bags to attract luck in love or add them to simmer pots to create an inviting and passionate atmosphere in the home. Whether used in oils, powders, or ritual blends, cinnamon infuses love magic with dynamic, heart-opening energy and ensures that intentions are fueled with both desire and clarity.

WARNING

If you're using cinnamon essential oil, dilute the essential oil with carrier oil before applying to the skin to avoid any potential skin irritation. Make sure to dilute all essential oils.

Damiana

Damiana (*Turnera diffusa*) is a small, aromatic shrub native to the dry, subtropical regions of Mexico, Central America, and the southwestern United States. Traditionally used by Indigenous peoples for its stimulating and aphrodisiac properties, damiana has a long history of use in love magic and sensual rites. When consumed as a tea or in a smoking blend, it produces gentle relaxing and euphoric effects, helping to ease anxiety, lift the mood, and open the heart to intimacy. In magical practice, damiana is often included in rituals to attract lovers, increase sexual energy, and enhance emotional and physical connection. Its warming, slightly spicy energy makes damiana a popular addition to love-drawing sachets, oils, and incense, where it serves to kindle desire and awaken pleasure on both a physical and energetic level.

TIP

Damiana can be infused into hot water and consumed for its euphoric, uplifting, and aphrodisiac effects. You can brew it by itself or combine it with other herbs, such as rose, passionflower, and vanilla bean.

Ginger

Ginger root (*Zingiber officinale*) has been used for thousands of years as both a culinary spice and a potent medicinal tonic. Revered in Traditional Chinese Medicine (TCM), ginger is considered a warming herb that stimulates circulation, dispels cold, supports digestion, and strengthens the body's vital energy, or *Qi*. Ginger is commonly used to treat nausea, colds, and fatigue and is often included in herbal formulas to invigorate and balance the system. As an overall health tonic, ginger promotes vitality and resilience, making it a staple in both Eastern and Western herbal traditions.

In love magic, ginger is prized for its fiery and energizing qualities. It brings the elemental energy of Fire to any magical working, boosting the strength and speed of spells, particularly those related to love, lust, and attraction. Ginger is frequently used in charms, ritual baths, and incense blends to ignite passion and encourage bold romantic pursuits. Whole dried ginger root can be kept as a powerful talisman, wrapped in red cloth or placed in a charm bag, anointed with love-drawing oils, and carried to attract romantic partners or to intensify an existing relationship.

Lemon balm

Lemon balm (*Melissa officinalis*) is a fragrant, lemon-scented herb in the mint family, known for its soft, heart-shaped leaves and delicate white or pale yellow flowers. Native to the Mediterranean and parts of Western Asia, lemon balm is now cultivated around the world for both its culinary and medicinal uses. As a gentle nervine, it is often used in herbal medicine to calm the nervous system, reduce anxiety, support restful sleep, and ease digestive upset. Taken as a tea, tincture, or infused into oils, lemon balm has a soothing and uplifting effect, making it a valuable remedy for stress and emotional turmoil.

In magical practice, lemon balm is deeply associated with love, healing, and emotional renewal. Its bright and comforting energy makes it especially helpful in spells to attract new love, bring luck in social situations, and support emotional recovery after heartbreak. Lemon balm's energy is not only emotionally supportive but also beautifying. It's commonly used in glamour magic and aura-cleansing rituals to enhance radiance and personal charm. By helping to lift heavy emotions and bring balance to the energetic body, lemon balm acts as both a spiritual tonic and a magical ally in cultivating self-love, confidence, and emotional well-being.

Orchid

Orchids (*Phalaenopsis* spp.) are exotic, sensual flowers that have long been associated with elegance, allure, and opulence. With their striking beauty and wide variety of forms, orchids symbolize sophistication and rare beauty, making them powerful allies in love magic. Traditionally regarded as herbs of attraction, certain species of orchids have also been used for their aphrodisiac properties, believed to stimulate desire and enhance romantic energy. In magical practice, orchids are often used to draw love, deepen passion, and increase one's personal magnetism.

With thousands of species to choose from, any variety of orchid can be worked with to attract romance, charm a potential lover, or cultivate sensual energy. Growing orchids in the home not only adds beauty to the space but also invites an atmosphere of romance and desire, subtly influencing the energy of the environment toward love and connection.

REMEMBER

Orchids only bloom once or twice a year. Store-bought orchids that are in flower will not flower again for some time, but it doesn't mean they are dead! Water them once or twice a week (don't use ice cubes!), and as long as the leaves are kept alive, the plant will flower again.

Patchouli

Patchouli (*Pogostemon cablin*) is a richly aromatic herb long associated with sensuality, attraction, and physical pleasure. Native to Southeast Asia, patchouli has been used in folk magic and spiritual practices for centuries, particularly in love spells and aphrodisiac preparations. Its earthy, musky, spicy-sweet scent is said to awaken the senses, stimulate desire, and draw lovers together.

In love magic, patchouli is often used to attract passionate encounters, deepen physical intimacy, and magnetize sexual energy. Its association with fertility makes it a favored herb in rites aimed at conception or enhancing reproductive vitality. Patchouli oil is commonly added to love-drawing oils, sprinkled in the bedroom, or worn on the body to exude an aura of sexual magnetism.

In folklore, patchouli was believed to stimulate lust and passion, making it popular in rituals designed to invoke romantic or carnal attraction. Its intoxicating aroma was thought to act on both the physical and etheric bodies, stirring deep, instinctual responses. Its grounding yet arousing energy helps balance the *root* and *sacral chakras*, the energy centers associated with sexuality, encouraging both stability and eroticism.

Whether used as incense, anointing oil, or in sachets and bath rituals, patchouli remains a potent botanical ally for those seeking love, pleasure, and fertile abundance.

Rose

The rose (*Rosa* spp.) has long been regarded as the quintessential symbol of love in all its forms — romantic, erotic, spiritual, and self-directed. With its soft petals, heady fragrance, and protective thorns, the rose embodies the complex and layered nature of the heart.

Associated with beauty, sensuality, and sexuality, rose is used in love magic to attract affection, deepen intimacy, and awaken the senses. There are thousands of cultivars of rose, each with its own unique color, form, and energy, but all are powerful allies in spells, charms, and rituals for drawing love, enhancing attraction, and creating emotional connection. From red roses for passionate desire to pink for gentle affection and white for spiritual union, every variety can be incorporated into magical workings to amplify love in its many expressions. Beyond its allure and charm, rose is also a gentle yet profound healer. It supports emotional restoration, encourages forgiveness, and strengthens the heart center, making it one of the most beloved herbs for self-love and heart healing. Rose tea can soothe anxiety and grief, while rose-infused oils and ritual baths help cleanse emotional wounds and restore one's sense of inner beauty. Working with rose in spiritual practice helps us to soften, to open, and to appreciate the beauty in ourselves and the world around us. It invites abundance not only in love, but in joy, creativity, and emotional fulfillment.

Creating Formulas for Attraction

Crafting formulas for romantic attraction involves more than simply combining ingredients. It is an act of intimacy that aligns the practitioner's desires with the energetic currents of love, sexuality and sensuality. Whether the goal is to influence the will of another, draw a lover closer, enhance one's own allure, or create a space charged with romantic energy, these formulations serve as powerful allies in love magic.

The formulas in the following sections provide foundational blends that you can adapt or enhance to suit personal workings, always crafted with focused intention and respect for the forces they seek to invoke.

Bend Over Oil

This Bend Over Oil is intended to bend others to your will or to get them to see things the way you want them to. You can wear it on the body or use it to anoint candles.

Calamus root, licorice root, and bergamot essential oil are the base of this classic hoodoo formula. Optionally, you can add Venusian ingredients, such as damiana, cubeb berries, or grains of paradise, to make this powerful formula better suited for love magic.

For Bend Over Oil, you need a glass bottle or jar with a lid, 60 ml carrier oil, 1 teaspoon calamus root, 1 teaspoon licorice root, and 20 drops of bergamot essential oil. If you'd like, you can add 1 teaspoon of any additional herbs, such as damiana, cubeb berries, or grains of paradise.

To make the oil, assemble all ingredients in a glass bottle and add the carrier oil of your choosing. Allow the ingredients to infuse in the oil for one entire moon cycle. Shake the bottle at least once a week while focusing on your intention. Depending on your preference you may choose to strain out the plant material using cheese cloth or allow it to remain in the bottle indefinitely to create a stronger infusion.

TIP

For love and romance-related workings, start making this oil on a Friday under a waxing moon to "grow" your influence. Apply Bend Over Oil to purple candles and burn to fill the room with your influence or apply the oil to the wrists and neck before coming into contact with the person you intend to influence.

Come to Me Oil

You can wear this formula for Come to Me Oil on the body or use it in rituals to influence a lover, ensure fidelity, and increase personal allure. You can use it in rituals to attract romantic partners in general or to get a current lover to call or show up.

You need a glass bottle or jar with a lid, 60 ml carrier oil, 20 drops of spikenard essential oil, and 1 teaspoon each calamus root, licorice root, rose petals, and orris root.

Bring all ingredients together on a Friday under a waxing or full moon and infuse them with your intention to attract what you desire as you add them to the bottle with the carrier oil. Allow the ingredients to infuse in the oil for one entire moon cycle. Shake the bottle at least once a week while focusing on your intention.

TIP

To cause a straying lover to return to you, apply Come To Me Oil to an article of their clothing (preferably clothing that they have worn recently that hasn't been washed). Wear nothing but this article of clothing to bed or place it in bed with you if it's not possible for you to wear it. Before you fall asleep, focus on your desire for this person to think of you until they return or reach out in some way.

Love-Drawing Oil

Once blended, you can add this Love-Drawing Oil to ritual baths to envelop the body in loving energy, wear it on pulse points to attract affection and attention, or use it to anoint red, pink, or green candles in spellwork to call in love in all its forms.

You need a glass bottle or jar with a lid, 60 ml carrier oil, 1 vanilla bean or ½ teaspoon of vanilla bean powder, and 1 teaspoon lavender flowers, 1 teaspoon of jasmine flowers or 20 drops of jasmine essential oil, 1 teaspoon of patchouli leaf or 10 drops of patchouli essential oil, and 1 teaspoon of orange blossoms or 20 drops of orange essential oil.

Then, On a Friday, the day ruled by Venus, during a waxing or full moon, combine all ingredients with a carrier oil of your choice.

Allow the ingredients to infuse in the oil for one entire moon cycle. Shake the bottle at least once a week while focusing on your intention.

TIP

Depending on your scent preference you may choose to increase or decrease the amounts of essential oil or use dried herbs instead. For example, if you find patchouli overpowering, use the dried herb instead of the essential oil.

Venetian Bath Salt

For a ritual bath blend to enhance your powers of attraction, glamour, and love, combine dried lavender, lemon balm, ashwagandha, chrysanthemum, rose, and dried strawberry with Epsom salt. This enchanting mix harnesses the calming and heart-opening properties of each herb.

To make enough Venusian Bath Salt for one bath, you need a jar or container for mixing, 1 cup Epsom salt and 1 tablespoon each of lavender, lemon balm, ashwagandha root, chrysanthemum, rose, and dried strawberry. Blend these dried botanicals into the salt and store in a jar until ready to use. For an added boost of fragrance and potency, you can add essential oils or other fragrance oils, such as rose, strawberry, or lavender, to the salt mixture before use.

When preparing your bath, add a generous scoop to the water, allowing the herbs to steep and infuse the space with their magic.

TIP

Fill a cloth or organza drawstring bag with the bath blend and place that in the water to avoid having to clean the herbs out of the bathtub when you're done.

Love-Drawing Incense

You can burn this Love-Drawing Incense for all forms of love magic. Finely grind and blend together 1 tablespoon each of dragon's blood resin, red sandalwood powder, cinnamon powder, and damiana herb. If you want, you can add 1 teaspoon honey, but make sure it's evenly distributed. Burn small amounts on incense charcoal in a firesafe vessel.

TIP

When burning any kind of loose incense, use a firesafe container on charcoal specifically meant for incense. Fill the incense container with sand to absorb the charcoal's heat.

Love Spell Candle Dressing

Candle dressing is a way of ritually preparing candles for spellwork using oils, herbs, and other ingredients to infuse your intention into the candle before burning it. Candle dressing is a simple but effective way to add layers of magical intention to your workings.

For a love spell candle dressing, you need a red, pink, or green candle, parchment paper, and a baking sheet or tray. Also gather your Love-Drawing Oil (see earlier formula in this chapter), honey, and finely ground love-drawing herbs, such as rose, cinnamon, red pepper, and basil.

TIP

Finely ground all herbs to a uniform consistency to better coat the candle.

Place the parchment paper on your baking sheet or tray to use as your workspace and then follow these steps:

1. **Focus on your intention.**

   Bring to mind the type of love that you're trying to attract, whether it's a new romantic partner or self-love. To focus on your intention, think about the qualities that this loving energy has and how it makes you feel.

2. **Hold the candle in your hands and rub the outside of the candle to warm it with your hands.**

3. **(Optional) Carve the candle with a toothpick or needle before applying the Love-Drawing Oil.**

   You can carve the name of a specific person or your desired intention into the wax.

4. **Pour some Love-Drawing Oil into your hands, rubbing your hands together, and apply the oil to the candle.**

   Work from wick to base to draw love in or to attract a romantic partner. Alternately, apply the oil from base to wick in upward movements to project seductive and alluring energies.

5. **Repeat Step 4 with the honey, washing your hands afterward.**

6. **Spread the powdered herbs on your parchment paper and then roll the candle in the powdered herbs to cover it completely.**

7. **Burn the candle on a firesafe surface to release your intentions.**

Casting Spells for Self-Love and Romance

Love magic begins within. Before you can draw meaningful connections into your life, you must first cultivate love, care, and compassion for yourself. Spells for self-love and romance help align your energy with the frequencies of affection, attraction, and emotional fulfillment. These rituals not only support romantic intentions but also heal the heart, boost confidence, and enhance your natural magnetism. Whether you're seeking to heal from past wounds, open yourself to new relationships, or simply celebrate the beauty of who you are, these spells offer gentle yet powerful ways to reconnect with love in all its forms.

Ritual bath for heart healing

The rose is a sacred symbol of the heart, offering gentle yet profound healing for emotional wounds, heartbreak, grief, and self-worth. This heart-healing bath ritual calls upon the nourishing power of rose and the illuminating energy of the full moon to cleanse and restore your emotional body. This spell is ideal for times of emotional heaviness, after a breakup, or whenever you feel the need to reconnect with the frequency of love. Performed over two nights, this ritual harnesses lunar energy to charge the sacred rose water and invites you to soak in its beauty, releasing pain and welcoming healing.

Make sure that you have a large bowl (preferably glass, ceramic, or wood), 1 dozen fresh red roses, 6 to 12 tea light candles, access to a window, balcony, or outdoor space, a bathtub, and warm water. Then follow these steps to perform a ritual bath for heart healing:

1. **On the night of the full moon, fill your bowl with clean water.**
2. **Gently pluck the petals from all 12 roses, focusing on your intention for heart healing, and add them to the bowl.**
3. **Place the bowl outside under the moonlight or in a windowsill where it can absorb the full moon's energy overnight.**
4. **The next morning, collect the bowl of charged rose water and keep it in a cool, safe place until evening.**
5. **That night, draw a warm bath and pour the rose water and petals into the bathwater.**
6. **Light your tea light candles and place them around the tub to create a sacred, soothing atmosphere.**

7. **Enter the bath, relax fully into the water, and focus on your heart space as you soak.**

   Imagine any emotional pain dissolving and being replaced by love, peace, and self-acceptance. Stay in the bath for as long as you feel called.

8. **When you're ready, thank the roses and Moon for their healing and release the water with gratitude.**

TIP

Repeat this ritual each full moon or whenever your heart needs gentle tending and spiritual restoration.

Spell for attracting a romantic partner

This ritual is a simple and focused way to attract a romantic partner by combining the magic of herbs with spellwork in an intimate setting. This ritual helps you clarify what you want in a partner and open yourself to receiving love. It's a meaningful way to connect with your own desires and invite new romantic energy into your life whether you are looking for a serious partner or just open to having fun!

You need fresh rose petals or other love-drawing herbs, such as jasmine, damiana, or lavender; four red candles, dressed with Love-Drawing Oil and/or herbs, and Love-Drawing Oil and Love-Drawing Incense (see earlier formulas). You also need a firesafe dish, piece of paper, a pen or a pencil, lighter or matches, a bathtub, and towel. Then follow these steps:

1. **Prepare your bath by filling your tub with warm water and adding fresh rose petals or a blend of love-drawing herbs.**

2. **As the herbs steep, speak your intention aloud or whisper softly to the water:**

   > *"Water warm and petals sweet, draw love to me, my heart to meet. With this bath, I cleanse my way, and welcome love with no delay."*

3. **Soak for at least 15 to 20 minutes, letting the water open your heart and wash away emotional residue.**

4. **Dry off and anoint your body with Love-Drawing Oil.**

   Focus on areas of intimacy and vulnerability: your wrists, neck, heart, and inner thighs. Remain naked throughout the rest of the ritual to honor your vulnerability and sensuality.

5. **Create your sacred circle.**

   On the floor or ritual space, form a circle large enough to sit in with the four red candles, placing them at the four directions (north, south, east, and west).

6. **Light the candles and burn your Love-Drawing Incense in a firesafe dish at the edge of the circle.**

7. **Sit in the center of the circle and call in your desire.**

   With incense smoke rising around you, write on your paper all the qualities you seek in a romantic partner. Be specific but emotionally open — for example, "My heart calls for one who is kind, passionate, loyal, and open."

8. **Charge your intention.**

   Once your list is complete, slowly and intimately rub the paper across your body, touching every part yourself with love and longing, as if your ideal partner were tracing those same lines. Feel their presence drawing near. Chant "As I touch, may love be near. Let my lover now appear."

9. **Bless and empower the petition.**

   Hold the paper in the incense smoke, letting it absorb the scent of your desire. Then anoint it with a drop of Love-Drawing Oil. "By Fire, scent, and sacred flame, bring my lover when I name. Let love be drawn to my embrace, with heart and soul and body's grace."

10. **Remain in the circle until the candles have burned most of the way down (or until you intuitively feel the ritual is complete).**

    Meditate, fantasize, chant, or simply bask in the glow of your own magnetism.

11. **Seal the spell.**

    When finished, extinguish the candles gently. Take the anointed paper with you to bed. Sleep naked, with the paper under your pillow to continue attracting love through dreams and the energetic body. "As I sleep, may love draw near. Heart to heart, I call you here."

Honey jar to bring the sweetness of love

Honey jars have been used in folk magic to "sweeten" people, situations, and energies. Traditionally used to soften someone's feelings or create harmony, honey jars are also powerful tools for self-love and attraction. When used to sweeten oneself, the honey jar becomes a vessel for magnetism, helping to radiate charm, affection, and romantic appeal outward into the world. This version of the spell focuses on cultivating a loving aura to draw in love by aligning your energy with warmth, beauty, and desire. As the Moon grows, so, too, will your personal magnetism and the energy you radiate, helping to draw loving, receptive, and harmonious connections into your life.

For this ritual, you will need a glass jar with lid, honey, cinnamon powder, vanilla beans or vanilla bean powder, and dried rose petals. Also make sure you have a piece of paper and red, green, pink, or white candles (one for each Friday). Then follow these steps:

1. **On a small piece of paper, write your full name and the phrase "I radiate the energy of love." Place the name paper into the jar.**
2. **Add honey, a pinch of cinnamon powder, a bit of vanilla bean or powder, and a few dried rose petals to the jar and then seal the jar tightly with the lid.**
3. **Place a red, green, pink, or white candle on top of the closed jar.**

   Use a candle holder or melt the bottom so that it adheres safely to the lid).
4. **Light the candle and allow it to burn all the way down.**

   While the candle is burning, meditate, visualizing your heart center glowing with love and light. Imagine this radiant energy expanding outward in the same color as your candle, surrounding your body and extending into the world.
5. **Repeat this process every Friday for one full moon cycle (roughly 28 days), using a new candle each time.**

Begin the spell on a Friday during a full moon or waxing moon, the ideal time for love and attraction magic.

IN THIS CHAPTER

» Combining intent with action

» Bringing together magical energies

» Speaking desires into existence

Chapter 10
Creating Your Own Herbal Magic

Creating your own spells, rituals, and formulas is what makes magic an art form. By bringing together all the components from herbal ingredients to ritual objects to match your intention and enhance the energies of your magic, you're engaging in a co-creative process with the Universe. While you'll want to follow some basic rules, creating magic is a highly individual process manifesting in different ways for everyone. This creativity is the beauty of magical practice. You can always accomplish a goal in more than one way.

In this chapter, I focus on all the different aspects to consider when creating spells and rituals for any magical goal.

Defining Your Own Ritual

Putting together a ritual is like selecting the perfect meal to make for guests. You may have an idea of what you're going to be cooking, but it's more about the feeling you're trying to evoke. Your intent may be a celebratory dinner, one intended to impress, or a romantic dinner. The occasion, what you're cooking, and who is going to be at the table all come together for a unique occasion.

This scenario is a lot like defining your own rituals. Setting your intention and understanding the desired outcome are the most important elements, but also important is bringing together all the moving parts — the ingredients, tools, timing, and energy — in a way that cohesively expresses the energy and intention of your desired outcome. The outcome of all these things coming together in a synchronous way is a successful spell or ritual.

Not every spell is going to manifest with all the bells and whistles; some manifest more subtly or in different ways than expected. Just like with cooking, magic is an artform. The spaghetti may not taste exactly the same every time, but you still love eating it.

REMEMBER

Writing your own spells and rituals is a highly individualistic process. While magical practice has some basic foundations, this ritual is yours, and it should reflect your own uniqueness.

Setting Your Intention

Setting your intention is what gives your magic a direction to aim at and is the entire point of doing the spell or ritual in the first place. Your *intention* is the entire energy of the working; it's the feeling you're trying to evoke, not just the object of manifestation. Just like an entrée is important, it's only part of the overall dinner; the atmosphere, music, type of cuisine and the outfit you wear all contribute to the dinner's overall vibe.

REMEMBER

When you're considering your magical intention, don't just think of the final outcome, but consider how it will make you feel and what it will take to get there.

For example, if you're writing a spell for prosperity so that you have the extra money to attend a concert you've wanted to see for a long time, imagine yourself at the concert having a great time and remember how that feeling feels. Also, consider how it feels to desire or need what you're working toward. Is it a hunger? A longing? A sense of excitement or desperation? Consider all these emotions, and channel them all into one energy. This is the energy of your intention. An intention is more than just a statement made or a vague idea of a spell's purpose. It's the very lifeblood that feeds it. An intention is the energy that you need to hold onto and focus toward your goal. Tapping into and directing this energy is what is meant when you hear "focus on your intention." It's not just thinking about it, but vibrating with the energy of it.

The tools that you'll use and the type of ritual you'll create will vary based on your intention, and the imagery of the spell will reflect what you're trying to achieve. The objects and imagery of a spell come down to the correspondences that you choose to work with and how you bring those different components together. Simply, a love spell will look like a love spell, and a money spell will look like a money spell. Following the dinner party analogy, the correspondences are what ties everything together, expressing your intention cohesively when all these individual components are brought together the intention of the ritual is communicated. (For a detailed explanation of correspondences, refer to Chapter 2.)

Timing Your Magic

Many different systems relate to magical timing, from the days of the week to the phases of the Moon to astrological timing. You can get complicated and mathematical with the timing of your rituals, but remember that there is no more magical time than now. If the moment calls for a specific spell or ritual, don't feel like you have to wait for the perfect magical time to perform it. That being said, magical timing offers the ability to further hone in on your intention and amplify it by pairing it with the most auspicious times for that particular working.

Astrological magic goes as far to match the phase of the Moon, day of the week, planetary hour, and even specific astrological transits to find the most optimum time for the working. Herb magic, especially the variety performed by folk practitioners, keeps things a little closer to home. In the following sections, we look at some systems of magical timing involving the Moon, the closest magical ally, as well as the days of the week to call upon specific planetary energies.

The Moon is likely the oldest and most reliable magical partner. Humans have watched the monthly journey of the Moon through the night sky, observing its ever changing shape since prehistoric times. By observing the changing Moon, along with the seasons and the events happening on Earth, humans have learned to associate the Moon's journey through the night sky with a variety of symbolic themes. You can see the influence the Moon has on the Earth just by observing the tides and the behavior of animals.

As magical practitioners, you can work in harmony with the Moon's energy at any given time to incorporate its power into your rituals. The simplest way to do so is by working with the phases of the Moon. The lunar cycle is about 29.5 days long from full moon to full moon, giving different energies throughout that cycle. The phase that the Moon is in dictates the type of energy that it's in alignment with.

Here are the moon phases:

- **New moon through waxing moon:** This period of the lunar cycle is when the Moon's light is increasing, making it the appropriate time for starting new things, building energy, inviting in new energy, increasing, attracting, and building.
- **Full moon:** The full moon lends its fully illuminated energy to any working, especially those involving culmination, blessing, healing, sending energy, manifesting, and bringing in extra energy. Full moon energy is available the day before, day of, and day after the full moon.
- **Waning moon:** The waning period begins after the Moon has reached its fullest and begins to grow smaller, losing its light. This time is good for cleansing, removing unwanted influences, diminishing what is undesirable, banishing, setting boundaries, reducing debt, and protecting.
- **Dark moon:** The three days the Moon isn't visible, known as the dark moon, is a time for more personal and private workings and a focus on rest, reflection, meditation, divination, and dreamwork.

For ritual timing Table 10-1 lists the magical correspondences for the days of the week.

TABLE 10-1 Magical Correspondences for Days

Day	Planet	Correspondence
Sunday	Sun	Confidence, success, recognition, creating peace and harmony, manifestation, gaining favors, accumulating wealth, victory, healing, abundance, creativity, purification, cleansing

Day	Planet	Correspondence
Monday	Moon	Care, intuition, healing, reconciliation, psychic ability, dream working, transformation, shadow work, love magic, safe travel
Tuesday	Mars	Courage, boundaries, decisive action, the defeat of enemies, protection, spell-breaking, barrier breakthroughs, creation of magical tools
Wednesday	Mercury	Commerce, messages, deals, spiritual development, influence, communication, business agreements, skill development, divination
Thursday	Jupiter	Growth, patronage, luck, wealth, abundance, social advancement, virility, health, success, goal achievement, spiritual development
Friday	Venus	Attraction, harmony, goodwill, love, romance, beauty, friendship, influence, glamour, enchantment, lust, connection with Nature, self-love, peace, partnership
Saturday	Saturn	Protection, banishment, binding, spirit communication, foundation strengthening, intention setting for new projects, planning

Selecting Your Herbs

After you become familiar with the different qualities of each herb and how those qualities change as you combine them in different ways, you can communicate complex intentions through the ways that you choose to bring those qualities together. Rather than mixing various herbs together without any reasoning behind why certain herbs go into a formula, a certain amount of logic and understanding is involved. Once these concepts become familiar, you'll develop the ability to work with herbs intuitively and create some powerfully personal formulas.

REMEMBER

Personal associations gained through experience are always more powerful than using a pre-existing formula or someone else's recipe. This is your magic, and it should feel personal!

When selecting herbs, think about the following:

- **Herbal energetics:** An herb's energetics and medicinal action will often give clues to an herb's magical uses, which you can apply to magical formulation. For example, an herb that is known for its ability to support heart health would be a good herb to choose for a formula intended for love magic or heart healing.

- **Magical correspondences:** Chapter 2 covers elemental, planetary, and astrological correspondences. These correspondences provide infinite possibilities when it comes to choosing and combining herbal ingredients for your magical intentions. You can use magical correspondences to create layered and nuanced formulas for virtually any type of magical working.
- **Traditional uses:** Traditional uses are the collective accumulated uses of herbs for specific purposes that have been passed on through ancestral, cultural, and spiritual lineages. Traditional uses may vary depending on the source of the information, as herbs may be used for different purposes depending on who is using them. Many of these traditional uses are passed on orally and are often part of initiatory spiritual traditions or cultural belief systems.

In addition, written historical sources have set a precedent for the uses of specific herbs. These written sources, such as Agrippa's *Three Books of Occult Philosophy*, have influenced herbal correspondences for centuries and are accessible to anyone.

WARNING

Avoid appropriating the herbal traditions of cultures and traditions that you're not part of. Look for ways to work with herbs in ways that are respectful of the traditions that maintain this sacred knowledge.

Listening to Your Intuition

By forming relationships with your plant allies and becoming familiar with them on an individual basis, you can begin to unlock the language that plants use to communicate.

Through meditation, regular contact, and practice, you can begin to tap into your own intuition when it comes to an herb's magical uses. Working with herb's intuitively is a highly individual process. While two people may come to similar conclusions, when it comes to an herb's potential magical uses, remember that not everyone will have the exact same uses for a particular herb.

Intuitive herbalism can draw from personal experiences, such as childhood memories or one's direct sensory experience of a particular herb. For example, if you don't like the smell of patchouli, you're probably not going to add it to formulas for attracting love or abundance.

Choosing the Right Formula

You have a variety of different herbal formulas and techniques to choose from when it comes to spellwork. These formulas make use of herbal ingredients in different ways that are appropriate for different types of workings and scenarios. For example, you may not be able to burn incense in your office at work, but you can discreetly use herbal powders instead. Many rituals will make use of more than one formula or technique. The formulas are vehicles to carry the energy and vibration of the herbal ingredients to achieve their desired effects. Table 10-2 lists the different formulas and their uses.

TABLE 10-2 Herbal Formulas and Techniques

Formula	Technique
Incense	Charge, cleanse, or impart influence over an object or an area. Changing environmental vibrations to correspond with ritual purposes. Offerings to spirits.
Powders	Sprinkling and scattering powders. Use to dust charm bags or sprinkle over objects, places, or people to impart a desired influence or effect. Finely powdered herbs and other ingredients often mixed with talc powder. Can also be added to oils, incense, or other formulas.
Washes and baths	A strong herbal mixture steeped in water added to floor cleaning solutions or ritual baths for cleansing, uncrossing, attracting business, and blessing homes. Herbal infusions and oils can be added to baths for a wide variety of ritual purposes.
Anointing oils	Used in spellwork to anoint candles, ritual tools, feed charm bags, and call forth a desired influence when used on the body. Made from dried herbs infused into an oil like grapeseed, sweet almond, or jojoba. Essential oils are also utilized either in combination or on their own to create different oils.

(continued)

TABLE 10-2 *(continued)*

Formula	Technique
Candle magic	Almost always part of spellwork. Contain a representation of all four elements. Can incorporate color correspondence and figure magic and create geometric forms conducive to rituals through their symbolism. Position the candles in ways that are in sympathy to the ritual and its desired effect. Often represent the relationship between the players and/or situation.

Gathering Ritual Objects

The ritual objects employed in herbal magic include the nonherbal tools that are part of the ritual. These tools take the form of a variety of different objects that are often the containers and anchors of the energy raised in the ritual. Oftentimes, these items are natural objects, such as special stones, but sometimes they're also human-made, including pieces of jewelry, or ritual tools like bells, cauldrons, and candles.

Selecting ritual objects is done on a case-by-case basis, depending on the type of spell or ritual you're performing. Some more universal ritual objects like candles (refer to Table 10-2) will be present in many of your rituals, while other objects will be specifically unique to one ritual alone.

You can charge the ritual objects with magical energy by using herbal formulas, such as anointing oils and incense blends, to carry a specific type of energy. You can recharge and use these objects on a long-term basis to achieve the desired outcome of your spell's intention.

Animal bones

Because bones were once part of a living thing, they're especially sacred and important in magical traditions around the world. Bones easily absorb the energies of herbal formulas when incorporated into rituals because they once contained the energy or spirit of a living being. Just as plant spirits have different magical qualities, animal spirits do, too, and you may choose a bone from a specific animal based on its spiritual qualities.

TIP

When sourcing bones, use only those that come from ethical suppliers. Better yet, use only those that you find personally out in nature. You will form a deeper magical connection to the bones that you find yourself compared to those that you purchase from someone else.

REMEMBER

When working with any spirit — plant, animal, or otherwise — it's of absolute importance to approach that spirit with respect and reverence. Making an offering of incense smoke or a special herbal powder or pouring some water on the Earth where you find these objects is a simple way of thanking the spirit for the gift it has given you.

Wood

Trees are just big plants, and, like plants, they each have their own unique magical correspondences depending on the type of tree. Collecting twigs and branches from trees to use in spellwork is a practice present in many magical traditions. You can make them into wands and other ritual tools, hang them over doorways, or incorporate them into wreaths for a variety of magical purposes. Some practitioners prefer to use only pieces of the tree that were naturally shed versus cut-off parts from a living tree. This choice is up to your personal preference. Either way, ask the tree for its permission before taking any part of it and leave some kind of offering in return.

TIP

Only leave offerings that are made from natural materials, biodegradable, and not damaging to the tree or the environment.

Stones and crystals

The mineral kingdom is the oldest kingdom on the planet, comprised of stones, minerals, and crystals that have been around for millions of years. These ancient spirits have been used for their magical properties since humans first learned how to make stone tools.

Stones and crystals are unique because while they each have their own magical correspondences, they're also easy to charge with the energy of one's own intention — just like a computer chip that contains minerals like silicon and quartz is used to hold information.

You can find countless beautiful crystals and minerals, ranging from affordable to prohibitively expensive, in metaphysical shops. While crystals are awesome and pretty to look at, you can use regular stones in magic as well.

You can carry stones and crystals as charms, place them around the home, or use them to decorate an altar space.

Ritual tools

Ritual tools include bowls, bottles, incense burners, spoons, knives, and more. Some ritual tools are simply utilitarian, while others have specific symbolic associations depending on different magical traditions.

REMEMBER

You may choose to reserve certain objects specifically for magical uses. These objects will build up an energetic charge over time through repeated use, but magic is everywhere, and you can find it even in your day-to-day activities. Speaking a blessing of health and abundance over a pot of chili that you have made for your loved ones is just as much a spell as brewing a potion made of witchy ingredients in an actual cauldron.

Writing Petitions and Incantations

Language is a powerful thing. It's sacred. It's what sets humans apart from other creatures and allows communication of complex concepts and ideas. Language is the power to create. A spell or incantation implies the use of language through writing or the spoken word to direct your intentions and create change in the world around you.

Petitions

A *petition* is an expression of your intention for the outcome of your spell or ritual in written format, typically written in the present tense — for example, "I have the job of my dreams that meets all of my needs."

Petitions are brief statements or requests directed toward a spiritual power, such as an ancestor, deity, or plant spirit or to the Universe in general. You can burn petition papers to release their energies or anoint them with the appropriate ritual oils. You can keep them on your person or add them to charm bags.

TIP

When writing petition papers, focus on your intention, holding it in mind the entire time. You can write the petition more than once, covering the entire piece of paper if you choose to further focus your intention.

Incantations

Spells or *incantations* are the words that you speak when performing magic. Incantations are the words that deliver your intention to the spirit world, awaken the magic in your rituals, and send your energy to affect change in the world around you.

Your incantations can be simple or complex. They're typically repeated over and over again during a ritual to raise energy and to alter your consciousness to achieve a sacred state of mind. To make this process more effective, incantations often rhyme, but they do not have to.

Incantations are typically spoken aloud, but they don't have to be. They can be whispered or shouted, but are also just as effective if you say them internally. Not everyone feels comfortable speaking incantations aloud. It is all about how you focus the mind and direct energy. The forces that you work with in magic hear your words whether they're spoken out loud or silently.

REMEMBER

When incorporating spells or incantations into your herb magic, the most important thing is that the outcome of your intention is expressed clearly. Expressing your intention will often be supported by naming the effects of the herbs you're working with to get all the energies that you are bringing together working on the same goal. An example of an incantation looks something like this:

> "By Moon's white light, and gentle peace. With this rose all pain release.
>
> In soothing water, and salt of earth. My heart be healed in love rebirth."

This example of a simple spell could be recited over a ritual bath for heart-healing working with the magic of rose. You don't necessarily have to name the plants specifically; simply referring to their qualities and how they support the outcome of your intention is sufficient. You can keep your incantations short like this one or, if you're a gifted poet, write something much longer. The important thing is that it resonates with you and the focus of your work.

Partnering with Nature

IN THIS PART . . .

Tend a magical herb garden.

Honor the land and its spirits.

IN THIS CHAPTER

» Deciding what to grow

» Tapping in to the energy of the Moon

» Working with seasonal cycles

Chapter 11
Growing a Magical Herb Garden

Any plant person will tell you that growing things is a magical, spiritual, and healing practice, whether you intend it to be or not! However, one thing that I always like to remind people is that you don't have to have a green thumb to practice herbal magic. You don't have to grow a single plant if you don't want to! You can connect with the magic of the green world in many ways, and if growing things is not your forte or not possible for you, don't let it discourage you from working with plants in other ways!

With that being said, in this chapter, I explore some ways you can incorporate magical gardening into your everyday life.

Choosing Which Herbs to Grow

Nothing is worse than the feeling of watching a bunch of plants die around you (trust me), so I take a very no-nonsense approach when it comes to growing things: grow what grows best for you (and if it doesn't, move on to something else!).

PLANTING WITH INTENTION

When growing herbs for magical uses, it always helps to ritualize the process. This may include planting certain herbs on the appropriate day of the week, working with moon phases, leaving offerings to the land, and communicating your intentions to the plants as you are planting them or bringing them into your home.

The nice thing about most herbs — whether used for culinary, medicinal, or magical purposes — is that they're relatively easy to care for. They're happy to grow in most soil conditions and aren't going to wither and die if you miss watering them for a day. Most herbs are as happy to grow in a kitchen window as they are in an outdoor garden. While there is something special about tending to an outdoor herb garden, it's not always possible, and maintaining a few small pots indoors can be just as rewarding.

When it comes to choosing what herbs to grow, choose whichever herbs speak to you. You don't have to grow rare herbs from faraway places, but can experience the magic of plants that grow locally to you. There is no better way to connect with a plant spirit than tending to it and being part of its life cycle.

You may choose to start herbs from seed, but you can also find a wide variety of herbs at your local garden store that are already started.

You may also choose to dedicate certain parts of your garden to herbs with specific magical correspondences, such as cultivating a garden of love-drawing herbs or keeping plants associated with prosperity in the home. The sky is the limit when it comes to how you may choose to construct your magical herb gardens. You may even choose to model yours after traditional monastery or physic gardens, which also provide a great place for outdoor meditation.

Planting with the Moon

Planting herbs in alignment with the Moon's phases is an ancient agricultural and magical practice rooted in the belief that the Moon's energy influences the growth and vitality of plants. Just as the Moon affects the tides, it is believed to affect the movement of water within the soil and the water within plants. By understanding and working with these lunar rhythms, herbalists and gardeners can cultivate herbs in harmony with nature's cycles, enhancing both their physical growth and their magical potency. Each phase of the Moon carries a distinct energy that can be harnessed for specific actions from germination and growth to harvesting and rest.

TIP

You can get more information on planting with the Moon and other techniques by picking up a copy of *The Farmer's Almanac*, which has been in print since 1792!

New moon

The new moon, which occurs when the first sliver of light is visible, is a time of beginnings, renewal, and setting intentions. In the garden, this phase is ideal for planting seeds of herbs that produce their magic or medicine above the ground, including annuals and leafy herbs like basil, mint, and parsley. The energy of the waxing moon that follows supports germination and upward growth, making it the perfect time to start new projects, plant new intentions, and infuse the soil with purpose. The new moon is also a good time to bless your garden tools, dedicate your growing space, and focus on what you want to cultivate both physically and spiritually.

Waxing moon

As the Moon moves into the First Quarter and Waxing Gibbous phases, its growing light corresponds to expansion, vitality, and strength. Herbs planted during this period tend to grow robustly, drawing upon the Moon's increasing energy. The waxing moon is an excellent time to transplant seedlings, fertilize, or perform spells for abundance, healing, and manifestation. Plants associated with growth, prosperity, and attraction thrive under this waxing influence.

Full moon

The full moon represents culmination, power, and illumination. The lunar pull is strongest, and so is the plant's internal flow of energy and moisture. The full moon is the best time to harvest herbs whose potency lies in their flowers, leaves, or essential oils. The full moon is also an ideal time to gather herbs for magical purposes as the moonlight infuses them with heightened spiritual energy. Many herbalists use this time to infuse dried herbs, tinctures, or oils with the Moon's power by exposing them to the light of the full moon.

Waning moon

Following the full moon, the waning moon begins a phase of release, reflection, and inward energy as the Moon decreases in light. The waning moon is the time to prune, compost, and focus on root development. Herbs with strong underground medicine, such as dandelion, valerian, and burdock, are best planted or harvested now, as the Moon's waning light draws energy down into the soil. Spiritually, this phase supports releasing what no longer serves and preparing for new cycles of growth. Working in rhythm with the waning moon helps bring closure and grounding to both garden and spirit.

Dark moon

The dark moon occurs when the Moon is not visible in the sky. It's a period of rest and regeneration and is typically not a time for planting. Traditionally, root vegetables would have been planted during the dark moon.

Working with the Seasons

Herbal practitioners are very in tune with the four seasons, just like the plants that we work with. Depending on where you live, your seasons may be slightly different — for example, if you live somewhere that is warm year-round, you may not know what a cold, snowy winter feels like. Everywhere has their own unique seasons as the Earth makes its journey around the Sun. It is the Sun and the Earth's position in relation to one another that creates the seasons, and most places (unless you live on the equator) experience changes in the Sun's angle and the length of day and night throughout the year. You will notice that even when grown indoors, plants will respond to the seasonal cycles in their own way.

Spring

For the herbal practitioner, spring is one of the most exciting times. It is when we get to start our seeds and plant the first plants outdoors. It is a time of growth, renewal, and excitement after the Sun returns to the world after a long, dark winter. Spring is the time when we get to plan our gardens and set our intentions for what we want to grow and cultivate in our lives for the rest of the year.

Summer

Summer is the time when plants are in peak season, and everything is in flower. Fresh flowers play a major role in Midsummer celebrations around the world. Summer is the time when the Sun is at its strongest, imbuing the green realm with life and vitality. It was traditionally a time when herbs would be harvested for medicinal and magical purposes, as they were considered to be at their highest potency when in flower. Summer is a time of celebration of the abundance that comes from the natural world.

Fall

Fall is such a magical time, but it is also bittersweet for the herbal practitioner because it signals the beginning of the end of the growing season. It is when we harvest fruits, vegetables, and the last of the herbs before the first frost begins to arrive. Fall is a time to give thanks for all that has been reaped during the growing season. Although winter is coming, fall is the time when you really get to enjoy everything that you've worked for over the spring and summer.

Winter

As the days grow shorter and the cold sets in, the green realm signals that it's time to rest. Perennials retreat underground into to their roots for the winter, and the annuals have shed their seeds for the next season. Winter is the time for drying the harvested herbs, storing seeds, and making medicines and magic to carry you through the winter months. It is also the time to start planning the garden for next year, because spring always seems to arrive so quickly!

Indoor/City Gardening

Not everyone is blessed with sprawling acres of land on which they can create their gardens, and country life is not everyone's cup of tea either (because that's a lot of grass to mow!). That doesn't mean that you can't have a magical terrace garden on your patio, or have one of the most amazing house plant collections on the block!

Indoor gardening is a great way to bring nature into our living spaces, and it also improves the quality of the indoor space as well both physically and energetically. Indoor plants help to purify the air, filter toxins and keep the energy of the space vibrant and alive. Some of my favorite plants to grow indoors that are easy to take care of include plants such as: lavender, mint, and basil. These are great if you don't have a green thumb, or if your schedule is to hectic to keep a Boston fern alive.

City gardening may have different obstacles to overcome than country gardening, but it is a powerful act of resistance and reclamation of our connection to Nature in the face of ever increasing urbanization of modern society. Even a small outdoor space can provide a much needed sense of peace and grounding, reminding us that while we may live in the city we are still part of Nature.

IN THIS CHAPTER

» Reconnecting with Nature

» Honoring what is sacred

Chapter 12
Protecting the Environment

As practitioners of herbal magic, you have a responsibility to the Earth and the health of the environment — not only because the earth is the very source of your herbal allies, but because you are very much a part of Nature. You can't practice herbal magic and ignore the environmental issues of today and the role that humans have played in creating and exacerbating those issues. In this chapter, I discuss the spiritual beliefs and practical approaches to re-evaluate your understanding of and your interactions with the land. Through these practices, you can become a better practitioner and better person.

Believing Everything Has a Spirit: Animism

Animism is the belief that everything has a spirit. It is the oldest form of human spirituality. The belief in animism can be held regardless of the spiritual tradition you belong to. Whether you conceptualize the animating force as spirit, consciousness, or a divine spark, animism is the recognition of the sacredness of all things. Animism also reminds you of your own sacredness and your connection to Nature. It is through this connection that herbal practitioners are able to work their magic.

Long before the rise of organized religion, ancient peoples perceived the world as alive, interconnected, and responsive. Every rock, river, star, and plant were understood to be ensouled, animated by an inner essence or spirit. Early cultures across the globe lived in harmony with this worldview, developing rituals and traditions that honored the spirits of place and the sacred presence dwelling within Nature itself.

In animism, the human and the natural world aren't separated. Instead, all beings exist within a network of reciprocity and respect. This understanding forms the philosophical and spiritual foundation of herbal magic. To the animist practitioner, herbs aren't merely tools or ingredients; they're living allies with distinct personalities, voices, and powers. Each plant spirit holds its own wisdom, healing vibration, and unique magical signature. When you engage in herbal magic through an animistic lens, you're entering into a relationship, asking for permission, giving offerings, and co-creating with the consciousness of the plant rather than simply using it.

Historically, the animistic beliefs of shamanism shaped the practices of cunning folk, wise women, and herbal healers. Shamanism is humanity's oldest belief system with animism at its core. It is still practiced by Indigenous people around the world, each with its own unique cosmology.

In the practice of herbal magic today, animism remains central. When crafting a charm, blending an oil, or brewing a tea, the practitioner invokes the spirit of the herb and aligns with its energy. For example, an herbal practitioner may call upon rosemary for protection and memory, while they may invite mugwort to open psychic sight. By forming a respectful bond with each plant ally, the magician strengthens the efficacy of their workings. The herb's spirit responds to intention, gratitude, and sincerity qualities that transform simple botanical work into living magic.

Ultimately, animism restores the sacred dialogue between humans and Nature. It reminds herbal practitioners that the plants they work with aren't inert substances, but conscious beings offering their wisdom and power. In herbal magic, this worldview fosters humility, reciprocity, and a sense of wonder — a recognition that the spirits of the green world are teachers, healers, and companions. Through animism, you rediscover the living heartbeat of the Earth and the sacred partnership that has existed since the dawn of humanity — the communion between people and plants, between spirit and matter — and without this understanding, herbal magic is not possible.

Earth as a Living System: Spiritual Ecology

Animistic belief informs the concept of spiritual ecology. *Spiritual ecology* is a philosophy and practice that recognizes the Earth as a living, sacred system in which all beings are interconnected, interdependent, and infused with spirit. Spiritual ecology merges ecological awareness with spiritual consciousness, understanding that the environmental crises of the modern age are not only physical or political but deeply spiritual in Nature. This worldview teaches that when humanity forgets its sacred relationship with the Earth, imbalance and suffering arise. By restoring reverence and reciprocity toward the natural world, spiritual ecology invites healing not only for the planet but for the human soul as well.

When applied to the practice of herbal magic, spiritual ecology becomes an act of conscious partnership. It reminds you that every leaf, root, and seed is part of a greater living web. Plants aren't merely resources for your use, but intelligent, sentient beings with whom you share relationship and responsibility. Approaching magic from this perspective transforms the way herbal practitioners gather and work with materials. Before harvesting, they may offer prayers, water, song, or gratitude, recognizing that they're taking part in a living cycle of sacred reciprocity.

Incorporating spiritual ecology into one's practice means cultivating awareness of the systems that sustain life. It asks you to honor the origins of your herbs and materials by understanding where they come from, how they were grown, and whether they were harvested ethically. Growing your own herbs, supporting sustainable sources, or foraging with reverence are tangible expressions of this philosophy. On a deeper level, it means aligning your magical practice with the rhythms of the land following the seasons, lunar cycles, and weather patterns and recognizing that the spirit of place has a voice in your work.

Practicing magic consciously through the lens of spiritual ecology also invites self-reflection and mindfulness. It encourages you to ask whether your workings are in harmony with the greater good and whether they bring balance, healing, and connection rather than control or harm. You can begin each ritual by acknowledging the land spirits, ancestors, and elements, asking for permission, and offering gratitude. Even simple acts, such as pouring libations of water, composting ritual remains, or tending to a small garden, can become expressions of devotion and ecological stewardship.

Ultimately, spiritual ecology is about remembering that your magic and spirituality aren't separate from the Earth but extensions of it. It teaches that true power comes not from domination, but from harmony and reverence. When you weave spiritual ecology into your herbal and magical practice, you act as caretakers as well as creators, working in balance with the natural world. In doing so, you restore the sacred covenant between humanity and the living Earth, ensuring that your magic nourishes not only yourself but the web of life that sustains all beings.

Avoiding Cultural Appropriation

Cultural appropriation within spiritual and herbal traditions occurs when sacred practices, symbols, or plant medicines are taken from their original cultural context without proper understanding, permission, or respect. Cultural appropriation often happens when people outside of a culture adopt its spiritual or healing traditions for aesthetic, commercial, or personal reasons while disregarding their historical, religious, and ancestral significance. It can manifest as using Indigenous, African, or Eastern plants and rituals without acknowledging their origins or the communities that preserved this wisdom despite colonization and persecution. Such misuse can perpetuate harm, erasing cultural identity and commodifying what is sacred, reducing living traditions to marketable trends.

To engage respectfully with herbal and spiritual traditions, practitioners must cultivate reverence, humility, and education. This means learning about the cultural and historical context of the plants and rituals you're using and recognizing that many of these traditions have survived centuries of exploitation and suppression. Instead of adopting ceremonies, prayers, or names that belong to living Indigenous or diasporic traditions, practitioners can focus on building authentic relationships with the plants available in their own regions and lineages. Honoring cultural boundaries and giving credit to the people and lands from which these practices originate is a powerful act of respect. Supporting teachers, healers, and authors from those cultures — and paying them for their knowledge — helps ensure that wisdom is shared ethically and that those communities retain agency over their heritage.

Colonization has deeply shaped the global trade and perception of plants, transforming sacred medicines into commodities. Herbs like sage, palo santo, ayahuasca, and cacao have been overharvested and commercialized for profit, often to the detriment of the ecosystems and Indigenous communities who stewarded them. This commodification not only damages the environment but also strips these plants of their spiritual context, turning sacred allies into consumer goods. Recognizing this legacy means confronting how colonial systems have historically extracted both natural resources and cultural knowledge without consent or reciprocity.

To decolonize your herbal practice is to re-establish relationship, accountability, and reciprocity. This begins by questioning where your materials come from and who benefits from their use. It may mean choosing locally grown herbs or cultivating your own, rather than relying on overharvested or culturally restricted plants. A decolonized practice also invites practitioners to connect with their own ancestral herbal traditions, rediscovering the healing plants and customs of their heritage, rather than borrowing from cultures still struggling to protect theirs.

Using Sustainable Practices

Sustainable practices in herbalism refer to methods of growing, harvesting, and using plants in ways that protect and preserve both the environment and the natural world's spiritual integrity. This means gathering herbs mindfully, taking only what is needed, respecting seasonal cycles, and ensuring that wild plant populations remain healthy and abundant for future generations.

It also includes supporting local growers, using organic or regenerative methods, and honoring the ecosystems that nurture the plants practitioners rely on.

From a spiritual perspective, sustainability is an act of reverence and reciprocity, acknowledging that plants are not resources to be consumed but sacred beings to be cared for in partnership. By practicing herbalism sustainably, herbal practitioners honor the spirit of the Earth, maintaining balance within the web of life and affirming their role as stewards rather than exploiters of Nature's gifts.

Eco-friendly harvesting is the practice of gathering plants in a way that minimizes harm to the environment and ensures the continued vitality of plant populations.

Bioregionalism in herbalism is the practice of working primarily with the plants, materials, and ecosystems native to your own local region.

Community herbalism programs are a powerful way to give back to the local community while deepening your connection to the land and to others who share a passion for plant medicine. These programs often provide free or low-cost herbal education, wellness support, and accessible remedies made from locally sourced plants, making herbal medicine more accessible.

ECO-FRIENDLY GUIDELINES

When harvesting, practitioners should take only from abundant stands, leaving enough behind for the plant to regenerate and for wildlife that depend on it. They should never uproot entire populations and always avoid harvesting rare or endangered species.

When harvesting, they should use clean, sharp tools to make precise cuts and leave the roots intact when possible so that the plant can continue growing. Lastly, they should harvest during the proper season when the plant's energy is at its peak for the intended use.

4 The Part of Tens

IN THIS PART . . .

Take your magic to the next level.

Create a home for your herbs.

IN THIS CHAPTER

» Meeting ten powerful plant allies

» Discovering the diverse ways that herbs are employed in magic

Chapter 13
Ten Herbs to Enhance Your Magic

This chapter covers ten accessible and versatile herbs that are important to magical practices and spiritual traditions around the world. They enjoy working with humans and are great allies for beginning to establish your relationship with the plant kingdom.

Basil

Planetary and elemental correspondence: Venus and Fire. Basil (*Ocimum basilicum*) has long been revered as one of the most sacred and versatile herbs in both culinary and magical traditions. Native to India and other tropical regions of Asia, basil has been cultivated for more than 5,000 years and is regarded as a sacred plant in many ancient cultures.

In folklore, basil has been used for both love and protection. In folk magic, basil is used to bring peace and fidelity between lovers, soothe tempers, and encourage affection. Sprinkling basil around the home is said to ensure domestic harmony and ward away harmful influences. Herbal practitioners often add basil to love potions or use it in ritual baths to attract romance and strengthen emotional bonds. As an herb of fidelity magic, basil protects relationships from jealousy and deceit, ensuring loyalty between partners. The scent of basil, especially when infused into oils or incorporated into food, stirs passion and heightens sensual awareness, making it a potent aphrodisiac and enhancer of sexual expression.

Magically, basil is also an herb of prosperity and success. Herbal practitioners commonly use basil in spells to attract wealth, draw in customers, and bring good fortune in business matters. Placing basil near the entrance of a shop or home is said to invite abundance while repelling negative energies. Its association with the element of Fire infuses it with vibrant life force energy, stimulating personal power, confidence, and eloquence. For glamour and influence, practitioners can add basil to ritual oils and incense to strengthen personal magnetism.

Medicinally, basil is rich in essential oils, such as linalool, eugenol, and methyl chavicol, which give it its distinctive aroma and therapeutic qualities. It has antibacterial, anti-inflammatory, and digestive properties and is traditionally used to treat headaches, colds, and digestive complaints. In aromatherapy, basil's scent clears the mind, sharpens concentration, and uplifts the spirit, making it an excellent ally for meditation, dream work, and mental clarity. Its fragrance helps to dispel mental fog and fatigue while grounding the senses in calm awareness.

Basil's high spiritual vibration also makes it suitable for offerings to deities of love and fertility, such as Venus, Aphrodite, and Lakshmi. In ancestor veneration and rites honoring the dead, basil is used to purify sacred spaces and aid the soul's transition. It promotes spiritual growth, peace, and happiness, linking the heart and higher mind.

Bay Laurel

Planetary and elemental correspondence: Sun and Fire. Bay laurel (*Laurus nobilis*), also known simply as laurel (where bay leaves come from), has been a sacred symbol of triumph, wisdom, and protection since ancient times. Native to the Mediterranean region, bay was deeply woven into Greek and Roman culture, where it was associated with Apollo, god of the Sun, music, healing, and prophecy.

TIP

A popular practice is to write wishes and desires on dried bay leaves and burn them to send your intentions out into the universe and tap into the powerful magic of bay laurel.

In folklore and magical practice, bay laurel is an herb of strength, purification, and protection. It was burned in ancient temples to cleanse and sanctify the space, and its leaves were placed above doorways to guard against lightning, disease, and malevolent spirits. In spellwork, bay is used to drive away negativity and restore spiritual balance. Carrying or wearing a bay leaf brings courage and confidence in times of challenge. It can also be included in healing rituals to strengthen the body's natural vitality and speed recovery. Because of its connection to the Sun and the element of Fire, bay laurel radiates warmth, renewal, and vitality empowering both body and spirit.

Bay laurel is equally valued in spells of prosperity, manifestation, and success. A traditional form of wishing magic involves writing one's desire on a dried bay leaf and burning it while focusing on the outcome. The smoke carries the wish to the spirit world. Herbal practitioners can add bay laurel to prosperity incense, charm bags, and ritual oils to attract abundance, enhance self-confidence, and ensure victory in endeavors. Bay laurel is particularly effective in legal or competitive situations; carrying a bay leaf in the pocket or anointing oneself with bay oil before a court case or business negotiation is said to bring success and favorable outcomes.

Medicinally, bay laurel contains essential oils rich in linalool and eugenol, giving it antiseptic, anti-inflammatory, and analgesic properties. Traditionally, herbal practitioners use the leaves and oil to treat muscle cramps, arthritis, rheumatism, and general pain relief. In aromatherapy, bay essential oil has a warm, spicy scent that relaxes the body and clears the mind. It helps relieve stress, anxiety, and nervous tension, creating a sense of clarity, security, and grounded peace. The fragrance also stimulates and relaxes the mind, making bay invaluable for meditation, prophecy, and dream work.

Placed beneath the pillow, its leaves can enhance psychic ability and invite prophetic dreams. Burned as incense, it purifies the atmosphere and awakens intuition. In both ancient and modern practice, bay laurel remains a symbol of victory, success, and inspiration.

Cinquefoil

Planetary and elemental correspondence: Jupiter and Earth. Cinquefoil (*Potentilla* spp.), also known as five-finger grass or tormentil, is a humble yet powerful herb steeped in centuries of magical and medicinal tradition. The plant's five-lobed leaves resemble the shape of a human hand, which inspired the belief that it could aid in "anything the five fingers can do." Native to Europe and naturalized throughout North America, cinquefoil was widely used in medieval herbalism for its healing and protective qualities, and it frequently appeared in old charms and amulets for good fortune and success.

In folklore, cinquefoil was considered an herb of power, luck, and divine favor. It was carried to attract love, money, health, protection, and wisdom (the five blessings of life) and worn to gain influence and victory.

During the Middle Ages, cinquefoil was often embroidered onto garments and banners for protection and success in battle. Its strong association with the human hand linked it to the ability to grasp or attract one's desires, making it a cornerstone of folk magic for attraction and manifestation.

Magically, cinquefoil is a remarkably versatile herb, lending power and success to nearly any spell. It is used in workings for love, prosperity, health, power, wisdom, and attraction. Because of its connection to the human hand, it helps to "draw" or "grasp" opportunities, guiding the practitioner toward tangible results. In money and success spells, cinquefoil expands one's sphere of influence and brings favor from those in positions of authority, aligning beautifully with the expansive energy of Jupiter. Cinquefoil is often viewed as a higher octave of Venus, combining the powers of attraction, charm, and eloquence with the benevolence and prosperity of Jupiter. Added to ritual oils, charm bags, or herbal blends, cinquefoil enhances the intention of the entire formula, ensuring that the magic manifests harmoniously and effectively.

Medicinally, cinquefoil is rich in tannins, flavonoids, and essential oils, giving it strong astringent, anti-inflammatory, and antiseptic properties. Traditionally, it was used to treat diarrhea, mouth and throat inflammation, wounds, and skin irritations. The root, known as tormentil, was often included in healing balms and decoctions for its soothing and restorative effects. In modern herbal practice, it is still valued for strengthening tissues and reducing inflammation.

Energetically, cinquefoil carries a bright, uplifting vibration that harmonizes with Jupiter and the element of Earth, offering both grounding and growth. It strengthens confidence, protects from jealousy and envy, and deflects negativity that could hinder one's success. Its aroma, though mild, is subtly invigorating and can be incorporated into incense or sachets to support spells for manifestation and protection. In essence, cinquefoil is an herb of empowerment helping the practitioner to grasp opportunity, repel harm, and ensure that all endeavors come to full and fruitful completion.

Dandelion

Planetary and elemental correspondence: Jupiter and Air/Earth. Dandelion (*Taraxacum officinale*) is one of the most familiar and underestimated plants in the world. Often dismissed as a weed, dandelion is revered in herbalism and folk magic as a plant of extraordinary healing power. Native to Eurasia but now found across the globe, dandelion has been used for centuries in both food and medicine. In traditional Chinese and Indigenous American medicine, it is valued for treating digestive disorders, liver ailments, and inflammation. Despite its humble appearance, every part of the plant from flower to root possesses potent medicinal and magical properties.

In folklore, dandelion holds a special place as a plant of wishes, transformation, and resilience. Its golden flower mirrors the Sun's warmth and vitality, while its airy, globe-like seed head carries its magic and medicine far and wide. Many people share the childhood memory of blowing on a dandelion puff to make a wish, sending their hopes on the wind. This custom connects dandelion to the element of Air, the realm of communication, inspiration, and thought. Its seeds travel great distances, carried effortlessly by the breeze, symbolizing the spreading of ideas and the fulfillment of desire, making dandelion a natural ally in manifestation and wishing magic.

Yet beneath dandelion's light and airy nature lies a deep, grounding strength. Dandelion's roots are thick, tenacious, and deeply embedded in the Earth, granting it a powerful connection to stability, nourishment, and endurance. Because of this duality of Air above and Earth below, dandelion bridges the two realms. Dandelion stands as a link between the material and spiritual worlds, making it an ideal herb for spirit communication, ancestral work, and connection to the Otherworld. Dandelion is also used in divinatory practices; drinking dandelion tea before divination or meditation is said to enhance psychic ability and open intuitive channels. Its presence on the altar can help strengthen communication with spirits or deities, especially when seeking clarity or guidance.

Medicinally, dandelion is a powerhouse of nutrients and restorative compounds. It contains vitamins A, C, and K, as well as minerals like calcium, iron, potassium, and magnesium. Its roots are rich in inulin, a prebiotic fiber that supports gut health, while its bitter constituents stimulate bile production and aid digestion. Herbalists use dandelion as a liver tonic, blood purifier, and detoxifier, helping the body eliminate waste and restore vitality. Both medicinally and magically, dandelion is a cleansing herb, clearing stagnation, removing toxins, and purifying both body and spirit.

In magic, dandelion's essence embodies resilience, transformation, and renewal. Herbal practitioners can use dandelion to banish negativity, strengthen determination, and promote spiritual growth. Whether blown into the wind as a wish, brewed into a tea for insight, or burned as an offering in summoning or purification rites, dandelion is a potent and compassionate ally. Rooted in Earth yet lifted by Air, it teaches balance between what is above and what is below.

Juniper

Planetary and elemental correspondence: Saturn and Earth/Fire. Juniper (*Juniperus communis*) is an evergreen native to Europe, Asia, and North America, long valued for its protective and purifying powers. Its sharp, aromatic needles and blue berries have played an important role in folk medicine, ritual, and magic since ancient times. The Romans burned juniper as incense in their temples and used it as a fumigant for cleansing sacred spaces. In medieval Europe, it was hung over doors and windows to keep out disease and evil spirits, while in Indigenous American traditions, juniper was burned in purification ceremonies and used to bless the home. Its strong association with fire and smoke marks juniper as a plant of transformation, bridging the earthly and spiritual realms.

In folklore, juniper has long been a plant of protection and potency. It was believed to repel ghosts, demons, and the evil eye, and its branches were burned to drive away sickness and misfortune. At the same time, juniper's berries were offered to spirits and ancestors, reflecting its connection to both life and death, the physical realm and the otherworld. This link to the Underworld makes juniper an important plant for those who work with the spirits of the dead, providing both protection and a bridge for communication.

Magically, juniper is a multipurpose ally. Herbal practitioners use juniper for breaking hexes and curses, banishing negativity, enhancing psychic ability, and promoting love, luck, and health. Its dual association with the elements of Earth and Fire speaks to its nature, grounding yet energizing, protecting and purifying. The woody, earthy scent of juniper's branches connects one to stability and endurance, while the bright, resinous aroma of its berries ignites passion, courage, and willpower. Burning juniper as incense purifies the air and drives out unwanted energies, making it one of the best herbs for spiritual and energetic cleansing. Juniper berries may be carried as charms for good fortune, especially in romantic pursuits, or added to magical formulas to draw in love and positive influence.

Medicinally, juniper has long been used for its antiseptic and stimulating properties. The berries contain volatile oils rich in terpenes, such as alpha-pinene, sabinene, and myrcene, which give juniper its distinctive pine-like fragrance. Juniper is a warming herb that increases circulation, eases pain, and helps the body fight infection. Juniper tea and tinctures have traditionally been used as diuretics to flush toxins and treat urinary tract infections. When added to baths or steam treatments, juniper stimulates sweating, clears the lungs, and cleanses the skin.

In aromatherapy, juniper essential oil is known for its cleansing, calming, and restorative qualities. Its scent helps clear mental fog, ease anxiety, and soothe an overstressed nervous system. Diffused or added to ritual baths, it promotes clarity, renewal, and inner peace. Whether burned as incense, used in a floor wash, or carried as a charm, juniper is a potent herb for purification and protection. It guards the threshold between worlds, banishing negativity while inviting in good spirits and beneficial energies.

Lavender

Planetary and elemental correspondence: Mercury and Air. Lavender (*Lavandula* spp.) is one of the most beloved and recognizable herbs in both the botanical and magical worlds. Native to the Mediterranean region, lavender has been cultivated since ancient times for its fragrance, beauty, and healing properties. Through the centuries, lavender has remained a symbol of peace, grace, and protection, woven into folklore and spiritual practice across cultures.

In magical traditions, lavender is considered one of the most versatile herbs, suitable for almost any type of spell or ritual. Lavender is especially prominent in love magic, where it's used both to attract romance and to promote fidelity and chastity. Its calming, uplifting energy fosters harmony between partners and encourages affection while dispelling jealousy or resentment. Lavender is also a powerful herb of protection and purification; when burned as incense or sprinkled in baths, it cleanses the body, spirit, and home of stagnant or negative energies. Its soothing influence promotes peace, happiness, and spiritual well-being, making lavender a favorite in household rituals meant to invite tranquility and joy.

REMEMBER

Lavender is a great example of how you can use one herb for a multitude of purposes. While one tradition may use lavender to promote peace and attract love, another tradition may use it for protection and purification.

Medicinally, lavender has long been valued for its calming and restorative effects. Lavender is known to ease anxiety, promote restful sleep, and reduce tension headaches. The herb contains essential oils rich in linalool and linalyl acetate, compounds that contribute to its distinctive floral aroma and sedative qualities. Herbal infusions or sachets of dried lavender flowers are often used to aid sleep and relaxation, while the essential oil is applied in aromatherapy to calm the nerves and ease emotional distress. Its gentle action on the mind makes lavender an excellent herb for dream magic, divination, and psychic work, enhancing intuition and helping to open channels of spiritual perception.

Lavender's delicate yet grounding energy makes it a valuable ally in meditation and spiritual practice. It raises vibrations, clears the mind, and centers the spirit, creating the perfect atmosphere for introspection and sacred work. Traditionally, lavender was harvested and burned during the Summer Solstice to honor the Sun's zenith and to ensure abundance and peace for the coming seasons. Its connection to Mercury and the element of Air aligns it with clarity, communication, and mental agility. Because of this alignment, lavender is often included in charm bags or oils for business success, eloquence, and diplomacy, helping to put others at ease and facilitate positive interaction.

In both magic and medicine, lavender represents purity, serenity, and higher consciousness. It bridges the practical and the spiritual, the mind and the heart, bringing stability and light wherever it's used. Whether diffused for relaxation in aromatherapy, added to ritual baths for purification, or incorporated into spells for love and harmony, lavender continues to be one of the most enduring and essential herbs in the witch's apothecary.

Mint

Planetary and elemental correspondence: Mercury and Air. Mint (*Mentha* spp.) is one of the oldest and most widely used herbs in the world, treasured for its refreshing aroma, cooling properties, and vibrant energy. Since ancient times, mint has symbolized hospitality, vitality, and purity. Across cultures, mint has been a cleansing and invigorating herb, used to stimulate the senses and bring renewal.

In folklore and magical practice, mint is considered an all-purpose herb governed by Mercury, the planet of communication, intellect, and swiftness. As a mercurial plant, mint embodies versatility and movement, aiding in spells related to learning, writing, business success, and magical skill. Mint is often used to break hexes, dispel negative energies, and purify sacred space. When added to baths or floor washes, mint cleanses the aura and environment, inviting freshness and clarity. Carried in the wallet or kept near the cash register, mint attracts prosperity and ensures that money flows abundantly. Mint is a favorite in prosperity magic, aiding in finding employment, increasing business, and drawing customers.

Magically, mint is both protective and attractive. It wards off harmful influences while inviting good spirits, blessings, and luck. Mint is often included in charm bags for travel safety, health, and success. Because of its refreshing, invigorating scent, mint also stimulates the passions and can be used in lust or attraction spells. Its bright green color and energetic vibration connect it to the element of Air and to Mercury's powers of eloquence, intellect, and persuasion — qualities that make it particularly effective for those seeking to improve communication, charm, and influence.

Medicinally, mint has long been valued for its cooling and calming properties. Its key chemical constituents include menthol, menthone, and rosmarinic acid, which give it its characteristic scent and flavor as well as its therapeutic effects. Mint relieves nausea, indigestion, and headaches, and its antispasmodic qualities soothe muscle tension and cramps. The aroma of mint stimulates the brain and enhances alertness, relieving mental fatigue and promoting clarity. In aromatherapy, mint essential oil is used to awaken the senses, improve concentration, and refresh both mind and body. Its scent clears stagnation and uplifts the spirit, helping to restore mental balance and vitality.

Mint's magical and medicinal virtues align perfectly as an example of the connection between the physical and spiritual properties of an herb. It promotes groundedness while keeping the mind sharp and alert, linking body and intellect in harmonious flow. Whether used to bless a home, protect a traveler, inspire clear communication, or attract wealth and success, mint serves as a faithful ally in both practical and spiritual pursuits. Under the influence of Mercury, it embodies speed, intelligence, and charm, offering protection, prosperity, and freshness to all areas of life.

Mugwort

Planetary and elemental correspondence: Moon and Fire. Mugwort (*Artemisia vulgaris*) is one of the most ancient and revered herbs in magical and medicinal traditions. Its lineage stretches deep into human history, appearing in the Anglo-Saxon *Nine Herbs Charm*, a powerful healing incantation dating to the tenth century, that already called it the "oldest of herbs." This title honors mugwort's status as a timeless ally, one whose virtues were known to healers, seers, and wise women across generations. Native to Europe and Asia, mugwort has been cultivated and wild-harvested for thousands of years. Mugwort was used in ancient Greece and Rome to aid digestion and ward off fatigue during travel, while in traditional Chinese medicine, mugwort remains a key herb in moxibustion therapy, burned over specific points on the body to stimulate circulation and balance energy.

Throughout history, mugwort has been closely linked to the realms of magic, protection, and prophecy. In medieval Europe, it was considered one of the great witch's herbs, sacred to the Moon and the goddess Artemis, the protector of women and goddess of the wild, who was believed to bless the plant with its healing and visionary powers. Mugwort was a staple in women's medicine, used to regulate menstrual cycles, ease childbirth, and support the female reproductive system, though it must be avoided during pregnancy. Because of these associations, mugwort became tied to both fertility and independence and of course witchcraft.

Magically, mugwort is a cornerstone of the witch's apothecary. Herbal practitioners use mugwort in spells for strength, protection, purification, psychic ability, and prophetic dreaming. Its silvery-green leaves, which shimmer under moonlight, link it intimately to lunar magic. When burned as incense or infused in ritual baths, mugwort cleanses the aura, removes toxic energies, and wards off harmful spirits. Practitioners also use mugwort to purify and charge tools for divination, such as tarot cards, pendulums, or scrying mirrors, making it an essential companion for those who walk between worlds. Drinking mugwort tea (for those *not* pregnant) or burning it before divination is said to open the psychic senses and promote prophetic dreaming.

WARNING

Do not consume mugwort if you are pregnant, nursing, or trying to get pregnant.

Medicinally, mugwort contains essential oils such as thujone, cineole, and borneol, compounds that contribute to its aromatic, slightly bitter profile and its stimulating effects on the body. Traditionally, it has been used as a digestive tonic, nerve relaxant, and uterine stimulant. In aromatherapy, the scent of mugwort has a grounding yet ethereal quality, promoting relaxation while also heightening awareness, a dual action that mirrors its magical role as one of the most powerful allies for dreaming, divination, and psychic enhancement.

Mugwort stands at the threshold between worlds as a bridge between waking and dreaming, the physical and the spiritual. Mugwort is a protector of travelers, a purifier of spaces, and a bringer of dreams and visions. Combined with its relative wormwood (*Artemisia absinthium*), it forms a potent banishing and cleansing blend, capable of dispelling negativity. To work with mugwort is to align oneself with the cycles of the Moon and the wisdom of the unseen, guided by an ancient spirit that continues to whisper through its silvered leaves, offering strength, protection, and illumination to all who honor it.

Rosemary

Planetary and elemental correspondence: Sun and Air. Rosemary (*Salvia rosmarinus*), whose Latin name means "dew of the sea," is one of the most beloved herbs of both kitchen and temple. Native to the Mediterranean region, rosemary has been revered since antiquity for its fragrance, healing power, and mystical potency. Over centuries, it became a symbol of remembrance, vitality, and enduring love.

In folklore and magic, rosemary holds a place of deep reverence as an herb of protection, purification, and blessing. Rosemary is one of the oldest known ritual incenses, burned since ancient times to sanctify sacred spaces and invoke powerful vibrations. Its rising smoke is said to banish malevolent energies while calling forth ancestral spirits and divine guardians. Rosemary protects the home and those within it, making it a favorite ingredient in cleansing rituals, charm bags, and protective bundles hung above doorways. Herbal practitioners also use rosemary to enhance psychic ability, cleanse the aura, and restore spiritual energy, making it an indispensable ally for healers, seers, and spiritual practitioners. When carried as a charm or worn as an amulet, rosemary offers courage and strength, especially in moments of confrontation or adversity.

Rosemary's association with the Sun gives it an energetic, radiant quality that vitalizes body and mind. Rosemary is a warming herb with stimulating properties that promote circulation and vitality, making it valuable in healing and purification baths. Spiritually, this solar energy translates into illumination, confidence, and clarity, traits that make rosemary ideal for mental work and study. Its fragrance awakens the senses and sharpens concentration, bringing lucidity to the mind and improving memory. Because of its effects on memory, rosemary is often used in magical formulas and aromatherapy blends to strengthen focus, aid in meditation, and enhance recall. This same quality of remembrance extends into matters of the heart, where rosemary supports love, fidelity, and emotional clarity.

Medicinally, rosemary is rich in essential oils, such as cineole, camphor, and borneol, which give it antiseptic, anti-inflammatory, and stimulating properties. Rosemary has long been used to improve circulation, relieve muscle pain, and support digestion. Its invigorating aroma clears the respiratory passages and refreshes the mind. In aromatherapy, rosemary essential oil is celebrated for enhancing memory and cognitive function, relieving fatigue, and promoting a sense of alert calm. Diffused in the air, rosemary uplifts the spirit, balances energy, and encourages motivation and clarity.

Rosemary is truly a multifaceted magical herb — a guardian, healer, and illuminator. Rosemary embodies remembrance, protection, and purification while nurturing love, longevity, and spiritual insight. Whether burned as incense, brewed into healing tonics, or worn as a charm, rosemary carries the warmth of the Sun and the wisdom of the ancestors. It invites blessings, strengthens intention, and empowers both mind and spirit with its fiery, purifying light.

Yarrow

Planetary and elemental correspondence: Venus/Mars and Water/Fire. Yarrow (*Achillea millefolium*), also known as arrowroot or warrior's wound wort, is one of my personal favorite herbs to work with. Its Latin name honors the Greek hero Achilles, who, according to legend, used yarrow to treat the wounds of his soldiers during the Trojan War. This association with the warrior archetype (Mars) reveals yarrow's enduring reputation as a plant of courage, resilience, and restoration. From ancient battlefields to household apothecaries, yarrow has served as a guardian of health, a charm of protection, and a bridge between the physical and spiritual realms.

In folklore, yarrow was carried or worn as a talisman to ward off harm and bring courage in the face of danger. Its presence in battlefield lore earned it a place among the most sacred healing plants of antiquity, and its common names "woundwort" and "herba militaris" reflect its value for staunching bleeding and speeding recovery. Yarrow was also considered a charm for love and divination; in some European traditions, sprigs were placed under a pillow to reveal one's future lover through dreams. The plant's ability to both protect and attract, to fortify and open the heart, reflect its dual connection to both Mars and Venus, blending strength with tenderness, and courage with compassion.

Magically, yarrow is a remarkably versatile herb used for protection, courage, love, divination, and psychic development. Yarrow enhances sensitivity to subtle energies while maintaining strong energetic boundaries, making it an ideal ally for empaths, healers, and diviners. Yarrow strengthens the aura, creating a shield that allows one to perceive spiritual currents without becoming overwhelmed by them. In ritual work, herbal practitioners use yarrow to banish harmful energies, exorcise spiritual intrusions, and safeguard sacred space. Yarrow's gentle, balancing vibration helps integrate the spiritual and physical aspects of healing, ensuring that the practitioner remains both open and grounded.

TIP

Yarrow flowers make wonderful dried flower bundles that last for a long time and maintain their color and beauty. You can hang these bundles around the home to protect and purify the space, as well as attract good energy.

Medicinally, yarrow's reputation as a healer is well deserved. It contains alkaloids, such as achilleine, flavonoids, and volatile oils, including azulene and cineole, which contribute to its anti-inflammatory, antiseptic, and astringent properties. Traditionally, yarrow was used to stop bleeding, promote wound healing, reduce fever, and relieve digestive discomfort. Herbalists also use yarrow as a tonic for circulation and as a remedy for colds and flu. Its soothing and restorative qualities mirror its magical role as a fortifier of body, mind, and spirit.

In aromatherapy, yarrow essential oil has a deep, herbaceous scent that calms the nerves, stabilizes emotions, and promotes psychic awareness. Yarrow helps release energetic blockages and restores harmony to the subtle body. Spiritually, yarrow embodies the balance of Mars and Venus, the courage of the warrior and the grace of the healer. Whether used in healing rituals, love charms, or divination rites, yarrow continues to stand as a timeless protector, a sacred herb that shields, heals, and guides those who walk the green path of the magical herbalist.

IN THIS CHAPTER

» **Preserving and storing herbs for magic**

» **Awakening the spirit of your herb cabinet**

Chapter 14 Ten Tips for Building Your Magical Apothecary

Nothing conjures that feeling of enchantment more than a dimly lit shop lined with shelves holding jars of mysterious ingredients. While the term apothecary is associated with the sale of ingredients for medicinal purposes, apothecaries have been associated with the magical and mysterious since the early days when the lines between magic and medicine were much vaguer. The connection between mundane and spiritual remains true in the magical community where apothecaries not only supply herbs with medicinal properties but a wide variety of other items intended for use in magical practice. In this chapter, I go over ten tips for assembling your own "apothecary" or magical herb cabinet at home.

Choosing Your Shelving

Your apothecary can be as fancy or as utilitarian as you like. It can be a repurposed bookshelf, an antique hutch or China cabinet found at a thrift store, or something completely unique that you build yourself. The place where you store your magical ingredients is the thing that brings them all together creating a special and sacred space.

TIP

I recommend having a separate place to store your magical herbs, apart from the kitchen pantry or spice rack (although, those herbs are magical, too!). The apothecary is a sacred space that represents your unique magical practice. You can decorate it however you like, painting it with leaves and flowers or carving magical symbols into the wood.

Dedicating Your Magical Herb Cabinet

The apothecary cabinet is as much a magical tool as are candles, incense burners, and spell components. Because all the items contained in the cabinet are for magical uses, dedicating the magical apothecary to spiritual purposes makes sense. This dedication may mean anointing it with ritual oils, smoking it with incense, or speaking blessings over it. Dedicating the storage space in this way sanctifies the space and creates a magical energy of its own that will continue to accumulate in power the more that it is used.

Storing in Bottles, Jars, and Vials

Like many magical practitioners, you, too, may have an obsession with seeing things stored in bottles. If there is one thing that is true about herbal magic practitioners across the board, it's that we have a lot of bottles!

TIP

Having extra empty containers on hand for various projects is always a good idea. Mason jars, upcycled pasta sauce jars, baby food jars, and just about any other glass container with a lid are as valuable as gold to the herbal practitioner.

I recommend using glass containers instead of plastic. Make sure that the lids seal properly and that the containers have been thoroughly cleaned before use. Of course, you can also buy new containers that have a more magical vibe, and reserve ornate containers for special formulas.

Drying Your Herbs

Something is so satisfying about growing, harvesting, and drying your own herbs for magical and mundane purposes. Nothing screams old-world kitchen witch like having bundles of fragrant herbs hanging around the house to dry.

TIP

To dry your herbs the old-fashioned way, simply harvest a bundle of herbs by cutting their stems so that they're about 10 to 12 inches long. Avoid making the bundles too thick so that they'll dry faster. Tie the bottom of the stems with a natural cord, leaving some extra so that you can hang them. Hang the herbs upside down in a cool, dry place until they're crispy to the touch and all the plant material, including the stems, is completely dry. (See the section "Mitigating Mold and Insects," later in this chapter, for additional information on drying your herbs.)

Autumn is traditionally the time for harvest, and most herbs will be completely dry by the end of winter. If you live in a warm, humid climate, this process will take longer, and you may want to opt for using a dehydrator.

Storing Your Herbs

To get the longest shelf life, one of the most important things is how you store the herbs. Most herbs will maintain their freshness for about a year. Only harvest or buy what you know you'll use so that you don't wind up with a shelf full of dead scentless plant material.

WARNING

Light, heat, and humidity are the enemies of herbal ingredients. Avoid storing your herbs in places that receive direct sunlight. You could even choose a cabinet with its own doors. Keep everything stored in a cool, dry place. Ensure that all the seals on your jars are tight and that no moisture is left in the jar when you add your herbs to it.

If you live in an extremely humid area, you can also find silicon desiccant packets that you can put in the jar with your herbs to absorb any moisture. In addition to ensuring that your containers are free of moisture, make sure that any plant material that you have harvested is bone dry. It should be crispy, not soft in any way.

Labeling Your Containers

Labeling your containers is a good practice to get into the habit of right from the beginning because it will make your life easier when you have accumulated a fully stocked apothecary.

TIP

The labels should include both the common name and scientific name of the contents of the jar. Using both names will help avoid any discrepancies because common names can be misleading. Some herbs have similar common names, while the scientific name is unique to one specific species. Using both names is also good practice so that you can remember the scientific names of your herbs.

The labels should also include the date that the herbs were harvested or purchased so that you can keep track of their shelf life. Including information like the herb's magical correspondences as well as common uses is also helpful for memorization and quick reference. This way, your magical herb cabinet will serve as a learning tool as well as a home for your physical ingredients.

Checking Your Herbs

As herbs break down over time, they'll lose their color and their scent. Discoloration and lack of scent also indicate that their magical potency is waning.

If you're not using all your herbs on a regular basis, check them regularly (preferably on a monthly basis) for freshness. Open each of your herb jars and give them a smell. If they still smell fragrant, then they're still good.

Also, make sure no insects are making a meal of your herbs, especially those that you've harvested and dried yourself. Because most herbs are grown outdoors, you always have a chance of bugs stowing away in the plant material. Even herbs purchased from reputable companies are not 100 percent free of infestations. If you find an insect, throw away all the plant material and thoroughly clean the jar.

Mitigating Mold and Insects

One way to help ensure that herbs are completely dry and insect-free before storage is to either use a dehydrator or, if you're drying herbs the old-fashioned way, put them in the oven at 100 to 150°F for 5 to 10 minutes. The heat will remove any residual moisture and kill any bugs that are hiding in the plant material.

REMEMBER

The idea here is to kill the bugs, not cook the plant material. I recommend leaving the oven door cracked to allow moisture to escape. If your plant material seems like it's cooking or starts to smoke, lower the temperature.

Using the Cabinet as an Altar

Depending on the height and style of the cabinet, many practitioners will use the cabinet's top surface as an altar or workspace for their magical projects. This area has the added benefit of not only having all your herbal ingredients at your fingertips while you're working, but also serves to add to your cabinet's magical energy.

How you set up your altar or workspace is up to you. You may include an incense burner, candles, mortar and pestle, spell bottles, or other items that are part of ongoing magical workings.

Working with the Magical Apothecary

After you've assembled all the components of your herb cabinet, if you're like me, you'll find yourself gazing in wonder and satisfaction at the beauty of all your magical allies sitting in one place. Something is innately magical about a fully stocked herbal apothecary, and it makes a great place to sit and meditate.

Spending time with your herbs is a great way to get to know them. You may find that certain herbs call out to you. Take their jars off of the shelf, hold them, and connect with their spirits and energy. Open the jar and smell the contents. Say the plant's names and read its label, and over time, you'll develop a detailed mental map of each jar, its contents, and its uses. This approach is a great way to memorize information about your herbs, communicate with the plant spirits, and maintain an intimate connection with them.

Index

D

E

F

G

H

I

Q

R

S

T

U

V

W

Y

About the Author

Coby Michael is an occult herbalist and plant medicine practitioner, specializing in poisonous and psychoactive plants, particularly for their magical and spiritual uses. He is the owner of The Poisoner's Apothecary (thepoisonersapothecary.com), a blog and online shop where he makes a wide array of formulas working with plants like deadly nightshade and fly agaric mushroom. Coby creates ritual formulas and talismanic jewelry, inspired by poisonous plants and their use in witchcraft and ceremony. Coby has a background in religious studies, traditional witchcraft, North American folk magic, and phytochemistry. He also is the founder of Botanica Obscura Conference, an annual gathering of magical plant practitioners from around the world sharing their plant spirit knowledge. He writes prolifically and teaches workshops on The Poison Path, flying ointments, and occult herbalism.

Since a very young age, Coby Michael has felt the call of the natural world. He took an early interest in plants, specifically medicinal herbs, and worked in the garden with his family every summer. It was here, in the fertile soil and deep forests of Indiana, that a connection was made. The unseen, hidden, and subtle forces of nature reached out, getting this young boy's attention. Coby felt a strange relationship with the land of his birth, feeling out of place and tethered at the same time. More comfortable with the company of trees over the company of other humans, he made countless silent discoveries. One of those led to the discovery of magic, through the practice of Witchcraft.

It was this discovery of the magic within and around him and this budding relationship that would keep him alive and guide him through the darkness. Many times there was only darkness and the sense of a greater purpose. His teen years were tumultuous, dealing with coming out of the closet, an abusive alcoholic father, and his own issues with substance abuse. Coby never let any of this stand in his way, and there was one thing that provided inner refuge: reading. Although Coby had his own personal battles, he always felt a sense of a greater purpose, of helping other people. Throughout his 20s, Coby continued his studies, practicing and accumulating information.

In 2016, while attending Arizona State University for Religious Studies, this solitary witch of 20-plus years, started blogging, sharing his ideas with an audience for the first time. This was a major turning point, and it was during this time that a vision of the future began to crystalize. It was at *Patheos Pagan*, under the editorship of Jason Mankey, that Coby began his career in writing. He continues to maintain his blog on Patheos Pagan and also has written for *The House of Twigs*, *This Witch Magazine*, and *The Witches' Almanac*. He released his first of three self-published booklets called *The Poisoner's Pocket Guides* in 2018 and began the work that would become his first book, *The Poison Path Herbal* (Park Street Press, 2022). He has currently written two more books on the subject of the Poison Path, including *The Poison Path Grimoire* (Destiny Books, 2024) and *The Poison Path Oracle* (Destiny Books, 2026).

Coby currently resides in St. Petersburg, Florida, but you can see him at events across the United States. He is currently working on some top-secret writing projects, including the manuscript for his second book. When Coby isn't writing or working with plants, you can find him doing yoga and connecting with the natural world. Follow Coby's work on social media @poisonersapothecary.

Dedication

I would like to dedicate this work to my parents, Kelley and Juan. Thank you for always believing in me and supporting me through this crazy journey! We have been through a lot together and learned so much along the way!

Author's Acknowledgments

I would like to thank the following individuals without whom this work would not have been possible. Thank you, first and foremost, to my friend and fellow author, Lorraine Monteagut, author of *Modern Witchcraft For Dummies* (Wiley Publishing). Thank you for not only suggesting me for this project, but also for doing the peer review. You have been a great friend and supportive in so many ways, and I have so much appreciation for you! Also thank you to my Associate Acquisitions Editor, Alicia Sparrow, for all the work you've done behind the scenes to make this book happen, and a huge thank you to my editor, Kelly Ewing, for all the technical support and insight that has shaped this into a *For Dummies* book! I would also like to acknowledge all the herbalists and plant people, past, present and future, for your inspiration and support. Thank you for carrying this important knowledge down through the ages. It is a great honor to walk this green path with all of you! I would also like to specifically acknowledge Harold Roth, Paul Beyerl, Scott Cunningham, and Christian Rätsch without whom I never would have found my way to the place I am now. Your work has inspired and influenced the world of magical herbalism in ways that will echo through the ages!

Publisher's Acknowledgments

Associate Acquisitions Editor:
Alicia Sparrow

Development Editor:
Kelly Ewing

Technical Editor:
Lorraine Monteagut

Senior Managing Editor:
Kristie Pyles

Production Editor:
M. Athiyappan Lalith Kumar

Cover Image: © Dmitriy/stock.adobe.com